The German Peasants' War 1524–26

Douglas Miller

Helion & Company Limited
Unit 8 Amherst Business Centre
Budbrooke Road
Warwick
CV34 5WE
England
Tel. 01926 499 619
Email: info@helion.co.uk
Website: www.helion.co.uk
Twitter: @helionbooks
Visit our blog http://blog.helion.co.uk/

Published by Helion & Company 2023
Designed and typeset by Mary Woolley, Battlefield Design (www.battlefield-design.co.uk)
Cover designed by Paul Hewitt, Battlefield Design (www.battlefield-design.co.uk)

Text © Douglas Miller 2023
Illustrations © as individually credited
Colour artwork drawn by Gorgio Albertini © Helion & Company 2023
Maps and graphics created by Anderson Subtil © Helion & Company 2023

Every reasonable effort has been made to trace copyright holders and to obtain their permission for the use of copyright material. The author and publisher apologise for any errors or omissions in this work and would be grateful if notified of any corrections that should be incorporated in future reprints or editions of this book.

ISBN 978-1-804512-02-9

British Library Cataloguing-in-Publication Data.
A catalogue record for this book is available from the British Library.

All rights reserved. No part of this publication may be reproduced, stored in a retrieval system, or transmitted, in any form, or by any means, electronic, mechanical, photocopying, recording or otherwise, without the express written consent of Helion & Company Limited.

For details of other military history titles published by Helion & Company Limited contact the above address or visit our website: http://www.helion.co.uk.

We always welcome receiving book proposals from prospective authors.

Contents

Acknowledgements		v
Preface		vi
1	Introduction	11
2	Warfare at the turn of the Sixteenth Century	18
3	Military Organisation of the Peasants	30
4	1524 The Outbreak of the War in the Southwest	51
5	1525 The Rise and Fall of the Revolt	58
6	Aftermath	162
7	Conclusion	170
	Colour Plate Commentaries	176

Appendices:
I	Extracts from the Ochsenfurter Field Ordinances, 24–27 April 1525	181
II	Ordinance Of the Upper Swabian Peasantry, March 1525	183
III	Extracts from the Ordinance of the Rhineland Peasants,10 May 1525	185

Bibliography   187

Acknowledgements

A number of people have been particularly helpful in making this book possible. I owe the members of the Association of German Peasants' War Museums a debt of gratitude for their assistance. Specifically, Dr Thomas T. Müller, Dr Ulrich Hahnemann, Dr Nora Hilgert, Bernd Breyvogel, Franz Liesch, Susanne Anwander, Gernot Peikert and Cornelia Wenzel. Dr Rainer Leng kindly provided me with a copy of his research on the siege of the Marienberg as did Michael Bletzer on the battles of Königshofen and Giebelstadt, and Michael Klebon on developments in the Kraichgau.

Thanks, are also due to Uli Becker who whisked me off to Pfeddersheim and to Jürgen Pfitzner for his guided tour there. Finally, a special credit to Geoff Laws who has assisted me over the years with various aspects of artwork.

Preface

The German Peasants' War was one of the most momentous events in European history,[1] viewed as both a decisive moment in the development of German parliamentary democracy[2] and at the same time as a 'revolution of the common man'.[3] Some doubt that this conflict ever constituted a 'war' since the insurgency began with a series of overlapping localised insurrections in central and Southern Germany which some contemporary observers and subsequent historians have dismissed as the actions of riotous mobs. However, as we shall see, there were organised human beings behind this popular revolt. Moreover, conventional definitions of war – armed conflict between organised armies – most certainly apply. The Swabian League – the mutual defence pact of the Holy Roman Empire's imperial estates – did in fact declare war against the peasants on the grounds of breach of the peace[4]. What continues to remain problematic is the description of this armed conflict as a 'peasant' war since farmworkers were joined in many cases by other groups such as miners, artisans, and the citizens of municipalities. Since all classes became involved and took up positions on both sides it is probably more accurate to describe the events of 1524 through to 1526 as in effect a 'civil war'. I have been tempted to retitle this book as the 'Great German Civil War', but such is the embeddedness of the term 'peasant' in general historical consciousness that I have stayed with the existing title.

The speed at which these incidents occurred and spread between July 1524 and April 1525 caught the authorities completely unawares and evolved from local protests into a potential overarching revolution which addressed a common set of grievances based in Reformation thought. By the summer of 1525, however, the insurgency was everywhere in retreat.

---

1. Robert Scribner, Tom Scott, *The German Peasants' War: A History in Documents* (London: Humanity Books 1994).
2. Johannes Rau, '475 Jahre Zwölf Memminger Bauernartikel" <http://www.bundespraesident.de/SharedDocs/Reden/DE/Johannes-Rau/Reden/2000/03/20000310_Rede.html> (accessed 26 September 2022)
3. Peter Blickle, *Der Bauernkrieg: Die Revolution des gemeinen Mannes* (München, C. H. Beck, 2002)
4. Peter Blickle, *der Bauernjörg, Feldherr im Bauernkrieg* (Munich: Beck Verlag, 2015) pp.100–105.

PREFACE

This has raised a series of specific questions for military historians. Are answers to this turnaround to be found within the changes which were occurring in the conduct of warfare at this time? How robust was peasant military organisation given the presence of Landsknechts within their ranks? Given the absence of a standing army how were the authorities able to successfully respond to the insurgency? Are the reasons for the military failure of the rebels to be explained by non-military factors? These themes will be explored in this book.

I first became interested in the military aspects of this conflict having undertaken research for an Osprey book on the Landsknechts back in 1973–1975,[5] the years of the 450th anniversary of the conflict. My research for what was to be a somewhat superficial account of the conflict in a second Osprey title (Armies of the German Peasant Wars) in 2003[6] led me to two museums in Mühlhausen and Bad Frankenhausen in Thüringia where the reformist preacher Thomas Müntzer had been particularly active. Retirement awakened my interest again and I decided to publish a detailed account of a decisive but enigmatic 'battle' in that war which took place in Frankenhausen.[7] Latterly, with the support of Helion, I had the opportunity to do an in-depth treatment of a mercenary army on campaign – namely the armed forces of the Swabian League under the command of Georg Truchsess of Waldburg.[8] That book focuses primarily on the campaign by the ruling elites against the rebels of Southern Germany (Swabia, Württemberg and Franconia). However, the Peasants' War played out in other well-defined regions beyond Thüringia and Upper Swabia – notably the Black Forest, Alsace, the Palatinate, and the Alpine lands (Tyrol, Salzburg, Styria and Carinthia). With the benefit of some 20 years research since the first Osprey title, the opportunity provided by Helion to revisit this conflict is timely as we approach the 500-year anniversary in 2025.

The events occurred during a period of massive political, economic, technological, cultural, and military upheaval and against the backdrop of a 'Reformation' of religious worship and belief. Comparison between the beginning of the sixteenth century and events which are occurring in Europe today permit some interesting observations – concern about an impending apocalypse, political tensions within the largest political territory in the European space – the Holy Roman Empire – the rise of religious division and intolerance and the role of high finance. Alongside these we must compare the tectonic social and cultural impacts of technological changes in the production of print media in the Early Modern Era leading to a rise in literacy and an attendant political unrest.

---

5   Douglas Miller, *The Landsknechts* (Oxford: Osprey Publishing, 1976)
6   Douglas Miller, *Armies of the German Peasant War 1524–1526*, (Oxford: Osprey Publishing, 2003)
7   Douglas Miller, *Frankenhausen 1525* (Seaton Burn: Blagdon Publishing, 2017)
8   Douglas Miller, *The Army of the Swabian League 1525* (Warwick, Helion & Company 2019).

An additional issue originating from the historiography of the German Peasants' War is that our understanding of the events is based predominantly on documentary evidence taken from the correspondence, descriptions, diaries, and commissioned art of the ruling elite. Moreover, the peasants were depicted in these accounts as a grotesque, uninhibited, mob of animals[9] devoid of any humanity. There is little by way of accounts of those men and women who fought to tear down the evils of feudalism at the time. Attempts were made by East German historians of Marxist persuasion in the mid-1970s to engage with the military aspects of the war from the peasant's perspective.[10] I have attempted to build on this tradition – not in the political sense – but in seeking to provide a perspective on the ways in which this popular revolt was organised militarily by shedding light on the various dimensions of peasant organisation, weaponry, and actions.

For those wishing to delve deeper into this conflict I can recommend Tom Scott and Bob Scribner's history in documents of the German Peasant's War. This stands alone as the go to source in the English language on the conflict with excellent summaries of events and translations of key texts preceded by concise commentaries. In addition to translations of key texts from this work I have attempted to provide as rich a set of contemporary illustrations as possible to assist in the visualisation of the military aspects of the war. As Hale has shown us, these must be viewed with a degree of caution.[11] Chapters 2 and 3 address changes occurring in the conduct of warfare at the turn of the sixteenth century and how these were or were not assimilated by the peasant bands. Chapter 4 covers the onset of the war in the Southwest in 1524. No effort has been made to provide a single chronological narrative as much of what occurred happened in parallel in each of the theatres of the war. Consequently, Chapter 5 consists of a series of sub sections each with its own chronology dealing with the conflict in each region. Since the events in Swabia, Württemberg and Franconia are covered in Helion's Army of the Swabian League, No. 3 in the 'From Retinue to Regiment' series, more emphasis has been placed in these sections on peasant actions as well as those military engagements not covered in the above title.[12] For a more holistic view of the conflict it is recommended to read this as a companion title. Chapter 6 discusses the aftermath including

---

9 Florian Welle, Die Körpermassaker im deutschen Bauernkrieg von 1525: Kulturgeschichte des menschlichen Körpers im 16. Jahrhundert 2005 <http://www.societyofcontrol.com/ppmwiki/pmwiki.php/Main/KoerperMassaker> (accessed 13 September 2022).

10 Siegfried Hoyer, *Das Militärwesen im Deutschen Bauernkrieg* (Berlin: Militärverlag der Deutschen demokratischen Republik 1975). Manfred Bensing, Siegfried Hoyer 1970 Der Deutsche Bauernkrieg 1524–1526 (Berlin: Militärverlag der Deutschen demokratischen Republik 1970).

11 John Rigby Hale, *Artists and Warfare in the Renaissance* (Yale University Press, 1990).

12 Similarly, for those wishing to dig deeper into the events in Thüringia these are summarised in Miller, *Frankenhausen*

PREFACE

the measures taken by the authorities to punish the insurgents, while Chapter 7 concludes with an assessment of the strategy and tactics of the opposing forces.

Lastly, this book has required piecing together events from a variety of sources in the German language and I take full responsibility for details which may have been lost in translation and for any attributions to image sources I may have missed.

Doug Miller
Newcastle, October 2022

1

Introduction

At the time of the Peasants' War, what we know today as Germany was part of the Holy Roman Empire, an elective monarchy which straddled Central Europe at this time. The most significant power brokers within this territory were the German prince-electors and their respective dynasties. Although these princes owed their Emperor Charles V their allegiance, they enjoyed a de facto sovereignty, functioning within their territories as autocratic rulers, recognising no other authority, and levying taxes and borrowing money as they saw fit to maintain their administration and military presence. The temporal princes were not the only ones to govern the Holy Roman Empire; there were also territories presided over by the prince bishops. (See Plate A)

Within each of these principalities, however, was a myriad of smaller subunits: counties, free imperial cities and other domains. The existing social order was pronounced but it was a hierarchy undergoing profound change. The lesser nobility (the knights), for example, now faced an evolving military technology and tactics which placed an increasing importance on firepower and the use of infantry and were beginning to see their social and political significance wane.

At the time of the Reformation, 80 percent of the population lived in the countryside with the economy highly dependent on agriculture. Metal mining, in particular silver, and salt extraction were also important industries, but the centres of processing and distribution – the municipalities – were generating new classes – wealthy patricians and burghers (merchants), an artisan class and urban day workers, with each becoming interest groups in their own right. Such developments in social hierarchy inevitably brought new tensions.

In the countryside, the peasants – who were mostly tenant farmers – had to support the nobility and the clergy with taxes and tributes. This was a major source of grievance, as were the feudal dues or rents imposed on agricultural workers, which could account for as much as 40 percent of production, plus a further 10 percent in tithes. Taxes were often levied at five to 10 percent of assessed property. Some levies were also payable on special occasions, such as the death of a landowner. The so-called taxes in kind often included what had been produced off the land.

THE GERMAN PEASANTS' WAR 1524-26

This woodcut caricature depicts the class system in the Holy Roman Empire which existed in a marked fashion at the time. At the top of the tree sit the Emperor and the Pope, beneath the princes, feudal nobles, and clergy, then come the artisans and other middle classes while the peasants crawl out of the roots but also interestingly sit at the very top of the tree. This suggests the political leanings and aspirations of the artist Hans Weiditz who went by the pseudonym Petrarca Meister. *Ständebaum* from *Von Artznei, beydes des guten vnd widerwertigen Glücks* Frankfurt 1596, (Bavarian State Library, with permission).

In addition, peasants were often forced to perform other services, (*Frondienst*) which amounted to de facto forced labour for their landlords. As the upper class expanded, the burden on the peasantry became increasingly unbearable. Moreover, the nobility had drastically curtailed their 'ancient rights'. No peasant could hunt, fish, or chop wood freely and they were powerless to prevent crops being destroyed by wild game and the hunt. Should a peasant wish to marry, he required not only his lord's permission, but had to pay a tax. There was also a death tax payable to the lord – usually in kind. There was little redress against feudal injustice since the courts were operated by the clergy or wealthy burgher and patrician jurists and the social order was kept in place by the most horrific forms of physical punishment.

INTRODUCTION

Peasant resisting a bailiff, Woodcut from *Von Artznei, beydes des guten vnd widerwertigen Glücks* by Hans Weiditz, (Bavarian State Library, with permission).

Resistance to this situation had simmered for years with disturbances in the Rhineland and beyond being recorded as far back as the first half of the fourteenth century.[1] In the early fifteenth century during the reign of Holy Roman Emperor Sigismund, a reform document known as the *Reformatio Sigismundi* was published by an anonymous author in 1439 referring to the injustice of the German rulers and calling for reform of the church. Then, in 1476 a shepherd and street entertainer by the name of Hans Böhm who lived in the German town of Niklashausen (in present-day Baden-Württemberg) began to preach on the sins of the clergy urging peasants not to pay taxes to the church. Further he promoted the abolition of forced labour and levies to the nobles. Böhm's sermons called for a levelling of society and a return of the commons to the people. When thousands began to converge on Niklashausen to listen to the 'Drummer Boy', the authorities sensed a real and imminent threat and when a revolt began in early May 1476, they intervened and arrested Böhm who was tried for heresy in July that year.[2]

---

1   *Der Aufstand des kleinen Mannes : Bauernrevolte und Bauernkriege* in Geschichte Vol. 2/2009, Nuremberg: Sailer Verlag.
2   Richard Wunderli, *Peasant Fires: The Drummer of Niklashausen* (Indiana University Press 1992).

THE GERMAN PEASANTS' WAR 1524-26

Miniature painting of the pilgrimage to see the drummer of Niklashausen and his ultimate execution from a chronicle written by Lorenz Fries (1489/91-1550) for the Prince-Bishop of Würzburg. (Universitätsbibliothek Würzburg, with permission).

Böhm's demands never receded, however, and resurfaced in a series of uprisings towards the end of the century. In 1493, a small group of conspirators chose the Bundschuh as their symbol when they planned to revolt against the unjust and opaque legal and tax system in Schlettstadt, Alsace. At the beginning of the sixteenth century this movement resurfaced under the leadership of Joss Fritz from Untergrombach and there were attempts at revolt in 1502 in the archdiocese of Speyer, in 1513 in Breisgau and in 1517 on the Upper Rhine. These uprisings were all crushed before they could take shape, as Joss Fritz was repeatedly betrayed by his comrades-in-arms. Early woodcuts show Joss Fritz holding a banner and depicts a shoe which was typical of peasant footwear—the so-called leather Bundschuh.[3] Since it stood in sharp contrast to the high boots worn by the higher classes it became an important symbol around which the aggrieved could organise.

Prior to the final Bundschuh insurgency in 1514, unrest broke out along the Rems valley to the east of Stuttgart. The Duke of Württemberg had been at pains to deal with an ever-worsening fiscal crisis brought on by his lavish lifestyle and in 1513 he had raised taxes on meat to finance his planned war against Burgundy. At the same time, he reduced the unit of measurement of weight, which aroused general indignation throughout his territory. A

---

[3] Joß Fritz continued his clandestine agitation into the early months of the Peasants' War. According to reports from the Hegau, among the rebels there was also Fritz from Grombach in the bishopric of Speyer, with an old greybeard, who continued to proclaim he could or would not die until the Bundschuh had run its course.

INTRODUCTION

year later in protest at this measure, a certain Peter Gais of Beutelsbach (aka Gaispeter) decided to borrow the new weights from his local butcher and submit them to 'ordeal by water', a trial usually reserved for witches.

Although conceived as a light-hearted stunt, this soon snowballed into a popular movement which gave itself the title of 'Poor Conrad'. Encouraged by the town priest, Dr Rainhard Gaisslin the movement grew, and the peasants assembled before the gates of Schorndorf, the seat of the district court. Ulrich, who was intent on nipping any possible uprising in the bud, sought military assistance from Duke Ludwig of the Rhineland Palatinate und Philipp, Marquis of Baden, and convened an emergency Parliament in Tübingen where a treaty was signed establishing privileges and co-determination rights for the estates but precious little for the peasantry. As news of the duke's approaching force reached the peasants who had established a camp on the Kappenberg near Weinstadt, the rebellion began to lose momentum. Although no blood had been shed, a show trial – a so-called *Blutgericht* – was convened in Schorndorf at which the ring leaders of the movement were deemed to have committed an arch crime and, following prolonged torture to extract the names of their accomplices, were sentenced to death.[4]

The Poor Conrad movement may have been the last major secular uprising before the Peasants' War but much broader movements were occurring at this time which some have described as the Northern Renaissance. Many areas of the arts and sciences were being influenced at the turn of the sixteenth century, and the spread of Italian Renaissance humanism to the various German states and principalities led to two major developments in the German Renaissance which were to dominate Europe in the sixteenth century: the Protestant Reformation and the invention of printing. Both were to play a significant role in the Peasants War.

The challenges to the political authorities at the time were mirrored by the doctrinal turmoil within the established church as a new wave of clerics began to question the authority of the Catholic faith. Foremost amongst these was Martin Luther who felt compelled to denounce the practice of

Cover of the second edition of a pamphlet dated 1514 by the printer and social commentator, Pamphilus Gengenbach describing the Bundschuh uprising. Purporting to be the only contemporary image of Joss Fritz standing before a group of his follows who are swearing an oath before one of the banners he had made. The motif on the banner was or remerge as an icon on the banner of several bands in the 1524–1525 uprisings. From: Adam T. 2002 *Joß Fritz – das verborgene Feuer der Revolution, Bundschuhbewegung und Bauernkrieg am Oberrhein im frühen 16. Jahrhundert* (Publications of the Historic Commission of the city of Bruchsal: Ubstadt-Weiher, vol.20), p.188.

---

4 Stadt Fellbach *500 Jahre Armer Konrad – der Gerechtigkeit einen Beistand tun.* (Fellbach: 2014).

THE GERMAN PEASANTS' WAR 1524-26

Woodcut depicting all the forms of state sanctioned punishments from the Laien-spiegel – a book of law and punishment published in 1509 by Ulrich Tengler. The power over life and death was originally exclusively held by the Holy Roman Emperor but had gradually been usurped by the territorial nobles by this time. The social order was kept in place by extreme forms of torture and punishment. Generally, the death sentence would be pronounced for criminal deeds such as murder and robbery, rape and homosexuality, witchcraft as well as infanticide. For the nobility, however, a lesson needed to be taught to those peasants who had dared to challenge the status quo and the ring leaders were to face the full weight of the state system of punishment. Coloured woodcut from Ulrich Tengler: *Laijen Spiegel: Von rechtmässigen ordnungen in Burgerlichen vnd peinlichen regimenten*, Straßburg: Hupfuff, 1510. (Bamberg State Library, with permission).

selling so-called paper indulgences to absolve individuals of their sins. In 1517, Albrecht of Brandenburg Archbishop of Mainz, who was heavily in debt, had received permission from Pope Leo X to conduct the sale of a special indulgence, the proceeds of which were to contribute in part to the reconstruction of St. Peter's Basilica in Rome. He appointed the Dominican friar Johann Tetzel as the General Commissioner of indulgences. It was this practice which Martin Luther took issue in his famous 95 theses which he nailed on the doors of the All-Saints Church in Wittenberg in 1517 thus heralding in the Protestant Reformation.

In 1521 an imperial ban was pronounced on Luther and his followers at the Diet of Worms but since a number of princes had begun to question their Catholic faith and embrace the Protestant Reformation, he was able to find protection from none other than the Elector Frederick the Wise of Saxony. As a fugitive hiding from the papal authorities in Wartburg Castle, Luther began translating the Bible into German. By 1525, as the Reformation progressed, Luther's doctrine of spiritual freedom and his focus on *Sola Scriptura* began to take hold. This posited the word of the Bible as the sole infallible source of authority for Christian faith and practice, thereby challenging the idea that anything other than 'Godly law' could not command the allegiance of the people. The availability of the recently invented movable type printing press, coupled with an improvement in literacy meant an increase in the publication of Bibles and polemical tracts. The greater accessibility of texts, and the need for informed interpretation of the Scriptures meant that attendance at public preaching and lecturing events grew as the 'new' clergy had become the intellectuals of their time. Reformist preachers began to multiply, latching on to the peasant manifestos which were beginning to emerge as religious unrest spread in Southern and Central Germany. One of the key demands was that the common people

INTRODUCTION

Protestant reformers developed a new apocalyptic understanding, focused on the historical interpretation of astrological prediction, which they saw as inseparable from political events. A series of anonymous so-called *Practica* pamphlets, published between 1515 and 1525, prophesised that in the years 1522 and 1524 there would be much discord and treason and the peasants would organise against the nobility. This title page from such a 1523 prognostic by Leonhart Reynmann takes as its central theme the prediction of the Great Flood expected in February 1524. It shows the conjunction of several planets in the sign of Pisces, producing a deluge which sweeps away a town and its inhabitants. On each side stand the opposing forces of the peasantry and the church. Although this may have appeared prophetic there had been serious floods in the years running up to the war and tensions between the peasantry and the clergy had been simmering for decades.[5] (Artist unknown) Coloured woodcut from Leonhard: Reynmann, *Practica vber die grossen vnd manigfeltigen Coniunction der Planeten, die im jar M.D.XXiiij. erscheinen... werden* (Bavarian State Library, with permission).

should have the right to choose their own pastor. As we shall see Luther went on to have a contradictory relationship with the peasants whereas other reformist clerics – most notably Thomas Müntzer – began to preach a more radical theology which prophesied the end of days and a coming conflagration between the people and the clergy.[5]

In the same way that all areas of society were undergoing change, so too was the 'art and science of war'. Since this was to have a decisive impact on the impending conflict, it is to this that we must now turn.

---

5 Cf. Scribner R. Images of the Peasant in Janos Bak (Ed.) 1976 *The German Peasants War 1525* (London: Routledge, 1976).

2

Warfare at the turn of the Sixteenth Century

The Peasants' War took place during a transitional period of change in military technology and battlefield tactics. From the mid-fifteenth century the Renaissance had begun to have a major impact on the science of warfare. Scholars in Italy and Germany had begun to concern themselves with questions of ordnance, military organisation, tactics, and close quarter combat, having developed a newfound interest in the ancient world – particularly that of the Romans. Military literature emerged, which in turn influenced military affairs and the works of Albrecht Dürer,[1] Leonardo da Vinci[2] and Nicolo Machiavelli,[3] were in circulation albeit in some cases not yet in printed form at the time of the Peasants' War.

New Battlefield Tactics

On the battlefield old institutions of chivalry, which had developed over centuries and were considered traditional, were gradually falling into obsolescence, but still coexisting alongside the emergence of new military science, hardware and tactics. New firepower (handguns and artillery), the replacement of heavily armoured knights by lighter 'cavalry' and the rise of the infantryman – mercenary soldiers (often from peasant stock) drilled in the use of polearms, specifically the pike, posed new tactical challenges to the mounted knight. During the fifteenth century two nations had risen to prominence in this latter respect – Bohemia and the Swiss Confederation.

---

1 Cf. Dierk Hagedorn, Daniel Jaquet, *Dürer's Fight Book* (London: Greenhill,2022). Albrecht Dürer, 1527 *Befestigungslehre,(A Study of Siege Warfare)* (Uhl, 1980).
2 Bern Dibner, *Leonardo as a Military Engineer,* (Burndy Library, 1946).
3 Ian King I. Niccolò Machiavelli: the father of Renaissance warfare in *Military History* < https://www.military-history.org/feature/machiavelli-renaissance-warfare.htm> (accessed 24 September 2022).

WARFARE AT THE TURN OF THE SIXTEENTH CENTURY

Despite their different origins, they posed an alternative to this classic feature of the feudalistic army. In both cases the new armies were recruited from the peasantry and the urban middle and lower classes. Each, however, developed their own specific tactics for dealing with the heavily armoured mounted man-at-arms.

In Bohemia it was the Hussites[4] under the command of the very capable Jan Ziska, who developed the use of the war wagon and the wagon fort as a particular tactic against mounted horse. It is no accident that the development of the war wagon emanated from Bohemia for it was here that Konrad Kyeser (1366–1405) a German military engineer wrote his major treatise Bellifortis (c. 1405),[5] a book on military technology while in exile at the beginning of the fifteenth century.

Under Ziska special wagons were constructed utilising the open sides as a framework against which boards bearing slits could be fixed. Before a battle, they would be circled or formed into a rectangular defensive structure, pushed together, and interlocked with chains. The sides of the wagons would serve as parapets from which crossbows and handguns could be trained on the advancing enemy. Since such a structure acted as a defence against a charge of knights, who, unable to get into hand-to-hand combat, would be forced to circle round the wagon fort from which they could be picked off with firearms or dismounted with the skilful use of a long bill hook. Initially protected inside the wagon fort, the Hussite infantry could counter-attack at the appropriate moment.

These new tactics gained popularity on German soil. There are records of the use of war wagons as early as 1427, with some cities such as Frankfurt am Main and Nuremberg establishing special ordinances to regulate their use. In the German lands, the adoption of the wagon fort was an attempt

Although the *gens d'armes* within the princes' armies were fast losing their effectiveness in conventional warfare due to the emergence of squares of pikemen, they would have thrown themselves into the fray as a matter of knightly chivalry despite their relative weight vis-à-vis the lighter cavalry. (Photo: Metropolitan Museum of Art, with permission).

---

4 Followers of the reformist Jan Hus who fought in the Hussite Wars 1419–1434
5 The original codex is kept in the Göttingen University library (Cod. Ms. philos. 63).

THE GERMAN PEASANTS' WAR 1524–26

This recreation from the Hussite Museum in Tabor, the Czech Republic) shows how the war wagon had been specially constructed. A peasant wagon fort is likely to have been a more improvised affair. Wagon forts were no longer deployed on the battlefield by the armies of the princes since they could rely on the squared formation of pikes to provide defensive cover. However, on campaign the baggage wagons would have been drawn up into tightly arranged circular or squared Laager encampments.[7] They still had tactical value for the infantry dominated peasant armies although their weakness soon showed through. (Image: Geoff Laws).

to adapt a military system which was, however, still feudal at its core.[6] As we shall see, the wagon fort became a preferred tactic of the peasants in the Central and Southern Germany theatres of the war, a point to which we must return.

What we know today as Switzerland emerged after the long struggle of the Swiss Confederation of cantons against the ambitions of the Habsburg dynasty of Austria. Swiss independence from the Holy Roman Empire was finally achieved after the battle of Dornach – the culmination of the so-called Swabian Wars (1498–1499). Here an army of Swiss infantry decisively beat Maximilian I's army skilled in the use of the halberd and pike in close quarter combat. One of the major factors contributing towards their military effectiveness was the ability of the Confederation to put a considerable number of men swiftly into the field. This had been greatly facilitated by the introduction of conscription in the middle of the fifteenth century. There were three categories which the local councils in the cantons could draw on – the *Auszug* – the elite fighters drawn from young unmarried men; the *Landwehr* – older men able to leave home when requested, and the *Landsturm* the open levy used in times of emergency whereby all men would be called up. In the cities, the guilds and the outlying communities, the local councils were expected to finance their own contingents with each soldier obliged to carry four to six days supply of food to the place of muster.[7]

Given the composition of the Swiss armies, which consisted of many poorer peasants, it is not surprising that in the second half of the fifteenth century the Swiss cantons responded more and more to the offers of pay from foreign powers. Members of the '*Auszug*' would be hired out, but soon these individual men realised they could become soldiers of fortune and the so-called '*Reisläufer*' (a journeyman warrior) was born. The final transition to a professional mercenary army coincided with the boom in precious metal mining and with it the possibility of higher taxes and easier access to credit – creating the economic conditions for such armies to be acquired. This change in the economics of warfare was far reaching. Each

---

6 Hoyer *Das Militärwesen*, p.21.
7 Cf. Miller, *The Army*, p.71.

individual soldier contracted by a mercenary commander or directly by a ruler was responsible for providing his own weapons and armour and for his own subsistence while on campaign.

In battle, the Swiss had been hailed as the 'New Romans' (Machiavelli) deploying tight formations of pike in front of a core of skilled halberdiers. By combining long stabbing and short slashing weapons, they gained a newfound security on the field of battle against the mounted man-at-arms. Such was their effectiveness that Maximilian gave orders to his field commander Georg von Frundsberg to raise and train such an army on German soil thus paving the way for the development of the Landsknecht armies of the Holy Roman Empire. In 1507, at the Imperial Diet of Constance, mercenary pay was regulated in a national agreement and fixed at four Rhenish guilders (Gulden) per month for an infantryman with the

This image by Albrecht Dürer was created 30 years before the war but gives a good representation of how a demi lancer would have appeared. This knight is clad in late gothic armour which was to be superseded by Maximilian style fluted armour. The breastplate is covered by a slashed tunic. He is wearing a sallet, some examples of which were highly decorated with heraldry. Note the lance which bears a fox tail which was often awarded for specific achievements. As a member of the *Rennfahne* such a knight would have carried no barding on his steed. (Graphische Sammlung, Albertina, Vienna, with permission).

rate doubled for experienced fighters who could serve in the front ranks – the so-called *Doppelsöldner*.[8]

The Development of Cavalry

The tactical deployment of Landsknecht or Swiss pikemen in squares became highly effective against the armoured knight. However, the warlords of the day understood the importance of mobile squadrons of light horse able to strike before such formations could be positioned.[9] The Imperial Diet of Constance noted the distinction between those fully armoured mounted men-at-arms and the more lightly armed free lancers.[10] These horsemen generally were to be found in the so-called *Rennfahne* – the vanguard. Contemporary illustrations show these mounted troops to be half armoured and their steeds devoid of bards (protective armour plates). Other depictions show these demi-lancers clad in their surcoats only or with surcoats covering armour.[11] During the campaign in Swabia and Franconia, the League army relied heavily on the deployment of horse to break up the peasant bands.[12] Although the wheellock pistol had been developed by this time with some commentators attributing its invention to Leonardo da Vinci, gun control laws decreed by Maximilian in 1517 and 1518 had retarded their use amongst the nobility. This did not prevent the inspired use of mounted hand gunners, as at Saverne, where the Duke of Lorraine used light horse to carry Italian arquebusiers into the fray at the village of Lupstein who were able to deploy tactically to create maximum damage to the rebels.[13] For those more heavily armoured knights in the ranks it was still a matter of chivalry to be engaged in the fray. The Truchsess of Waldberg, commander of the Swabian League army, provides a case in point having been wounded in the thigh in close combat at Königshofen.[14]

---

8   Miller, *The Army*, pp.98–99.
9   For a full discussion of changes in the use of mounted horse cf. Hans Delbrück 1920: *Geschichte der Kriegskunst im Rahmen der politischen Geschichte. Vierter Teil: Neuzeit* (Berlin: Georg Stilke, 1920) (Reprint Berlin: Walter de Gruyter, 1962) available at <http://www.zeno.org/Geschichte/L/Delbr%C3%BCck+Gdk+4.+Teil> (accessed 17 June 2022)
10 Cf. Hoyer *Militärwesen* p.30
11 Cf. Miller, *The Army*. p.v
12 As at Leipheim, Königshofen and Böblingen cf. Peter Blickle *Der Bauernjörg*, pp.157–165, 236–240, 199–202.
13 Nicolas Volcyr de Sérouville, 1526 *The History and Collection of the Triumphant and Glorious Victory Won Against the Seduced, Abuse Lutheran Mescreants of the Land of Daulsays and Others,* Paris, Galiot du Pré, Ch. 12 Available at: <https://gallica.bnf.fr/ark:/12148/bpt6k324157v/f46.item.r=volcyr%20de%20s%C3%A9rouville.zoom> (accessed 13 September 2022)
14 *Ibid*. p.238

WARFARE AT THE TURN OF THE SIXTEENTH CENTURY

This drawing by former mercenary Urs Graf pits the German Landsknecht together with a Swiss 'Reisläufer.' Generally distinguishable by the cross of St Andrews slashing on the hose and doublet on the part of the Landsknecht and the St George's cross slashing for the Swiss mercenary this may have required additional recognition marks for the heat of the battle particularly where these men were on opposing sides. It is possible that a white armband improvised with a tied piece of cloth around the upper arm was used in the case of those Landsknechts in the service of the peasants to distinguish them from those mercenaries in the pay of the princes, who may have worn a red cross sewn either on their doublet or bonnet. Woodcut by Urs Graf 1524. (Kunstmuseum Basel, Kupferstichkabinett, with permission).

Artillery

Although it is held that the peasants eschewed the use of cavalry on the field of battle (See Chapter 4) this was most certainly not the case as far as artillery and firearms were concerned. Both in Germany and Italy great strides were being made in the physics behind the construction of cannon and the science of ballistics.[15] Johannes Formschneider, some 30 years in the service of the city of Nuremberg as a master gunner (1440–1470) penned a '*Feuerwerks – und Büchsenmeisterbuch*'[16] that was passed on to his successor. Martin Merz appointed supreme commander of the artillery by

Various handwritten versions of a treatise on all aspects of ordnance written at the beginning of the fifteenth century by an unknown author had circulated but was finally printed in 1531 as *von der Büchsenmeisterey* (Matters of ordnance). By this time major advances in artillery and ballistics had been made. Title page of *Buechsenmeisterey von Geschoß, Büchsen, Pulver, Salpeter und Feurwergken* (Bavarian State Library, with permission).

---

15 For an exhaustive treatment of ordnance during this period cf. Jonathan Davies, *The Art of Shooting Great Ordnance* (Warwick: Helion Publishing, 2022).
16 Munich, Bavarian State Library Cgm 734.

Frederick I, Elector Palatinate in 1469, created his *Feuerwerksbuch* around 1460–1480[17] and is credited amongst other inventions with the development of the movable carriage for the cannon barrel. In 1496 the master gunner Philipp Mönch (born in 1457) produced his illustrated book '*büch der stryt vnd buchßen*'.[18] In 1510 Ludwig von Eyb zu Hartenstein wrote his *Kriegsbuch*[19] as a copy of the *Bellifortis*.[20] All these treatises were handwritten and illustrated and closely guarded but copied where possible until the first printed versions began to appear after the Peasants' War.[21]

Despite this renaissance in the science of warfare,[22] there was tremendous diversity in the typologies of cannon and methods of measurement which cried out for standardisation. According to one historian, by the onset of the sixteenth century some consensus amongst European gunmakers was beginning to emerge:

> the smallest and specialised types aside, artillery should be muzzle-loading and cast of bronze in one piece; a gun should have a high ratio of length to bore (from about 12:1 to powder 40:1) and it should fire iron balls using corned. Ordnance came to be classed by proportion and size, with individual pieces rated by the weight of their projectile: full half and double cannon for close siege work, with longer barrelled culverins of similar ball weights for more distant battery…while essential to the siege, heavy cannon and culverins were awkward in the open field. Battlefield use was therefore mostly restricted to the quarter cannon, the lighter culverins, sakers, falcon(et)s and other types firing balls of roughly 12–15 pounds and under.[23]

There were other design improvements. Trunnions (*Zapfen*) – horizontally cast lugs cast into the barrel at about the balancing point – allowed a cannon to be easily elevated and depressed with wedges. Gun carriages (*Lafetten*) also markedly improved with two wheeled carriages with a solid trail rendering aiming, firing and recoil more stable and permitting the attachment of a two wheeled limber for easy transport in the field. Lighter

---

17 Munich, Bavarian State Library Cgm 599.
18 Heidelberg University Library Cod. Pal. germ. 126.
19 Erlangen University Library, Ms. B 26.
20 The first illustrated manual of military technology written and illustrated by Conrad Kyeser of ä, Germany, and covering a thousand years of European weaponry.
21 1528 – Franz Helm wrote his '*Buch von den probierten Künsten*', Heidelberg, Cod. Pal. germ 128 and *Von der Büchsenmeisterey* finally made it into print in 1531 some 60 years after the invention of printing.
22 a particularly useful reference on the development of the science of combat and warfare <https://talhoffer.wordpress.com/2011/07/07/engineers-and-masters-of-warfare/> (accessed 22 June 2022).
23 Thomas Arnold, *The Renaissance at War* (London: Cassell 2001), p.28.

THE GERMAN PEASANTS' WAR 1524-26

Artillery nomenclatures are particularly confusing during this period.[24] With the exception of the Tyrolean peasants the rebels had no artillery at their disposal and had to rely on castles and city arsenals for their ordnance. Where they laid siege, heavy cannon (*Kartaunen*) were called forth, as at Würzburg, although these arrived too late. The Swabian League generally deployed lighter artillery pieces (falconets and sakers) into the field – they were counting on a relatively short campaign and heavy siege guns would have slowed down their mobility. Philip of Hesse included heavier pieces in his train as his initial target was the city of Mühlhausen in Thuringia. Selected images from *Zeugbuch Kaiser Maximilians 1502 Cod.icon 222* (Bavarian State Library, with permission).

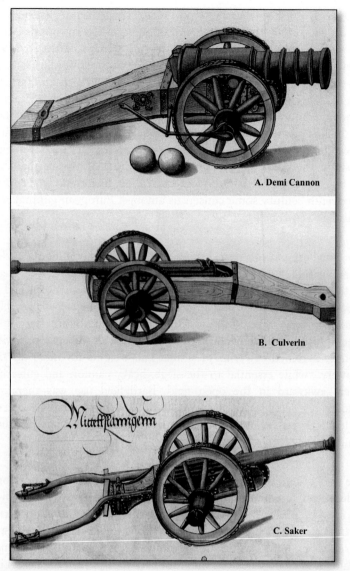

A. Demi Cannon

B. Culverin

C. Saker

pieces with two trails pulled by a single horse or for handling by a gun team had already developed during the fifteenth century. Some falconets, for example, had stumpy carriages on which a forked trail could be attached for quick transport by a single horse.[24]

Despite this standardisation it must be recognised that municipal and castle arsenals – which would become the main source of heavy armaments for the peasants – could contain old artillery pieces. Although wrought iron guns with a barrel of long iron staves joined edge to edge and held tight by a reinforcing outer casing of iron hoops had been technically superseded

---

24   Cf. Arnold T. *The Renaissance at War* (London: Cassell, 2001), pp.28–34. And Davies J. *The Art of Shooting Great Ordnance* (Warwick: Helion & Company, 2022)

WARFARE AT THE TURN OF THE SIXTEENTH CENTURY

by bronze cannon, many of these dangerous pieces, which were prone to explode, were still in circulation. In such situations the expertise of the master gunner was crucial. Such men came at a premium.[25]

Firearms

Firearms underwent a fast pace of development during the 1419–1434 Hussite Wars and became primary offensive weapons following the Battle of Kutná Hora in 1421. The so-called *píšťala* and the heavier *hákovnice* and *tarasnic* were cast iron 'handgonnes'. While adding a new dimension to infantry combat, loading and firing with a burning fuse or a glowing hook remained very cumbersome. A jet of fire shot out of the fuse hole after the fuse was lit, which greatly impaired aiming. Moreover, high humidity or rain could render the handgun useless.

Matters improved by the latter half of the fifteenth century with the replacement of the 'handgonne' by a lighter wooden arquebus – a barrel on a wooden stock capable of projecting round lead shot with considerable force. The word arquebus derives from the Dutch word *Haakbus* (German word *Hakenbüchse*) and originally referred to 'a handgun with a hook-like projection or lug on its under surface, useful for steadying it against battlements or other objects when firing'.[26] The addition of a shoulder stock, priming pan and matchlock mechanism in the late fifteenth century turned the arquebus into a handheld firearm and eventually the first firearm equipped with a trigger. The heavy arquebus, with a greater calibre (19mm) which was then called a musket, was developed to better penetrate plate armour, and appeared in Europe around 1521.[27]

A wood cut, probably by Erhard Schön (*circa* 1513), showing an arquebusier loading his matchlock. Note the powder horn and 12 wooden cartridge holders on a bandolier.

---

25 Miller, *The Army*, p.37.
26 Joseph Needham, *Science & Civilisation in China, vol. V:7: The Gunpowder Epic* (Cambridge University Press, 1986), p.426.
27 Bensing & Hoyer, *Der Bauernkrieg*, p.33.

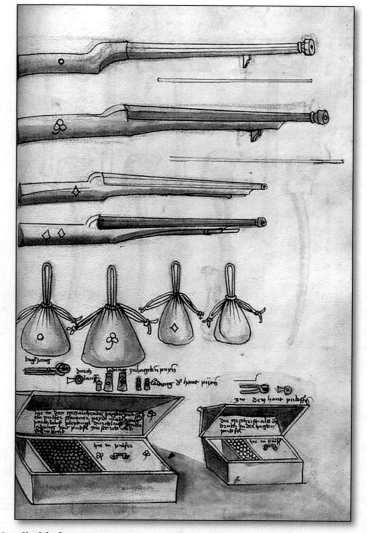

Hackbuts (hook guns) were recognisable by the lug at the end of the barrel which allowed for steadying on a parapet, bipod, or a forked stand. These varied in length and calibre. From Ludwig von, Eyb's *Kriegsbuch*, (University Library Erlangen-Nürnberg, MS.B 26, fol. 276r with permission).

Handheld firearms were generally ineffective in close combat (see box below). They needed to be deployed in concentrated formation and protected as part of a square of pikes and halberds to have any effect against the enemy. Such 'sleeves' of handgunners were relatively easy to manoeuvre compared to the chequered 'horns' of hand gunners positioned at the four corners of an infantry square.[28]

---

28 Cf. Arnold, *Renaissance*, pp.79–81.

WARFARE AT THE TURN OF THE SIXTEENTH CENTURY

Loading Handguns

To load the weapon, the arquebusier would unplug a wooden container (never called an apostle because there were 12 of them) from his leather bandoleer. He would then pour a pre-measured amount of loose gunpowder from the container into the muzzle of the handgun. Then a lead ball from a sack at his waist was placed into the muzzle and rammed home into the chamber with a wooden scouring stick (ramrod). The powder pan on the side of the barrel was opened and loose gunpowder from a powder flask was poured into it. A glowing match made from cord soaked in saltpetre was placed in the hammer of the lock. The arquebusier would aim his weapon. The trigger was pulled forcing the match into the pan, igniting the powder. The flash from the pan would travel into the chamber through a hole and ignite the powder. The expansion of gases would force the ball on its way to the intended target. Reloading took a long time, involving some 48 distinct movements.[29]

This woodcut from manoeuvres on the 'Arrival of Charles V in Munich in 1530' by Hans Sebald Beham shows wings of handgunners at the side of the squared formation of pike. The infantry was deployed in deep squared formations rather than phalanxes to prevent them from being run down by the heavily armoured cavalry. Handgunners had to stay close to the pikemen for defence against the cavalry but also for their concentrated volleys to be effective since accuracy could not be guaranteed with a matchlock. (Munich City Archive, with permission).

---

29 Irons L. smoothbore musketry. Available at http://scotwars.com/equip_smoothbore_musketry.htm last accessed 24 June 2022.

3

Military Organisation of the Peasants

Formation of the Band

Since the marketplace in a nearby town was the cornerstone of peasant social activity this defined the extent of such activity beyond the confines of the village or farmstead. However, there were other points of contact – manorial administrative courts, collection points for tax deposits and parish councils. According to one commentator the radius of contact for organising peasants was unlikely to exceed 10 to 15km of a marketplace.[1] The basic organisational unit of the peasants was the so-called *Haufe* – a derogatory term in German normally denoting a disorderly pile or heap which as we shall see was by no means the case and *Haufe* has come to be translated as band or troop. There was a discernible process by which a band came into being. Given the nature of the reasons for such organisation, a coming together would be deemed by the authorities a conspiracy of individuals and therefore had to take place in secret. Some meetings may have taken place in taverns, but the risk of eavesdropping pushed such gatherings out into the countryside. As numbers and confidence swelled, religious festivals became important meeting points where grievances would be openly discussed. Beyond a certain magnitude the core group would call a meeting at a prominent, traditionally distinguished location, for example, the Allgäu peasants assembled at the Leubas courthouse, the Rappertsweiler detachment of the Lake band came together at the hall in the monastery of Langnau.[2]

---

1   Elmar Kuhn < http://elmarlkuhn.de/aufsaetze-im-volltext/oberschwaben-und-bodenseeraum/bauernkrieg-in-oberschwaben/die-organisation/index.html> (accessed 16 June 2022).

2   Kuhn E. < http://elmarlkuhn.de/aufsaetze-im-volltext/oberschwaben-und-boden-

MILITARY ORGANISATION OF THE PEASANTS

At such meetings those present would swear their covenant and commit themselves to mutual assistance. Such an act rendered the *Haufe* a compulsory community and a military organisation beginning with the raising of a banner and the election of officers and ranks. Since some leaders and members were former Landsknechts, the military organisation mirrored in many respects that of a typical mercenary army of the day with companies known as (*Fähnlein*) and their subunits or squads known as *Rotten*. The word *Fähnlein* means a small flag which was used in a Landsknecht army to designate the origin of the company and was carried by an individual holding a special rank, the company ensign. Each *Haufe* and sub troop would have had their own banner which had a greater function than simply identification. (See section on peasant banners).

There were, however, differences in the way that Landsknechts and peasants were recruited. Whereas the nobility would use a contractor to recruit men to come to an appointed place of muster to join a specific company,[3] the peasant *Haufe* on the other hand would coalesce usually around a village from which the band established its identity. These might soon grow as men from other villages joined by means of pamphlets or threats. In this way, previously passive villages were urged to join thus expanding the reach of the peasant band. As a result, the insurgent armies were not fixed to a certain number and varied according to the number of local *Haufen* which could be mustered. The Hersfeld troop, for example, was 4,000 strong, whereas at Frankenhausen the troop numbered between 7,000 and 8,000. The Lake (Constance) band had 12,000 men while the

Village festivals were important gatherings at which peasants would discuss their grievances and organise their struggle. This is an extract from *'die Dorfkirchweih'*. Woodcut by Hans Sebald Beham 1539, (University Library Erlangen Nuremberg, Creative Commons).

---

seeraum/bauernkrieg-in-oberschwaben/ablaufmodell/index.html >(accessed 16 June 2022).

3   Miller, *The Army* pp.31–32.

Alsatian rebel army at Saverne (Zabern) ran to 18,000. Moreover, the bands and therefore armies were never at full strength, given the presence of a rotation system which allowed every third of fourth man to return home to tend to his crops. Given that the rebels were not static, seeking to unite with other troops and/or attack specific targets, there was always fluidity in the size of any specific contingent.[4]

Despite the presence of Landsknechts in their ranks who were clearly responsible for the adoption of the template of military organisation of the day, there was a practice which developed in certain bands which contributed to a major organisational weakness. Similar to a method of recruitment which had developed in the local militias, wealthier peasants could buy themselves out of the duty to serve in the ranks and send a substitute at the cost of 15 Kreuzer per week. This payment would increase at the second call up. This was reported for the peasants of the Ries and in the Tauber Valley and Allgäu bands.[5] The internal cohesion of a band could also be compromised by the practice of rotation (see Box below). In the Alsace the villages had to provide contingents which were replaced following a certain period (2–4 weeks). After the course of eight days, these men were relieved. In some areas there was a degree of coercion applied in recruiting peasants to the cause. In the Black Forest band, for example, those who refused to join would be punished with a secular ban (a stake would be driven in front of the door of the individual peasant's house). No one was allowed to have fellowship with him. The banned person was also denied any use of the commons.[6]

---

4   Blickle, *Der Bauernjörg*, p.322.
5   Oliver Gerstacker, *Was waren die Gründe für das Scheitern des 'gemeinen Mannes' im Bauernkrieg 1524–1526?* (Grin Verlag, 2016) p.6.
6   Balthasar Hubmaier had threatened refuseniks with the 'secular ban'. The consequences were then detailed in the manifestos of the peasants, see Heinrich Hug's Villinger Chronicle from 1495 to 1533, ed. by Chr. Roder. Tübingen 1883, p.117f. Also E. Müller, *Der Bauernkrieg im Kreise Waldshut*, Ettikon 1961, p.71.

MILITARY ORGANISATION OF THE PEASANTS

Gerber's Proclamation of 29 April 1525

I, Erasmus Gerber, commander, and the entire assembly of those at Altdorf and now at Marmoutier, proclaim with this letter to all, be they of high or low estate, rich or poor, that we shall and will stand by one another in the name of Jesus Christ our Lord, to the praise and honour of God, to confirm his Word, and for the consolation and aid of the poor common man, previously so badly led by the priesthood. It is therefore our friendly and earnest desire that each town, market, and village should send to us immediately, on receipt of this letter, their 'fourth man.' Those who are now with us in the army shall go home in order care for their wives, children, and properties; those who are now called up should remain in the army for eight days and change over again in eight days' time. Thus, we can remain assembled, and all be treated alike, so that this affair will take place for the good, consolation, and aid of the common man. The same (groups shall serve) all together if there is a general alarm in the land or an army march against us, when bells will be sounded one after another, so that we might retain our land, if God wills it. [We request a written reply]. Dated Saturday after Low Sunday, (29 April), anno '25].[7]

Organisation

The peasants were by no means lacking in their efforts to establish a rigorous organisational structure despite the disparate nature of the band. One of the most detailed set of articles was drawn up by the Franconian bands in a field ordinance at their camp at Ochsenfurt on 27 April. (See Appendix I) It established the articles of war; rules of engagement and martial law based on the Landsknecht model and established the hierarchy within the band specifying ranks and responsibilities.

At the head of each troop was a supreme field commander with four bodyguards. The commander had two lieutenants. The court-martial was presided over by a military magistrate (*Schultheiss*) but the policing of the band was assigned to a provost (*Profoss*) who had two bodyguards for protection and four officers for maintaining discipline within the ranks. A master of the ordnance (*Oberster Zeugmeister*) had overall responsibility for the procurement of artillery, shot and powder. The actual gunnery masters (*Büchsenmeister*) were highly sought after for their expertise at this time by both sides. When Florian Geyer, commander of the so-called Black Band

---

7   Franz, Quellen, 244 (no. 75) in Scott and Scribner p.244.

THE GERMAN PEASANTS' WAR 1524-26

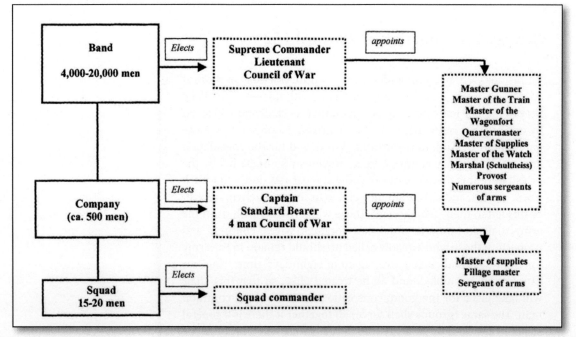

Peasant organisation mirrored that of a Landsknecht army, not unsurprising given the presence of numerous mercenaries in their ranks. (Author).

approached the city of Rothenburg ob der Tauber for its best artillery he also requested the services of the city's master gunners. Supervision of the baggage train was provided by the office of the wagon master (*Wagenmeister*) an important role given the tactical importance of the ability to quickly form a Laager or a wagon fort which would also require a master of the watch (*Wachtmeister*) to organise the camp guards. Logistics were covered by a commissary (*Proviantmeister*) who was expected to distribute the food impartially in the camp and was assisted by the foragers (*Quartiermeister*) and the master of the booty (*Beutemeister*).

As already stated, the organisational units deployed in a typical Landsknecht army – company (*Fähnlein*) and squad (*Rotte*) could also be found in the *Haufe*. A company, usually numbering between 400 to 500 men would be commanded by a captain (*Hauptmann*) and would be identified by the banner(s) raised by the band to which a colour sergeant (*Fähnrich*) would be assigned. Sergeants of arms (*Weibel*) were responsible for maintaining the battle orders which were drawn up collectively in the council of war. Such ranks would be occupied by seasoned Landsknechts. Each squad could number between 10 and 15 men and would be led by a corporal (*Rottenführer*).

In addition to these ranks, a figure of particular importance in the peasant army was the preacher whose role in sustaining morale and commitment was considerable. In Swabia, the political, economic, and religious basis for the peasant uprisings was the so-called 'Christian Union', the association of those villages, towns, judicial districts and individuals, including nobles, which accepted the 12 articles of the peasantry agreed in Memmingen. The three main Swabian bands were in effect the military instrument of this 'Christian Union' and as such constituted a direct challenge to the authority of the existing feudal and religious order. The pastors in the ranks were expected to preach the word of God and give righteous justification to the rebel cause. In central Germany, the most notable cleric in this respect was Thomas Müntzer who at Frankenhausen gave a rousing sermon to the rebels in the wagon fort above the town[8] to prevent capitulation to the combined armies of Philipp of Hesse and George of Saxony. Müntzer was not the only preacher at Frankenhausen, a further five were executed following the peasants' defeat.[9] Similarly the Franconian rebels had numerous preachers in their ranks who allegedly even formed their own 40 strong troop.[10]

Peasant Weaponry

Since *Frondienst* – the provision of labour at the request of the lord – also included military service, peasants and artisans were far from militarily deficient both in terms of available weapons and their use but could find themselves torn between allegiances during the conflict. Most territories and municipalities had adopted defensive ordinances which detailed numbers of required men and weaponry and laid down the periods of service. In the Palatinate, Württemberg, Franconian and Ortenau regions conscription to the local militias was a common practice.[11] A defensive ordinance laid down in the district of Worms, for example, obliged all adult males, except for certain village tradesmen, to make themselves available for defensive service. The village was expected to maintain a small arsenal of weapons containing six sets of light armour, pot helmets and handguns as well as 10 halberds all of which were to be subject to annual inspection. It is not unreasonable to assume therefore that every peasant household was in possession of at least simple cutting and stabbing weapons and/or that they had some experience in their use.

In some regions there were above average defensive systems. The best-known example was the Rothenburg militia (*Landwehr*) in Franconia. Here the villages around Rothenburg ob der Tauber were protected by a series of ramparts, ditches, and towers all of which required manning. The head of each village was appointed as captain and given the responsibility of mustering units capable of defending the territory. There was an expectation that weapons and armour were to be acquired at the peasant's own expense.[12] Typical weapons were the boar spear, the pitchfork, a long knife, a flail, sickle, and a scythe (here the blade was detached and refixed to the end of a staff to make into a polearm). Some weapons were improvised

---

8   Miller, *Frankenhausen*, pp.94–95.
9   *Ibid.*, p.112.
10 Scott and Scribner, p.60.
11 Hoyer, *Militärwesen* p.40.
12 Hans Wolterding, *Die Reichsstadt Rothenburg ob der Tauber und ihre Herrschaft über die Landwehr*. Rothenburg ob der Tauber 1965.

– a flail studded with nails could prove lethal for example – or a morning star fashioned from nails driven through a wooden club.

> ### Peasant Weaponry
>
> Representative example of weapons and armour carried by 20 of the Aichstetten contingent numbering 113 men in the Lake Band.[13]
>
> | | |
> |---|---|
> | Conz Metzler: | halberd and pike |
> | His Squire: | halberd |
> | Hans Stainli: | halberd |
> | Hans Futer: | boar spear |
> | Bailiff: | boar spear |
> | Henchell: | halberd, matchlock |
> | Michel Ungler: | pike, matchlock, two crossbows |
> | Jäck Scheich: | matchlock, boar spear, breastplate |
> | Hans Dreier: | matchlock, spear, halberd, two pikes, breastplate |
> | Crista Bander: | matchlock, halberd |
> | Conz Dingler: | matchlock, halberd, breastplate |
> | Müller: | pike |
> | Hans Genflin: | halberd, breastplate |
> | Jäck Stricher: | matchlock, breastplate |
> | Hans Rietmeyer: | halberd, dagger, breastplate |
> | Hans Ziggeler: | halberd |
> | Old Hans Gelter: | breastplate, matchlock |
> | Habs Wibner: | pike and body armour |
> | Young Crista Rott: | breastplate, boar spear |

The municipalities had weaponised by the end of the fifteenth century. Records from Strasbourg, Hagenau and Würzburg mention skilled marksmen (*Schützenmeister*) from the first third of the century. City inventories also give a sense of the size of an arsenal. In Nordhausen the city arsenal contained 164 handguns, 175 crossbows and 45 trained artillerymen. In the district of Dachau there is a record of a parade attended by 2,000 men with 452 in breastplates and 64 in jacks.[14] Almost all cities employed mercenaries from outside their territory. In 1504 Nuremberg, for example,

---

13 Blickle pp.173–174.
14 Hoyer, *Militärwesen*, p.41.

MILITARY ORGANISATION OF THE PEASANTS

This section from *Battle of the Naked Men and Peasants* by Hans Lützelberger shows the array of basic farming implements which those rebels who were not part of the local militia would have armed themselves with during the uprising. (National Gallery of Art, Washington licensed under Creative commons).

recruited soldiers from the Lake Constance area for deployment in the Palatinate war.[15] Cities thus became important sources of weapons and men during the conflict. As the rebellion grew and castles were stormed and city councils pressured to open their arsenals, a wider range of polearms became available – halberds, glaives, partisans, poleaxes, billhooks, bardiches and pikes. There is a record of the 'Eternal Council' in Mühlhausen ordering 225 pikes from a carpenter in Eisenach – initially for the municipal levy but these could have constituted part of the weaponry which Thomas Müntzer's band carried from the city to Frankenhausen.[16]

Handling such weapons required skill since their use required different fighting styles which differed between small scale skirmish warfare and larger scale mass combat.[17] The use of a pike necessitated considerable proficiency and training in formation, Similarly an arquebus or a crossbow

---

15   *Ibid.*
16   *Ibid.*, p.83.
17   Eckart Opitz, Militärgeschichtliche Aspekte des Bauernkrieges in Deutschland *Militärgeschichtliche Mitteilungen 28*. (Militärgeschichtliches Forschungsamt, vol. 28/2 1980) p.11.

THE GERMAN PEASANTS' WAR 1524-26

Mounted peasants must have been used as couriers and scouts but arguably the single most tactical reason for the defeat of the peasants was the absence of any mounted men-at-arms. Woodcut from Hans Burgkmair from the Triumph of Maximilian. (Public domain).

would not have been unfamiliar to certain peasants but since hunting was taboo for the lower classes, such weapons were not common unless the owner was a poacher and/or had acquired a firearm while in military service. As the handgun developed during the fifteenth century, some cities formed clubs for practising marksmanship so those townsfolk who joined the rebel ranks would have brought this expertise to the fray. Most certainly the peasant contingents which were enhanced by the presence of Landsknechts, would have brought considerable firepower to bear. The Lake Constance band was particularly well-equipped and it is said to have counted 4,000 hand gunners in its ranks.[18]

However, since this period predated the wheellock firing mechanism, the use of firearms, in particular the arquebus, as we have seen, could be a frustrating affair. Although handguns had become lighter as they developed through the fifteenth century and powder grinding devices had improved the range of an arquebus, loading and firing the gun with a glowing wick became quite cumbersome not to mention the problem of damp equipment.

Since most mounts were used as draught horses for pulling hay wagons and other farming equipment there was little hope of mounted peasant troops on mobile steeds ever emerging. There is only one mention of a troop of mounted rebels under the command of Claus Pfannenschmidt in the combined Mühlhausen band.[19] Ideological reasons may have been decisive. As expressed in some of the field ordinances mounted men symbolised the oppressors and as such were frowned upon in the ranks. In Müntzer's confession (under torture) he had argued that princes should ride out with a maximum of eight horses and 'knights with two'.[20] Nevertheless, mounted rebels were most certainly have been given scouting and messenger duties.[21]

---

18 Blickle, *Der Bauernjörg*, pp.173 and 180.
19 Bensing & Hoyer, *Bauernkrieg*, p.147.
20 Müntzer, Thomas in Matheson, Peter (ed.). *The Collected Works of Thomas Müntzer* (Edinburgh:T&T Clark, 1988).
21 Ordinance of the Rhineland Peasants Para 31. Cf. Appendix III.

MILITARY ORGANISATION OF THE PEASANTS

Paulus Hector Mair (1517-1579) was a sixteenth century German aristocrat, civil servant, and fencer. Like his contemporary Joachim Meyer, Mair believed that the medieval martial arts were being forgotten and was interested in preserving historical teachings intact. At some point in the latter part of the 1540s he commissioned what would become the most extensive compendium of German martial arts retaining Jörg Breu the Younger to create the illustrations for the text. Significantly a part of this treatise is dedicated to the handling of peasant weapons – notably the scythe, sickle, flail, and club which suggests that these had been used skilfully in mortal combat before.[24] This is a composite of plates available from the Wiktenauer collection (Bavarian State Library Cod. icon. 393(1) with permission).

The rebels had to rely on plunder to acquire artillery or by requisitioning pieces from city arsenals and were able to assemble considerable trains. Inventories of pieces taken following peasant defeats give an indication of this. After the battle of Königshofen, 49 wheeled artillery pieces were counted, plus 12 larger hook guns, 39 hook guns and 15 half calibre firearms. After the battles at Sulzfeld and Ingolstadt, 20 falconets, two bombards, two wall guns, five double hook guns, 43 hackbuts and four half hackbuts were recorded.[22] The rebels in the Alpenlands made their own cannon fashioned from drilled out lengths of tree reinforced by wrought iron bands.[23] [24]

Logistics

In general, the peasants were dependent on the plunder from castle and priories for weaponry and food. When it came to municipalities, supplies would depend on the political stance of the city council, the Rothenburg

---

22 Rainer Leng, Bauern vor den Mauern: Technische und taktische Aspekte des Sturms auf die Festung Marienberg in Würzburg in Fuchs F. and Wagner U. *Bauernkrieg in Franken* pp.141–180, (Würzburg: Königshausen & Neumann 2016), p.166.
23 According to the Wittenberger Chronik of 1730 a wooden cannon is supposed to have been seized from the peasants besieging the archbishop's Hohensalzburg fortress.
24 Translations of the methods of their use can be accessed via the Wiktenauer pages of the Historical European Martial Arts Alliance (HEMAA) <https://wiktenauer.com/wiki/Paulus_Hector_Mair> accessed 17 June 2022.

Contemporary images show that the design of the so-called 'ladder wagon' (Leiterwagen) has not changed since medieval times. There would have been variations in size (cf. the exaggerated wagon in Hieronymus Bosch's Haywain triptych) and some would have been boarded out in planks or with wickerwork. In attempting to fashion the hay wagon into a war wagon, reinforced boards were suspended from the side facing the enemy attack. The image to the left depicting a peasant wagon bristling with polearms is taken from Sheet five of Jacob Mürers Weissenauer Chronik. (Photo: Sonia, Zwickau with permission).

council, for example, repeatedly declined requests from the peasants to furnish them with field artillery, ammunition and weapons. However, faced with other city councils in Franconia opening their gates to the rebels, the ruling caucus finally relented on condition that they withheld the provision of any manpower.[25] Müntzer's march to Frankenhausen with a troop of 300 men was armed with only eight cart guns (*Karrenbüchsen*) provided by the Mühlhausen council but his call to arms which had included a request to the outlying areas to provide reinforced wagons and earthwork materials, failed to materialise. In the few instances where the rebels were able to triumph – as at Schladming in the Tyrol for example – the booty of eight falconets, three demi-culverins along with 30 hundredweight of gunpowder was not inconsiderable.[26]

Maintaining and distributing supplies of food for ever growing bands was a major logistical problem however.[27] The poor harvests of 1523 and 1524 which had both contributed to the outbreak of the war meant that food supplies in the villages and towns at this time were quite limited. Feeding a massive peasant army left the rebels with no other alternative but to plunder from those that had. The combined Mühlhausen and Eichsfeld Band's activities illustrates this well:

> The Cistercian abbey of Volkenroda ... was plundered and destroyed, the fishponds emptied and the livestock and food brought back to the peasant camp at Görmar, where they had erected two tents and a field kitchen. As they were distributing the booty, a large contingent of Eichsfelders arrived with eight or nine wagons full of cured meat, church bells, household goods and ironware, which they said they had taken from the convents in the Eichsfeld. Müntzer warmly greeted and admitted them as brothers. Seated on a horse he then

---

25   Franz Ludwig Baumann quoted in Hoyer *Militärwesen* p.84.
26   Hoyer *ibid.*, p.86.
27   Cf Volker Bach, Markets for Mercenaries: Supplying Armies in Sixteenth Century Germany in McWilliams M. (ed.) *Food & markets: proceedings of the Oxford Symposium on Food and Cookery* 2014 (London: Prospect Books, 2015) pp.33–45.

delivered a sermon to the camp and afterwards distributed the booty equally amongst the Mühlhausen and Eichsfeld rebels.[28]

The Counts of Gleichen based in Thüringia complained that their cellars had been drained by the Langensalza band and, itemised in detail their losses for the purposes of demanding compensation: 200 casks of wine, dried meat from 35 oxen, meat from 70 pigs, 200 barrels of beer, another 70 tuns of wine and more beer and 1,920 loaves of bread. They further complained that their ponds had been drained of fish –at once both a political act given that fishing rights was one of the 12 Articles and a way of increasing food supplies. The same fate befell the monasteries. Hans Müller von Bulgenbach, leader of the Black Forest band, ordered that the fishpond of the Abbey of St Jörgen be drained to get to the 300 carp which it contained.[29] Some priories delivered up food to avoid further damage to their property by the insurgents. The 'common priesthood of Speyer' for example had to promise to deliver 200 bushels of bread, 25 tuns of wine and 100 florins worth of meat to the Rheinhausen rebels.[30]

In some cases, there were serious crises in the supply of the troops, because the enemy had devastated the area through which the peasants passed, or because the supplies were exhausted as a result of prolonged encampment in one place. In the Tyrol the rebels could not rely on the provision of food from the municipalities since for geographical reasons these were few and far between. The enemy tried to capitalise on this and while contemporary descriptions paint a picture of marauding peasants looting and ransacking properties in search of food, the bands were at pains to organise its collection and distribution in a systematic way.[31] Field ordinances show that special ranks were created whose task it was to oversee and account for the gathering and assortment of foodstuffs (*Pfennigmeister*, the paymaster and *Proviantmeister*, or commissary). This latter rank existed at company level.

The Use of Landsknechts

When in March 1493 the Bundschuh movement in the Alsatian imperial city of Schlettstadt was crushed by the authorities before the uprising broke out, several of its leaders were imprisoned. One of these leaders, a Klaus Ziegler von Stotzheim, confessed that they had planned to establish contact with Swiss mercenaries. A Landsknecht was to be appointed in the Scherwiller area to recruit other mercenaries. Ziegler named a Landsknecht by the

---

28 Quoted in Miller, *Frankenhausen*, p.31.
29 Villinger Chronik quoted in Hoyer, *Militärwesen*, p.87.
30 Peter Haarer, *Eigentliche und Wahrhaftige Beschreibung des Bauernkriegs* 1531, (Halle: Max Niemeyer 1881 Kessinger Legacy Reprint) p.34.
31 Hoyer, *Militärwesen*, p.89.

name of Walter Claus who had offered to recruit up to 6,000 mercenaries to aid the conspiracy.[32]

While such claims may have been exaggerated, the authorities took such statements quite seriously and when in 1502 fresh Bundschuh incidents occurred in the Upper Rhine region and in the Speyer diocese, these were crushed before they could take hold lest they took on a more military character. More than any other protest movement of the century, the Bundschuh spoke to the heart of the Landsknechts particularly those who had been stood down and were immiserated during this so-called period of stand down (*Gartzeit*). They in return could be a potential backbone of this popular uprising since they were more mobile, knew how to maintain secrecy and understood the importance of good organisation and discipline.[33] During the last two Bundschuh uprisings (1513 and 1517), the authorities grew genuinely concerned at the sight of hungry and unemployed but politicised troops of Landsknechts marauding through the countryside.

When in 1525 unrest spread across Southern and Central Germany the authorities had to consider whether armies of Landsknechts recruited from within the region would be the most appropriate troops to take on the peasants. The Bavarian chancellor Leonhard von Eck was not the only one to warn against their use, preferring recruitment to take place in Bohemia or the Balkans. Konrad von Leonrod, a Bavarian official, accused the Swabian League of trying to catch a fox with a fox.[34] These apprehensions soon proved to be well founded for when the League Commander Georg Truchsess of Waldburg sought to give his army new orders to proceed against the peasants of Upper Swabia at the League camp in Dagersheim in March 1525 there was a mutiny.[35] They justified their refusal with three arguments: firstly that the peasants were in many cases their own flesh and blood, secondly that they received support from peasant communities in hard times when they had been stood down and thirdly as indicated above, that they had great affinity with the peasant cause.

As the war unfolded Landsknechts would fight both for and against the peasants. In many cases, they formed the backbone of the army as in the case of the Lake Band where estimates have them numbering one-third of the 15,000 strong rebel troop. Several peasant commanders had served as Landsknechts on the battlefields of Europe, notably Florian Geyer with his Black[36] Band in Franconia, Hans Müller von Bulgenbach who captained

---

32   Reinhard Baumann, *Landsknechte* (Munich: C.H. Beck Verlag, 1994). p.187.
33   *Ibid.*, pp.188–189.
34   Joseph Edmund Jörg, *Deutschland in der Revolutionsperiode von 1522-1526* (Freiburg im Breisgau, 1851), pp.240–242 in Baumann, *Landsknechte*, p.189.
35   For details of the outcome cf. Miller, *The Army*, pp.55–58.
36   Claims that this troop were dressed in some form of black uniform could not be substantiated and may have been nothing more than a black ribbon to distinguish what was a unit of no more than 200 men from the so-called Bright band (*Heller Haufen*).

the Black Forest band and Walther Bach the supreme commander of the Allgäuer. Generally, the important ranks of ensign (Fähnrich) and sergeant (Weibel), would also be reserved for experienced mercenaries.

Opinion could be divided on the use of Landsknechts. Wendel Hipler, the commander of the Odenwälder Band and one of the leading figures of the revolution, argued for a cadre troop of Landsknechts responsible only for training, while Walther Bach, argued in the Allgäu Peasants' Council for the recruitment of Swiss *Reisläufer*.[37] Neither came to pass. A consensus emerged not to engage wholesale units of Landsknechts since these were not only expensive but would not in the end be fighting out of conviction.[38] Nevertheless those individuals who joined the peasant ranks could be regarded as the combat elite providing valuable know how in tactics, drills and the use of firearms.

A further group – the miners of Saxony, Bohemia and the Tyrol – presented a significant military boost for the peasants. Their occupation required great social cohesion and discipline and miners had the right to carry weapons subject to the permission of the mine agent.[39] Since miners were also subordinate to their respective territorial lordships, they also had to perform military service as part of the local militia. Ludwig the Rich of Bavaria-Landshut is reported to have recruited 100 of the straightest and best Rattenberg ore miners in 1468 in exchange for a week's pay to Sigmund the Wealthy of Tirol, who had requested that they be armed with pikes, firearms and halberds, in addition to a sword and throwing axe. For military identification purposes they were to be clad in a white smock and red hat.[40] Similarly in 1493 the Emperor Maximilian had included miners as part of his army and had mining laws changed to enable their release and payment. However, given that their labour was needed to extract the precious metals used to finance military campaigns, priority was given to other sources of mercenary soldier.

A complex picture emerges when considering those Landsknechts who served in the armies of the nobility. These mercenaries who played a significant role in defeating the peasants could wreak bloody carnage but could also show restraint since a dead peasant meant no potential ransom money. Since a number of the peasants had to leave the land, some aspects of the recruitment of soldiers were of special importance. Many young men from the Southwest German villages had followed the recruiters of the

---

37 Hoyer, *Militärwesen*. p.91.
38 Baumann, *Landsknechte* p.191.
39 Heinrich Achenbach, Die deutschen Bergleute der Vergangenheit in *Zeitschrift für Bergrecht*, vol. 12 1871 in Hoyer, *Militärwesen*, p.80.
40 Joseph Bühl, Urkundliche Mittheilungen aus dem gräflich Preysing'schen Archiv zu Hohenaschau, in: *Erster Jahresbericht des historischen Vereines von und für Oberbayern für das Jahr 1838* (München, 1839), p.416 in Karl-Heinz Ludwig Bergleute im Bauernkrieg 1525-1526: Salzburger zwischen Habsburg und Wittelsbach — oder politisch darüber hinaus? - *Mitteilungen der Gesellschaft für Salzburger Landeskunde* (2009): pp.191–248.

THE GERMAN PEASANTS' WAR 1524-26

By the sixteenth century, silver, copper, and iron ore extraction had become a major source of wealth for the Habsburgs and those nobles and merchants who had bought mining rights from the same. The most prominent of all the mining towns of central Europe at the end of the fifteenth and the beginning of the sixteenth centuries were Joachimstal in Bohemia, Mansfeld in the county of that name, Schneebergt, Annaberg, and Marienberg in Saxony, and Schwaz in the Tyrol. Common grievances – hazardous working conditions, irregular wage payments and overpriced foodstuffs could be added to those articulated in the 12 Articles. Less well known is the significance which mining had for the military by the late Middle Ages. Contemporary images also show that some form of breastplate was worn to protect the body from the harsh working conditions. As the military prowess of this group grew, scouts were often tasked with ascertaining the most accurate possible numbers of miners present in the ranks of the enemy in order to establish the numbers of mercenaries who would be needed to match them.[41] In the alpine uprisings a free company of miners was recruited in Styria numbering between 50 to one and two hundred men who were present at Radstadt.[42] Source: DE RE METALLICA LIBRI XII by Georg Agricola 1556 (Wellcome Collection, Creative Commons (CC BY-4.0).

peasant armies in the years before the Peasants' War.[42]This was related not only to the extensive use of mercenaries in place of the previous feudal army, but also to the increase in the population. In the villages, the employment of free labourers in agriculture and village trades increased thus providing a reserve army for recruiting mercenaries. According to the respective needs and the financing possibilities, a Landsknecht usually served for only a few months and after their discharge had to find either a new military service or another activity. The contact with their homeland was undoubtedly not completely lost during this period, even though the Landsknecht system

---

41   *Ibid* p.213.
42   *Ibid* p.218.

showed a tendency to gradually develop a class of professional warriors. The mercenaries acquired some characteristics that the peasants lacked: mobility and the military experience of fighting in a closed unit under fire and or attack from mounted men-at-arms.

Banners (See plates E - I and P1)

Since Roman times, the terms 'banner' and 'flag' had been used respectively to describe the attachment of a cloth to a crossbar or to a pole. The flag primarily represented a sign of authority and any violation of the same was tantamount to dishonouring a regent or noble. In civic uprisings in the Middle Ages the guilds, for example, carried their banners to the public assemblies.[43] In miners' revolts, the 'throwing up of the flag' was always seen as a sign of the miners' will to fight as in Schneeberg in 1498. In the Joachimstal treaty of 1525 the miners' banner was to be kept in a drawer with two locks for which the miners and the council each had a key. This meant that the miners would require the consent of the council before any rally could be properly organised.[44] The flag also had a tactical military function enabling the identification of specific units but also acting as a symbol of honour, unity, and attachment to that unit. To raise a banner was a major step for a group of peasants, cemented by swearing an oath of allegiance to the same rather than the authority governing the land. The flag thus had to be defended at all costs.

From the tenth century onward, there was an interchange of secular and ecclesiastical motifs. Evidence suggests that the cross of Christ and a flag were carried side-by-side as army standards. Since the written sources in most cases give no indication of the concrete graphic design of the peasant banners, the appearance of the flags during the peasant wars can only be surmised. The flags described in this section provide clues to the self-image and goals of the rebels, as they applied to the specific uprising. What we can glean from contemporary images is that the motif of Christ suffering on the cross played a significant role in banner design. Other reported designs used Latin lettering. The peasants of Sundgau in Upper Alsace for example carried a flag with the words 'Jesus Christus' in gold letters. In Strasbourg, two white flags with the letters NDMIA (*Nomen domini manet in aeternum*) were carried while the Ebersheimmünsterer Band bore a flag with the letters VDMIA (*Verbum domini manet in aeternum*): 'the word of

---

43 Barbara Huber, *Im Zeichen der Unruhe: Symbolik bäuerlicher Protestbewegungen im oberdeutschen und eidgenössischen Raum 1400–1700*, PhD Philosophisch-historischen Faculty of the University of Berne submitted 11 November 2005, pp.172–178.

44 Siegfried Sieber, Der Joachimsthaler Aufstand 1525 in seinen Beziehungen zu Sachsen, *Bohemia*, (München vol. 4, 1 January 1963) p.52.

the Lord endures forever'. This was the motto of the Lutheran Reformation, a confident expression of the enduring power and authority of God's Word.

In the county of Henneberg the peasants planned a design which would involve a crucifix:

> alongside it, fish, bird and wood shall also be painted; and the crucifix shall signify the eternal Gospel and the handling of the word of God; and by the birds and wood shall be understood that all these things shall be free.

Two other Peasants' War flags show simple crucifixes, one in Schwäbisch Hall and one from Schmalkalden. Similarly, the author of the Metz Chronicle mentions in connection with the outbreak of the Peasants' War in Alsace a flag with a crucifix and peasant implements. In the conflict in the Alpine lands the rebels carried a crucifix at the head of their army. The striking feature of these flags is that they do not bear any reference to heraldry which would denote affiliation to the nobility.

In the German Peasants' War, an additional motif was the St Andrew's cross which is detailed in the field ordinance of the Upper Swabian peasants: the banner shall be red and white and the cross shall be alternately red and white. The St Andrew's cross is a diagonal cross, the emblem of St Andrew, the patron saint of the house of Burgundy. This originally dynastic insignia was incorporated into the Burgundian coat of arms because of the marriage of Maximilian I with Mary of Burgundy and was adopted into the imperial insignia. While the Upper Swabian Band acknowledged this heraldic symbol, the imperial eagle remained absent from its banner.

Given the presence of Landsknechts on both sides it was inevitable that some form of field recognition would be necessary. We can surmise from the report of the priest Johann Herolt from Schwäbisch Hall who described how the peasants flagrantly wore white crosses sewn onto their headgear as a sign of their band membership, and that this practice would have extended to any mercenaries in their midst. One might be tempted to infer that the Swabian League's Landsknechts wore red crosses since the Swabian League banner was a red cross on a white banner.[45] However, the German imperial banner consisted of a red ensign with a continuous white cross. As the emperor's main army flag, such a flag had been used as the imperial cross flag since 1298, with other dynasties and rulers also adopting this flag motif. In contrast the Herbitzheim band in the Saarland is reported to have had eight white ensigns with a red St Andrew's cross sewn on them.

Two flags illustrate that the insurgents also chose to display 'self-portraits' to represent who was participating in the uprising. The Deiningen band in the Ries (between Donauwörth and Dinkelsbühl) bore a flag depicting a

---

45   Günther Franz (Ed.), *Quellen zur Geschichte des Bauernkrieges* (Tübingen, 1876) p.417.

MILITARY ORGANISATION OF THE PEASANTS

peasant and a Landsknecht extending their hands out to each other. This image expresses the strong presence of Landsknechts and their influence on the military organisation of the bands. In some cases, guild banners were used. The Appenzellers are reported to have carried a large red guild flag when they stormed the monastery at Rohrschach. Similarly, the scribe of the Truchsess von Waldburg reported a vintner's ensign being observed during his campaign against the peasants. These carried no emblematic meaning and would have been used solely for military signalling and identification.

It was a significant risk to have a flag painted or sewn and raised and this was seen as a clear act of resistance. Sittich von Berlepsch, Duke George's official in Salza (today known as Bad Langensalza), felt compelled to write to his lord in mid-April 1525 about Müntzer's raising of a flag in Mühlhausen, the neighbouring municipality:

> The Allstedter (i.e. Müntzer) has had a white flag made from 30 ells of coarse silk, on which has been painted a rainbow with the words Verbum Domini Manet in Eternum and a verse declaring 'This is the emblem of the Eternal League of God: let all those who will stand by the league assemble hereunder'. He has placed this pennant next to the pulpit in St Mary's and let it be known that he would be the first to carry it in the field. He also plans to recruit two thousand foreigners (as soldiers) …[46]

The rainbow motif seems to have taken hold amongst the peasants at Frankenhausen. Hans Hut who had escaped the carnage in the town confessed this upon his arrest in Augsburg in 1527:

> God was on the subjects' side for the peasants had painted a rainbow on every banner which they displayed to which Müntzer explained that (the rainbow) was a sign of God.[47]

Since the raising of a flag was an act of great importance during the uprising because it signalled a mobilisation in earnest, it is not surprising that terms of surrender included their handover if not physical destruction as was demanded as part of the Treaty of Weingarten.

In the summer of 1524, the first uprisings of the Peasants' War took place in the area of the earlier Bundschuh conspiracies in southwestern Germany, but this emblem depicting a form of leather shoe made held together by straps, seldom appeared during the war. Only two flags with the Bundschuh as a symbol have survived: one as a sole emblem from St Trudpert in the

---

46   Letter to Duke George of Saxony – translation from Scott and Scribner, p.146.
47   Quoted in Christian Meyer, Zur Geschichte der Wiedertäufer in Oberschwaben. Die Anfänge des Wiedertäufertums in Augsburg. *Zeitschrift des Historischen Vereins für Schwaben und Neuburg* (1874) pp.207–253 and p.241.

southern Black Forest and one from Mömpelgard combined with a stag horn. A third Bundschuh flag resembling the original commissioned by Joss Fritz is mentioned in the Metz Chronicle as having been observed at the end of April or the beginning of May 1525 in Northern Lorraine.[48]

Discipline and Decision Making

The Peasants' War archival sources pay special attention to the democracy practised in the peasant bands. The fact that the military leaders were elected and that the supreme commander could take certain measures only after consultation and with the agreement of the whole band via the so-called *Ring* were indicators of the rebel mistrust of the existing hierarchy. Peasant councils were set up as control organs as in the case of the Molsheim band in Alsace, which proscribed a majority of four peasants to two Landsknechts in a six-man war council.[49] However an examination of the leadership of the peasant bands reveals that they were often fronted by men who mediated between the peasant villages and the outside world such as parish clergy, innkeepers and even petty nobles. Military leadership might be delegated to former/existing Landsknechts but there could often exist an uneasy tension within the leadership regarding the direction of travel the band should take both politically, geographically and militarily.[50] From a military point of view such tensions resulted in delays and missed opportunities as experienced soldiers were unable to bring their expertise to bear.[51] It is highly likely that a system of delegation was employed with representatives attending the *Ring* having to report back – this was certainly the practice in the Landsknecht camp.[52] Only through delegation could the problem of communication in the open air be solved.

Internal discipline was an issue on several counts. The field ordinances give an indication of the extent to which this could escalate concerning the spoils of the expedition against a monastery or castle (see Appendices). In the case of the Franconian peasants, the Tauber Valley band showed considerable restraint after stripping out the contents of the castles and abbeys they ransacked, with the booty master laying everything of value out on a field for sale with the proceeds being handed over to the

---

48 Frieder Leipold, *Das Wappen der Revolution – Der Bundschuh als Symbol*, Hausarbeit Ludwig-Maximilians-Universität München 2015, p.23.
49 Baumann, *Landsknechte*, p.191.
50 Cf. Franz G. Die Führer im *Bauernkrieg in Bauernschaft und Bauernstand 1500–1970* Göttingen 1977 and Roy Vice, The Leadership and Structure of the Tauber band during the Peasants War in Franconia in *Central European History*, Volume 21, Issue 2 June 1988, pp.175–195.
51 Eckart Opitz Militärgeschichtliche Aspekte des Bauernkrieges in Deutschland *Militärgeschichtliche Zeitschrift*, vol. 28 Issue 2 1980 pp.13.
52 Miller, *The Army*, pp.56–57.

leadership council.⁵³ As events unfolded, questions would arise as to the extent to which retribution was to be exacted – some nobles and prelates offered up their food stores and other goods in return for safe passage and agreement to spare the fabric of their buildings. On numerous occasions such agreements were broken – a result of the inevitable mix of radical and moderate elements within any band.

The Role of Women

Given a male dominated historiography relying on source material written by male representatives of the nobility and clergy, the absence of a 'herstory' of the Peasants' War is palpable. It is inconceivable that women did not play their part in this most significant popular uprising by accompanying their men on their forays, plundering priories as at Heggbach near Baltringen and negotiating with the authorities as in efforts to spare the city of Mühlhausen after the defeat at Frankenhausen and in undertaking courier duties in Alsace.⁵⁴ A contemporary engraving by Lucas Cranach the Elder depicts a group of women attacking a group of clerics.⁵⁵ The most notable female protagonist during the rebellion was Margarete Renner who hailed from Böckingen – a suburb of Heilbronn. At the time of the war, she was the widow of a Peter Abrecht – a tenant farmer or *Hofmann* through whom she received the nickname *Schwarze Hofmännin*. In 1520, she had lodged a complaint with the lords of her manor regarding their refusal to pay a bond to release her husband and to perform *Frondienst* and had their entitlement to grazing, water and other rights denied by the Heilbronn council. During the war she accompanied Jäcklein Rohrbach and took part in the Weinsberg massacre and the battle of Böblingen. Legend has it that after the gauntlet of pike at Weinsberg she is said to have urged the peasants to use the belly fat of Count Ludwig von Helfenstein to grease their weapons against rust and to smear their shoes. It is reported that she herself did not engage in combat but spurred on the men in her band. In contrast to the fate of Rohrbach she was imprisoned in Heilbronn but released following an intervention by the lord of her manor who claimed her main crime was an 'unguarded mouth'.

---

53 Peasants' War documents from the State archive in Nuremberg as quoted in Vice, *The Leadership*, p.187 & p.189.
54 Kobelt-Groch, Marion. '*Von armen frowen* und, *bösen wibern*' – Frauen im Bauernkrieg zwischen Anpassung und Auflehnung' Archiv für Reformationsgeschichte, vol. 79, no. jg, 1988, pp.103–137. Franziska Neumann, Der selektive Blick. Frauen im Bauernkrieg zwischen Frauen und Geschlechtergeschichte, in: Schattkowsky, Martina (Hrsg.): Frauen und Reformation. Handlungsfelder, Rollenmuster, Engagement, (Leipzig Universitätsverlag 2016), pp.153–170.
55 <http://www.zeno.org/Kunstwerke/B/Cranach+d.+%C3%84.,+Lucas%3A+Frauen+%C3%BCberfallen+Geistliche+%5B2%5D> (accessed 21 October 2022).

THE GERMAN PEASANTS' WAR 1524–26

Engraving by Sebald Beham of a peasant couple carrying a distaff and flail dating 1537 Digital collection of the University Library Erlangen Nuremberg Signatur H62/AK 697 (Creative Commons 1.0).

4

1524 The Outbreak of the War in the Southwest

Chronology

23 June	Stühlingen Uprising
24 June	Band assembles in Bonndorf
18 July	Peasants ransack Charterhouse at Ittingen and free Reformist cleric
24 August	Stühlingen rebels ally with the town of Waldshut.
2 October	Hegau uprising in Hilzingen
	Stühlingen Band marches through the upper Black Forest
	Open rebellion in Klettgau
	Truchsess von Waldburg receives his commission from the Archduke Ferdinand of Austria to command the military response
November	(middle) Revolt spills over into Breisgau
	Thomas Müntzer the radical reformist cleric visits the Hegau and Klettgau regions – remains until January.
14 December	Black Forest peasants suffer a defeat at Donaueschingen

The Peasants' War broke out in the summer of 1524 on the southern fringes of the Black Forest near the Rhine River and the border of the Swiss Confederation. This primarily agricultural area which bordered on the regions of the Hegau, Klettgau, and Thurgau (see map) had seen seven lean years between 1513 and 1519, culminating in famine and plague and this had not been followed by better times.

The devastating storms and hailstorms of January and July 1524 in the Hegau region seemed to prove the astrological prophecies of Reynmann's Practica right – at least in the meteorological sense. For those who also believed in a coming storm between the peasantry and their overlords

THE GERMAN PEASANTS' WAR 1524-26

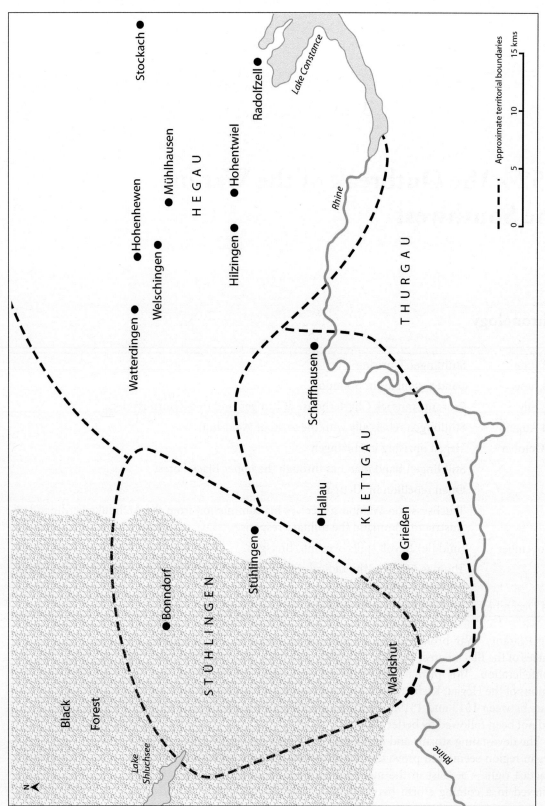

Map 1. Area of Outbreak 1524

1524 THE OUTBREAK OF THE WAR IN THE SOUTHWEST

there was also steadily mounting evidence. On 30 May for the first time the subjects of the monastery St Blasien refused to pay their tithes. On 23 June, the peasants in the County of Stühlingen rose up after the Countess of Lupfen demanded in the middle of the harvest that they should collect snail shells for her maids to spin thread. This proved to be the final straw. A day later the Stühlinger joined the villagers of Ewattingen and Bettmaringen and gathered in Bonndorf where they drafted a list of grievances, raised a banner[1] and appointed a captain by the name of Hans Müller from Bulgenbach, Then, on 18 July in the Thurgau region there were iconoclastic[2] acts by the peasants as they stormed the Ittingen Charterhouse to free the Protestant preacher Hans Oechsli who had been arrested by the authorities in the town of Stein am Rhein.

The incident at Ittingen resonated across the Swiss Confederation and as the Protestant doctrine in various forms appeared to be spreading alarmingly fast in the triangle between Waldshut, Zurich and Constance, the Archduke Ferdinand at the Habsburg headquarters in Innsbruck began to consider measures against the 'Lutheran sect' and the 'Bundschuh'[3] as he called it in the Hegau. He concentrated his attention on the town of Waldshut where the reformist preacher Balthasar Hubmaier was particularly active. Waldshut proved to be not only a hotbed of resistance to the authorities it also challenged the established church having expelled 12 Catholic priests in May. Ulrich von Habsberg, an Austrian military commander of the four Black Forest towns (Rheinfelden, Säckingen Laufenburg and Waldshut) felt compelled to write to the Archduke in June:

> There is serious trouble in Waldshut, where those who would obey his princely grace [archduke Ferdinand] dare not make a move. ... All those under my command are willing to help punish Waldshut for its disobedience, but it will take firearms at the very least ... If no action is taken, Laufenburg and Säckingen and the Black Forest will likewise shortly be in revolt. Most of the inhabitants of Rheinfelden are refusing to pay the prince the military composition fine (Wehrgeld) or the war levy (Hilfspfennig) and have threatened to kill the councillors if they are forced to pay.[4]

---

1   Described by Heinrich Hug from the Chronicle of the Villingen Town Council as 'A banner of white, red and black colours of the House of Austria', It may have carried an inscription in black since the colours of Austria at the time were red and white stripes, but this is not known.
2   Iconoclasm – Religious symbols were derided by a number of Protestant reformers who called for their destruction.
3   There had been a previous uprising in 1460 in the county of Hewen directed at Counts of Hohenlupfen cf. Tom Scott, *Town, Country, and Regions in Reformation Germany,*(Brill, 2005), p.105.
4   Translation from Scott and Scribner p.120.

THE GERMAN PEASANTS' WAR 1524–26

Archduke Ferdinand I, (1503–1564) Portait by Jan Vermeyen, (Bemberg Foundation, with permission).

In late July, the Bonndorfer (Stühlinger) Band under Hans Müller von Bulgenbach made its temporary base in the town and demanded from their lord, Landgrave Sigismund von Lupfen, a reduction of the tax burden, a reduction in their labour obligations, the right to freely use the forests and waters of his territory and the abolition of arbitrary prison sentences. On 24 August 1524, an 'evangelical brotherhood' was declared between the citizens of Waldshut and the Stühlingen peasants.

Within a week of the declaration, the Archduke summoned his councillors, the Counts von Lupfen and the other local nobles, to a meeting at Radolfzell on Lake Constance, to discuss the insurrection. However, his options were limited. The preferred military intervention was difficult since most of the available troops in the area were in Northern Italy in the pay of Charles V. Some form of negotiation was going to be necessary to buy time.

A meeting was arranged at Schaffhausen between the peasants and the lord to which the peasants sent a delegation. At the meeting they were asked to kneel before the count, surrender their banner, admit their wrongdoing, and swear their allegiance to the nobility. They refused. Eventually the peasants of Stühlingen accepted a standstill agreement lasting several weeks and arbitration proceedings in October which bought the authorities some time. Meanwhile in Hilzingen across in the Hegau region there was a separate flare up. The authorities there had become concerned at developments in the surrounding area and to control the situation had issued a strict ban on carrying weapons and ringing the storm bells.[5] The church festival on 2 October, to which about 3,000 people were expected to come, needed to be a peaceful affair but despite the ban, the storm bells were tolled and 800 armed peasants assembled there and formed an alliance.[6]

On 6 October, the Villingen town council learned that the peasants of Stühlingen had regrouped and were on the move, marching northward,

---

5   Karl Müller, Gernot Peikert, Die Rolle der Glocken im Bauernkrieg, in *Kriege, Krisen, Friedenszeiten im Hegau* Jahrbuch des Hegau-Geschichtsverein e.V (Singen/Hohentwiel, 2014), pp.49–64.

6   < http://www.bauernkriegsmuseen.de/hilzingen.htm > (accessed 24 June 2022).

1524 THE OUTBREAK OF THE WAR IN THE SOUTHWEST

via Wutach to Bachheim, where they camped and formed three troops. An emissary of the peasants sent word to the inhabitants of the town of Bräunlingen that they should certainly not oppose the peasants, otherwise they would have to be treated as enemies. During the night, the peasants continued their march which took several days and nights to assess the mood amongst the people and win support. By 10 October the band had grown to 3,500 peasants.

On Tuesday 11 October the insurgents marched 1,500 strong to Donaueschingen where they learned that a force of 1,800 foot and 200 horse under the command of Hans Jacob von Landau, Wolf Dietrich von Honburg and a Lord von Lowenberg was on its way. On receiving this news, the peasant troop moved to Erwattingen where they received a delegation from the authorities and an agreement was reached to set up a twelve-man court of arbitration to settle the peasants' grievances. Some days earlier the authorities had reached an agreement with the peasants of Hilzingen who were to have their grievances heard before a court in Stockach. Although hostilities were temporarily halted, there was a further insurrection in the middle of November 1524 where, at the mill at Klengen in the Brigach Valley, a number of dissatisfied peasants gathered and agreed on a reform programme of 16 articles.

Hans and Burkhart von Schellenberg – the lords of Hüfingen – fled their residences and brought their most valuable possessions to safety behind the walls of the city of Villingen. Hüfingen became the assembly point for the newly formed Brigach Valley band after the Schellenenbergs had fled. The people from the Brigach Valley had now elected two captains: Oswald Meder from Rietheim and Hans Hecht from Dürrheim. In addition, the captain of the whole peasantry, Hans Müller from Bulgenbach, suddenly

Villingen was a town under Austrian control. During the Protestant Reformation it remained Catholic and became a place of refuge for those nobles threatened by the actions of the Black Forest peasants. In 1530 the Archduke Ferdinand awarded the town a new coat of arms for its loyalty to both the regime and the Catholic faith. Engraving by Matthias Merian from Topographia Sueviae (Swabia), 1643 Bavarian State Library, with permission.

THE GERMAN PEASANTS' WAR 1524–26

appeared in Emmingen. Whether he had been summoned or appeared on his own initiative is unclear.

For the first two weeks of December the peasants roamed the countryside drumming up support which was not always forthcoming. On 9 December envoys from the imperial city of Rottweil, acting on behalf of the lords of Schellenberg, sought to negotiate with the leaders of the so-called 'New Band'. Their efforts proved fruitless. In the following days Meder and Hecht crisscrossed the land at the head of their band finally appearing before the gates of Donaueschingen. In Villingen the authorities had denounced the peasant cause and had been keeping track of events. Word was sent to Rudolf von Ehingen at Tuttlingen to raise a troop of horsemen:

Albrecht Dürer engraved several studies of peasants. Three peasants in conversation completed towards the end of the fifteenth century reveals some of the detail of peasant costume of the day. (Kulturhistorisches Museum Magdeburg, with permission).

He (von Ehingen) arrived here on the Wednesday 14 December around 8:00 a.m. with 40 horsemen, ... A council was held and the captains were told to be at the churchyard at 11:00 a.m. At noon they marched out with four hundred men. foot and horse, and five field guns. When the troop came to the Brigach Valley, the peasants got wind of our men and took flight towards Wolterdingen; the vanguard and the horse gave chase, but they had made a circle with wagons and carts. which greatly confused the horsemen, although some peasants were run through by the knights. Then they marched to Bräunlingen, in search of our enemies. but there was no one there, so we marched in order to Hüfingen, where we remained overnight, and in the morning 15 December we marched home. On Friday 16 December the horsemen rode off to Tuttlingen. and on the Sunday after St Lucy's Day 18 December a garrison of 50 men from Rottenburg and Horb arrived.[7]

---

7   Translation of the report by Heinrich Hug from the Chronicle of the Villingen Town Council. Scott and Scribner, p.119.

1524 THE OUTBREAK OF THE WAR IN THE SOUTHWEST

The surviving peasants disappeared where each could hide most quickly – in the remote valleys of the Black Forest. Thus ended the first bloody clash of the Peasants' War. Word soon spread that Villingen was nothing but a 'pit of murderers' (*Mördergrube*). Hans Mueller von Bulgenbach, however, was still at large and by now a wanted man with the Archduke Ferdinand ordering that he be despatched 'without much fuss and in secret'. It was clear, as 1524 drew to a close, that hostilities in the Habsburg territories were far from over and that for the wider region incorporating Württemberg and Upper Swabia there was a new additional threat for the Swabian League – the authority responsible for keeping the peace[8] – in the person of the exiled Duke of Württemberg determined to retake his Duchy – if needs be with the assistance of the peasants.

Ulrich of Württemberg 1487-1550, was a profligate and unpopular ruler of the Duchy which he lost in 1519 having been exiled by the Swabian League which they sold to Emperor Charles V. In exile he never lost sight of the possibility of recovering Württemberg and around 1523 also he announced his conversion to the Protestant faith. His opportunity came with the outbreak of the German Peasants' War where he posed as an ally of the lower classes garnering some support. He invaded Württemberg in February 1525, prompting the League to mobilise against him. However, the Swiss mercenaries in his ranks were recalled owing to the defeat of Francis I of France at Pavia and he was forced to return to his fortress at Hohentwiel. Woodcut by Hans Brosamer, public domain.

---

8   Cf. Miller, *The Army*, pp.11–19.

5

1525 The Rise and Fall of the Revolt

The outbreak of the rebellion in the southwest was sufficient to put the authorities across Southern and Central Germany on high alert and in a matter of months this part of the Holy Roman Empire was faced with a serious insurgency. Five main regions can be identified as centres of open revolt: Upper Swabia and the Black Forest, Württemberg and Franconia, central Germany (Thüringia and Saxony), Alsace (including the middle Rhine) and the Alpine lands (Salzburg and Austria). While events in these regions occurred at times in parallel, they broadly concur with the chronological development of the conflict. See Plate B.

The patchwork nature of political entities within the Holy Roman Empire coupled with Charles V's preoccupation with his war in Northern Italy against Francis I meant that the nobility and clergy could not rely on an overarching army to supress the uprisings. Thus the imperial government (*Reichsregiment*)[1] with its seat in Esslingen was ruled out as a potential headquarters from the outset. The true bearers of military power at this time were the larger and smaller territorial princes and some larger imperial cities with territorial possessions. They varied in their powers, finances and capacity to keep the peace. The most organised territorial unit at the time was the Swabian League.[2] This was a union of princes, ecclesiastical lords, lesser nobility and imperial cities of the area south of the Main River and was renewed several times during its 35 year existence until 1524. It brought together the often fragmented forces of the Southwest, German feudal nobility and the patrician class of the cities. Its members included not only numerous feudal lords and towns of Swabia, but also the Duke of Bavaria, the Landgrave of Hesse, the Archbishop of Mainz and the imperial towns

---

1   Created to provide a unified political leadership in the Empire with an input from the Elector Princes moved from Nuremberg to Esslingen following the Imperial Diet of 1521. Under the stewardship of Margrave Philip I of Baden, it developed diplomatic activities after the outbreak of the uprising, but in truth had no military means of power. Cf. Hoyer p.107.

2   Cf. Miller, *The Army*.

1525 THE RISE AND FALL OF THE REVOLT

of Nuremberg and Windsheim. As this was the first of the authorities to intervene it is to the rebellion in Upper Swabia that we must turn.

The Revolt in Upper Swabia, the Black Forest and the Hegau Upper Swabia – Chronology

23 January	Rebellion in the Allgäu – Peasant assembly at Leubas.
30 January	The Swabian League strikes agreement with the peasants of Villingen.
5 February	Ongoing meetings of the League Council in Ulm.
15 February	Georg von Waldburg appointed supreme commander of the League army. Declaration of War by the League.
16/17 February	Letter of Grievances submitted by the Baltringen band to the Swabian League.
21 February	Peasant Disturbances around Lake Constance. Duke Ulrich of Württemberg begins to mobilise an army for a march on Stuttgart.
24 February	Battle of Pavia. Landsknechts in Georg von Frundsberg's army begin to return from Italy.
27 February	Formation of the Christian Union in the Allgäu. Drafting of the 12 Articles commence.
1 March	Lake (Constance) band formed.
6 March	Peasant parliament convenes in Memmingen, Formation of the Christian Union.
7 March	The Federal Ordinance and 12 Articles are voted through at the Memmingen Peasant Parliament.
12 March	The exiled Duke Ulrich of Württemberg is forced to abandon retaking Stuttgart.
15 March	Second convening of the Parliament. Mutiny of the League troops at Dagersheim.
19 March	12 Articles are printed.
25 March	The Christian Union opens negotiations with the Swabian League in Ulm.
4 April	Battle of Leipheim
6 April	Renewed action by the peasants in Hegau and the Black Forest
14 April	Defeat of the peasants at Wurzach
17 April	Treaty of Weingarten Revolt spreads through Klettgau, Hegau and the Black Forest.
2 May	Renewed disturbances in the Allgäu. Uprising in Baden.
8 May	Peasant articles submitted to the town council of Villingen.
12 June	Peasants lay siege on Memmingen.
27 June	Allgäu peasants withdraw from Memmingen.
9 July	League commences campaign against the Allgäu peasants.
14 July	Defeat of the Allgäu peasants at Leubas.
16 July	Hegau and Black Forest peasants are defeated at Hilzingen.
25 July	The Treaty of Hilzingen.

THE GERMAN PEASANTS' WAR 1524–26

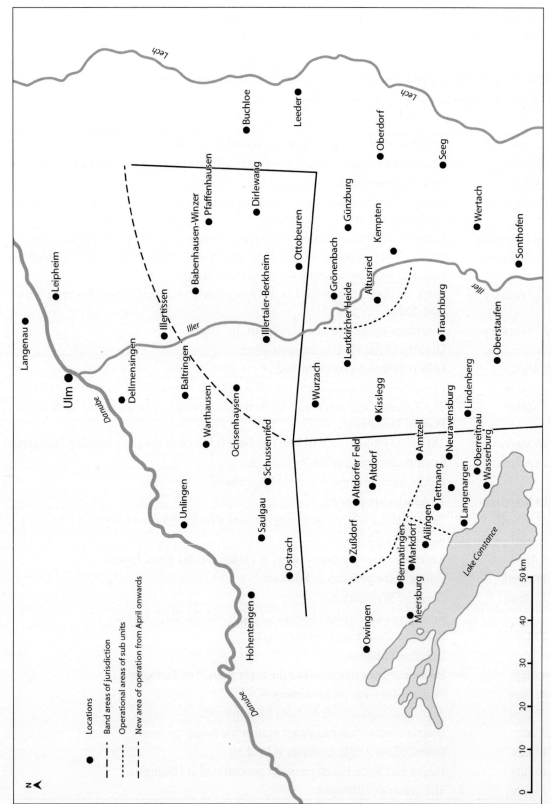

Map 2. Map showing the Peasant Bands of Upper Swabia

It was only a matter of time before the insurrection which had started in 1524 would spill over into the Southwest corner of what we now know as Germany. Throughout the territory known at the time as the Swabian Circle[3] three different districts rose in revolt between December 1524 and late February 1525. There was an uprising in Upper Swabia in the vicinity of the imperial cities of Ulm and Biberach, an insurgency in the environs of the Abbey of Kempten in the Allgäu and a series of disturbances in the area immediately above the northern shore of Lake Constance. Three peasant bands emerged respectively: the Baltringen band, the Allgäu band and the Lake band.

The Baltringen Band

Late in December 1524 the village of Baltringen some 30km south of Ulm became the centre for a series of peasant assemblies at which their collective grievances were debated. By February a troop of peasants numbering 7,000 to 10,000 men had organised. This so-called *Baltringen Band* elected as its leader Ulrich Schmid from Sulmingen, raised its own banner) and was conducting negotiations with representatives of the League by early February. Ulrich Schmid, a blacksmith by profession, was uncompromisingly guided by the word of God as the basis for the peasant demands and rejected any violence against the authorities. In arguing that theologians had to decide on the legality of the peasants' demands, Schmid managed to recruit Sebastian Lotzer, a journeyman furrier from Memmingen, to take on the role of clerk to the Baltringer Haufen who formally declared the band as a legitimate organisation to the imperial city of Ehingen on 28 February.

The Allgäu Band

Parallel to the Baltringen band a troop of peasants began to emerge from five distinct sub regions[4] of the geographical area known as the Allgäu. The main focal point were the historic tensions that had existed with the Abbey of Kempten primarily concerning the tax burden. When Sebastian von Breitenstein (*c.* 1465–1535) took up office as prince-abbot in 1522 the peasants had refused to swear an oath of allegiance to him. On 23 January 1525, the peasants of the entire area gathered under the leadership of Jörg Schmid in Leubas to the north-east of the imperial city. Mirroring the Baltringers they unanimously decided to submit a list of

---

3   See Miller, *The Army*, p.12.
4   Grönenbach, Leutkircher Heide, Altusried, Kempten and Wertach cf. Ulrich Crämer, Allgäuer Haufen im Deutschen Bauernkrieg und beteiligte Haufen in *Das Allgäu – Materialien und Anleitungen zur analytischen und synoptischen Raumbeobachtung* (Himmelstoß/Jahn, 1954).

grievances to the Swabian League. A notarially drawn up document was personally handed over by Jörg Schmid, their leader, to the League Governor Walter Hürnheim in Ulm. In addition to the issue of the tithe, the Allgäuer were also concerned with the restoration of the so-called old divine right and the itinerant reformer Christoph Schappeler took up their cause. On 14 February 1525, the subjects of the Kempten principality gathered in Sonthofen and decided to enforce what they called their divine right against the clergy, the Swabian League and the Emperor in Vienna. This band grew to between 7,000 and 9,000 men and included Landsknechts in their ranks.

The Lake Band

The peasants in the territories to the north of Lake Constance began assembling somewhat later than their counterparts in Upper Swabia. The authorities were however acutely conscious of the opposition which was steadily building. As early as January and February 1525, the imperial city of Ravensburg reinforced its arsenal and the monasteries of Weingarten and Weissenau brought their valuables and documents into the city for safekeeping. On 21 February, about 8,000 peasants – a majority of the subjects of the Counts of Montfort – gathered for the first time in the village of Rappertsweiler by the monastery of Langnau. Late in the evening they approached a squire by the name of Dietrich Hurlewagen on his estate in Gitzenweiler and asked him to become their captain.

In the adjacent area to the north, the subjects of the monasteries of Weissenau and Weingarten, the imperial city of Ravensburg and the Austrian bailiwick formed a large band of their own under the leadership of a miller by the name of Eitelhans Ziegelmüller. This became known as the Bermatinger band. These troops appear to have organised along the lines of local market catchment areas with the Bermatinger band drawn from the surrounding areas of the market town of Überlingen and the places north of it in the Ravensburg surrounding area. During the uprising, monasteries served as supply bases in each case: Langnau for the Rappertsweiler, Salem for the Bermatinger, Weingarten and Weissenau for the Altdorf detachment.[5]

The Christian Union

On the initiative of Lotzer and Schmid from Baltringen, representatives of the three Upper Swabian peasants' bands met in Memmingen where they decided to merge and, on 6 March 1525, form the Christian Union.

---

5   Elmar Kuhn *Der Bauernkrieg in Oberschwaben 1525* <http://elmarlkuhn.de/aufsaetze-im-volltext/oberschwaben-und-bodenseeraum/bauernkrieg-in-oberschwaben/die-fuehrer/index.html> (accessed 15 June 2022) p.24.

1525 THE RISE AND FALL OF THE REVOLT

In a letter they informed the Swabian League of the Union's formation and declared their intention to seek a peaceful resolution of their grievances and asked the League to refrain from any violence. Based on the demands by the Baltringer Band and with the probable participation of the Memmingen preacher Christoph Schappeler, the association worked out the most famous document of the German Peasants' War, the 12 Articles, establishing a basis for the peasant demands in 'Divine Law'.

Summary of the 12 Articles

1. Every town and village shall be entitled to elect and to dismiss its preacher

2. The small tithe shall be abolished, and the great tithe shall be used to pay the pastor the poor and our defence.

3. Serfdom shall be abolished

4. Hunting and fishing shall be permitted

5. All the forests shall be returned to the commoners for timber and firewood.

6. Compulsory labour (*Frondienst*) shall be reduced.

7. Additional services beyond that agreed should be remunerated

8. An independent re-assessment of rents and taxes shall be undertaken

9. Punishments shall be meted out in accordance with the old written law

10. The common land shall be returned to the people

11. Inheritance tax shall be abolished

12. The authorities shall recognise that all these demands originate from the word of God

THE GERMAN PEASANTS' WAR 1524-26

Cover of the 12 Articles resolved at Memmingen. Woodcut by unknown artist.

On 7 March 1525 Sebastian Lotzer, the Baltringers' notary, also drafted the Federal Ordinance (*Bundesordnung*), the Christian Union's constitution. On 15 and 16 March 1525, during their further deliberations a list was published of those individuals, who were supposed to evaluate and examine the peasants' demands and ascertain their basis in Divine Law. It contained 14 names including leading intellectuals and power brokers of the day: Martin Luther, Philipp Melanchthon and Huldrych Zwingli as well as Archduke Ferdinand of Austria and Frederick of Saxony. The Swabian League rejected the list leading to a second, amended version with less contentious individuals of more local and regional importance. They presented this to the League in Ulm on 24 March 1525. The following day, a new proposal, developed by the mayors of Kempten and Ravensburg, was handed over to the peasants' representatives. It called for the dissolution of the Christian Union, the formation of an arbitration court, a rejection of the notion of 'Divine Law ' and a re-assertion of obedience to the authorities. The peasants were given until 2 April to decide on these counter-demands.

The Response of the Swabian League

When hostilities broke out in what was effectively Outer Austria in the summer of 1524 it was the Archduke Ferdinand who had taken the initiative appointing George III Truchsess[6] of Waldburg in October 1524 to command the military response. The Truchsess already had experience in dealing with civil disobedience having been commissioned by Duke Ulrich von Württemberg to suppress the Poor Conrad uprising in 1514. In 1519 he had been deputy commander-in-chief of the League army which had expelled Ulrich from his territory. He was considered to have the requisite

---

6 Truchsess translates as Senechal or governor.

1525 THE RISE AND FALL OF THE REVOLT

Tradesmens' Hall in Memmingen, (Photo: Mrilabs, public domain).

experience given the twin threat of the peasants and the exiled duke. Archduke Ferdinand requested that the executive of the Swabian League convene in January as a matter of urgency:

> concerning the manifold disturbance withdrawal of previously performed services and obedience by his Highness's subjects in his county of Nellenburg, and the actions of the rebellious peasants of the Hegau. the Black Forest, the town of Villingen and other subjects of the worthy house of Austria, likewise the Württemberg peasants who have joined them and especially the subjects of the abbey of St Blasien in the Black Forest…[7]

The six appointed councillors and three captains feared that the revolt would in time concern all Estates of the League and that it should be suppressed with severe punishment as soon and as firmly as possible. Mindful that the weather would prevent any mass mobilisation on the part of the peasants, they nevertheless ordered a swift retaliatory expedition into the Hegau. On 10 February the Truchsess set off with 259 men

Leonard von Eck chancellor and 'hawk' within the leadership of the Swabian League. Engraving by Barthel Beham. (Metropolitan Museum of Art, with permission).

---

7   Klüpfel K. (ed) 1863, *Urkunden zur Geschichte des Schwäbischen Bundes* 1488–1533), Stuttgart: Bibliothek des Literarischen Vereins pp.285–287. Translation in Scott & Scribner pp.150–151.

THE GERMAN PEASANTS' WAR 1524-26

from Villingen to make an example of the village of Mühlhausen in the Hegau which had been the only community to have formally handed in a letter of grievance to the authorities at this time. On 15 February the Truchsess formally declared war on the peasants on the grounds of breach of the territorial peace (*Landesfriedensbruch*).

In the first quarter of 1525 the League began to assemble its command structure. It had a tightly organised system of military deployment, with proportional contingents precisely defined for each member.[8] In the autumn of 1524, the League Council had decided on the relative strength of each individual contingent. A quarter of the full League commitment was set at 463 horsemen and 2,746 footmen with each member providing their predetermined share of this or transfer money to the League in lieu.[9]

As the insurgency began to spread within the League's territory in early 1525, two factions formed in the League on the question of how to deal with the uprising. In general the city members, such as Augsburg, Ulm and Nuremberg, under pressure from the pro-peasant party within their citizenry, urged negotiations and a peaceful settlement of the conflict. The princes, however, represented by the Bavarian chancellor Leonhard von Eck, on the other hand, were much more hawkish,[10] although their main priority in the first instance was to deal with the exiled Duke Ulrich's attempt to retake his Duchy of Württemberg. While negotiating with the peasants would buy the League some time, the uprisings spreading through their territory constituted a serious breach of territorial peace and had to be met with a proportionate military response.[11]

While negotiations with the peasants were ongoing as early as 5 February 1525, the League Council proposed the summoning of the first third of the rapid response contingents (*Eilende Hilfe*); and determined 27 February as the deadline for the muster by Ulm. There was by this time real concern that the contingents would not be big enough against the peasants.[12] However, in late February the military situation

Portrait of the 'Bauernjörg', supreme commander of the Swabian League army tasked with the suppression of the peasant uprisings in upper Swabia, Württemberg, and Franconia. (Burg Waldburg (Württemberg), Photo: Andreas Praefcke with permission).

---

8   Cf. Miller, *The Army*, pp.11–34.
9   For the precise League breakdown cf. *The Army* p.24.
10 Hoyer, *Militärwesen*, p.109.
11 Blickle, *Der Bauernjörg* pp.100–105.
12 Ulrich Artzt informed his hometown that he was very worried that the members of the League would not be strong enough against the peasants in Vogt. W. 1880 Die Correspondenz des schwäbischen Bundeshauptmann Ulrich Arzt von Augsburg, *Zeitschrift des Historischen Vereins für Schwaben und Neuburg* vol. 6.p.304.

1525 THE RISE AND FALL OF THE REVOLT

changed rapidly in favour of the League. Following Charles V's victory at Pavia in Northern Italy those Landsknechts in the Emperor's pay began streaming home to Upper Swabia which had always been the Emperor's preferred recruiting ground. On 12 March, when news finally reached those Swiss mercenaries in the ranks of Duke Ulrich's army of the heavy losses of their compatriots at Pavia, they abandoned him before Stuttgart, forcing Ulrich to beat a retreat to his fortress at Hohentwiel. This meant that the League army could now be directed wholly against the peasant threat. However, there was a small matter of convincing the Landsknechts in their ranks to go after their compatriots – a matter which led to a serious mutiny in the League camp at Dagersheim before Stuttgart and which was to present the commanders of the League army with an ongoing issue – to what extent could the League depend on the loyalty of those mercenaries who were kith and kin of the peasants.[13]

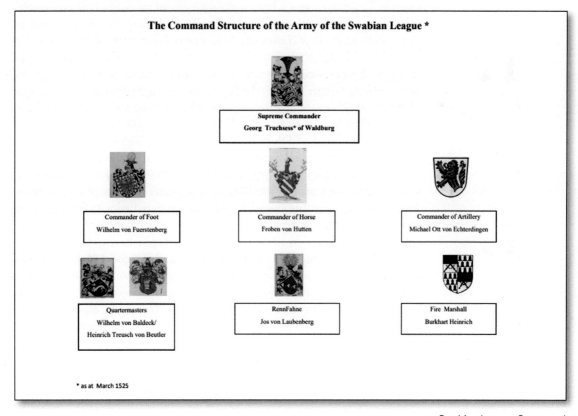

Swabian League Command Structure

In their efforts to resolve their grievances peacefully the Baltringer band complained in a letter to the League dated 25 March 1525 that soldiers belonging to the Swabian League had started to attack villages. They emphasised again that they demanded nothing but the application of the 'Divine Law'. The situation escalated after news that troops of the Swabian

---

13   Cf. Miller, *The Army*, pp.55–58.

League, consisting of 8,000 footsoldiers and 3,000 cavalry had arrived at Ulm. The same day more radical elements within the Baltringen band looted Schemmerberg Castle. The following day, as a reaction to the slaying by troops of the Swabian League of a landlord from Griesingen returning from Memmingen, 8,000 enraged peasants stormed and looted, amongst others, Heggbach Abbey, Laupheim Castle, Untersulmetingen Castle and Achstetten Castle with the latter two burnt to the ground. The monasteries of Gutenzell, Ochsenhausen, Wiblingen and Marchtal were forced to support the Baltringer Haufen by supplying the peasants with provisions. At the same time intense diplomatic activities by the Upper Swabian cities were instigated in order to prevent a military confrontation between the peasants and the Swabian League by appealing to both parties to refrain from violence. In the end all these efforts were to no avail.

On 31 March troops of the Swabian League based at Erbach moved towards Dellmensingen where a detachment of peasants had ensconced themselves. During the ensuing skirmish 50 soldiers of the Swabian League lost their lives. Further clashes took place near Achstetten, Oberstadion and Zwiefalten during which several villages, after having been looted, were set ablaze by League troops. Following these initial unsuccessful attempts to subdue the Baltringer Haufen, the Truchsess then turned to face the challenge of the seemingly more threatening peasant army that had dug itself in near Leipheim. During the ensuing battle (4 April 1525), the Leipheimer Haufen was utterly defeated and their leaders, Hans Jakob Wehe and seven others, were beheaded the following day.[14] On 10 April the Swabian League's army under the command of Georg Truchsess von Waldburg left Leipheim for Baltringen encountering a small band of peasants near Laupheim on their way. During the ensuing skirmish 150 peasants perished with the survivors scattering into the surrounding forests. However, when the Truchsess arrived in Baltringen on 12 April the enemy was nowhere to be seen.

Meanwhile, to the east of the River Lech the Duchy of Bavaria was particularly concerned about disturbances to the north in the prince-bishopric of Eichstätt[15] and by any possible incursions by the Allgäu peasants. He was the first to mobilise its own troops. In addition to his obligations to the Swabian League, Duke Wilhelm had to secure the border of the bishopric of Augsburg, which ran along the River Lech. Fearing an eastward advance by the rebels along the River Bach the duke ordered his militia (*Landwehr*) to muster fully armed on 3 March. His Chancellor Leonard von Eck, who was also the secretary of the Swabian League, had

---

14 Cf Miller, *The Army*, pp.58–64.
15 Between April and May a peasant band emanating from Thalmässing drew in support from the surrounding area threatening the Prince-Bishop Gabriel von Eyb who called upon the duke and the count palatine Friedrich to crush the uprising. Cf. Josef Seger *Der Bauernkrieg im Hochstift Eichstätt* (Friedrich Pustet Verlag, 1997).

little trust in the local militia and urged the duke to move a 100-strong troop of horse to Schöngau as an extra precaution.

Eck's fears proved correct – Bavaria had problems recruiting reliable men both from the cities as well as the countryside along the River Lech, as numerous peasants defected to the ranks of the Allgäu band or joined the insurgents in the archbishopric of Salzburg. By the beginning of April the duke felt obliged to seek military support further afield and began recruiting foreign mercenaries from Bohemia and stradiots from as far a field as Venice. A similar situation prevailed in the Tyrol. Here the government had increased its stockpile of weapons in January 1525, but it could not rely on mustering the militia (*Landsturm*) fearing that they would turn on the upper echelons of the the feudal clergy.[16] They too would need to recruit a mercenary army.

Landsknecht drummer, ensign, and fifer. Engraving by Barthel Beham, (Metropolitan Museum of Art, with permission).

Meanwhile the Truchsess pushed ahead with the League army into what was now his own territory (Waldburg and its environs). He had received a letter of grievances signed by a Florian Greisel, a pastor who had been appointed by the Truchsess himself and who now was commander of the Lower Allgäu band. This enraged von Waldburg and instead of marching west on Ravensburg he turned east towards Wurzach where he routed a 4,000 strong peasant troop.[17]

It was now time to suppress the Lake band. The League army left Wurzach on 15 April and after a march of some 12 kilometres encountered the peasants at Gaisbeuren 16km to the north of Ravensburg. When news arrived from the Hegau that Jörg Truchsess von Waldburg was approaching Gaisbeuren with the League army of 7,000 infantry and 1,500 mounted men-at-arms the leaders of the Bermatinger band ordered the storm bells to be tolled throughout the whole valley and around Lake Constance to mobilise the villages. On Good Friday about 10,000 men set out to confront the oncoming army. A squire by the name of Humpis von Senftenau had overall command. Eitelhans Ziegelmüller was captain of the Bermatinger troop and

---

16 Hoyer, *Militärwesen*, p.118.
17 Miller, *The Army*, pp.66–67.

THE GERMAN PEASANTS' WAR 1524-26

One of the very few contemporary depictions of the events at Weingarten was illustrated by the abbot Jacob Murer, the author of the Weissenau Chronicle. In his chronicle, he focused exclusively on the surroundings of his monastery at Weissenau near Ravensburg. His drawings reveal some understanding for the peasant cause but ultimately his perspective was that of the overlords. To the left is the Swabian League army with the cross of St George on its banner. Note the squared formations of the peasants who had large numbers of Landsknechts in their ranks. (Waldburg Zeil'sches Gesamtarchiv, Schloss Zeil ZAMs54, with permission).

the Rappertsweiler detachment which was in transit was led by Dietrich Hurlewagen.[18]

The Lake band had taken up a favourable position at Gaisbeuren – a wood to the rear and marshland to the front. The Truchsess was aware of the numerical superiority of the peasants and the presence of a considerable number of Landsknechts in their ranks with about a third armed with firearms. He held back from committing his vanguard of light horse to a frontal attack. Instead, there was an exchange of artillery fire which ceased as the Truchsess ran out of ammunition. Following this the Lake band moved back into their camp at Gaisbeuren. At the peasant council of war, a plan was drawn up to attack the League camp under cover of darkness, but on the night of Easter Saturday, Wilhelm von Fürstenberg, the League commander of the infantry, sent a small team into Gaisbeuren to set fire to the village causing the peasants to retreat through the Altdorf Forest in the direction of Weingarten, where they were still able to take up a tactically favourable position.

---

18   Elmar Kuhn Der Bauernkrieg in Oberschwaben 1525< http://elmarlkuhn.de/aufsaetze-im-volltext/oberschwaben-und-bodenseeraum/bauernkrieg-in-oberschwaben/die-fuehrer/index.html> (accessed 15 June 2022).

1525 THE RISE AND FALL OF THE REVOLT

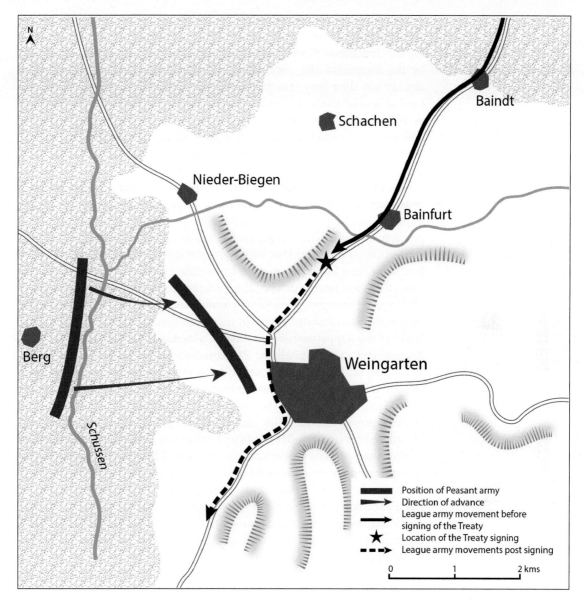

Map 3. The Confrontation at Weingarten 16–17 April 1525

The League army remained in their initial position and orders were given to rest on the Easter Sunday.[19] The situation had become difficult for the Truchsess. News arrived that the Lake band had been reinforced by the Rappertsweiler contingent and that other peasant groups were already on their way. Furthermore, new orders had arrived from the League headquarters at Ulm to proceed at haste to deal with the rebellion in Württemberg as soon as possible, since many of the League members had been threatened. Finally, a delegation from the neighbouring city of Ravensburg arrived with a mandate to negotiate a peaceful settlement with the peasants.

As League commander-in-chief, Georg von Waldburg had received orders on his appointment in February to suppress the insurgency with impunity, yet he sent a four-man delegation to the peasants to negotiate a peace treaty. This offer – a guarantee to submit the peasant grievances to arbitration on condition that they surrender their arms and ensigns bought him some time to take up a more favourable position. Within the peasant camp there was intense debate. The leaders occupied senior positions in the rural social hierarchy. Hans Jakob Humpis von Senftenau, was the son of a well-known Ravensburg patrician merchant family. Dietrich Hurlewagen, leader of the Rappertsweiler contingent, a landowner and merchant and the Bermatinger captain Eitelhans Ziegelmüller, owned several farms[20] were anxious to settle but the rank and file were in no mood to surrender their weapons. This was conveyed to the Truchsess when the negotiators returned to the League camp. A further parley involving only the handover of the artillery pieces extended the League's battle preparations but ultimately, he ordered his commander of horse, Frowin von Hutten, to stand his men down as the peasant numerical superiority and firepower persuaded him that he could not be convinced of victory as the Lake band was arguably the best armed band of all the Swabian troops with, it is estimated, one in five a Landsknecht. The arsenal of weapons at the band's disposal was also quite impressive. Every third man carried a matchlock and the band had a number of artillery pieces including cannon from the arsenals of the lake towns of Markdorf and Meersburg.[21]

The Truchsess had a draft treaty drawn up which stated that the peasants were guilty of breach of the peace and of violations of imperial law and the Papal Bull all of which had given due cause for the military actions of the League. No action, however, would be taken against them provided the peasants dissolved their alliances, disbanded and renounced all rebellion forever. All property from the plundered monasteries, cities and estates was

---

19   For the events of 15 April, see Günther Vogler, *Die Gewalt soll gegeben werden dem gemeinen Volk: der deutsche Bauernkrieg 1525* (Berlin,1983), p.88f.
20   Cf. Elmar Kuhn, < http://elmarlkuhn.de/aufsaetze-im-volltext/oberschwaben-und-bodenseeraum/bauernkrieg-in-oberschwaben/die-fuehrer/index.html   > (accessed 16 June 2022).
21   Blickle, *Der Bauernjörg*, p.175.

to be returned and the payment of taxes and other levies was to be resumed. The Truchsess demanded the surrender of the peasant banners and all arms and armour in return for a procedure tabled by the League some 3 weeks previously whereby three towns were to be appointed by the peasantry and three by their lords, to negotiate and settle all disagreements amicably, legally and bindingly. Negotiations dragged on for four days. The peasants declined to offer up their weapons – not only were these the (costly) tools of the trade of the 1,000 Landsknechts in the ranks, but they were also needed by those peasants who belonged to the local militias. For the militant members of the ranks this amounted to outright capitulation. The Truchsess failed to disarm the peasants although he secured the return of eight pieces of artillery to their rightful owners. Whereas he had demanded the handover of all the peasant banners as part of the dissolution of the individual bands – some 32 – only five were handed over – these he tore up symbolically in front of the leaders.[22] Nevertheless, securing the signing of the treaty meant the de facto neutralisation of the Upper Swabian rebellion.

Tensions ran high amongst the contingents of the Christian Union. The Allgäuer who had answered the Lake band's request for assistance were still in transit when the treaty was signed and were determined to continue the struggle. Along with leaders from the Hegau peasants they urged members of the Lake band to form a new alliance, but the League was able to rely on the peasant leadership to keep the peace. Ziegenmüller assembled his Bermatinger peasants at the beginning of May to impress upon them the necessity of keeping to the terms of treaty and to make them swear to uphold it. He was handsomely remunerated for this. Hurlewagen even endeavoured, in consultation with the imperial city of Wangen, to mobilise the Lake peasants against the Allgäuer, who were camped in Eglofs at that time. For this, the lords gave him a considerable sum. Yet Hurlewagen, was held responsible for a second plundering of the monastery at Langnau on 14 May, after the treaty had been concluded. The League placed a bounty on his head and he seems to have fled the region late summer of 1525.[23]

The arbitration courts promised in the Treaty of Weingarten never came to pass. To maintain the fragile situation in the territory, the authorities set up a troop of 500 mounted men-at-arms to police matters enabling the League army to push north to deal with the insurrection in Württemberg. Before heading north, the Truchsess needed to deal with the ongoing insurrection in the Hegau and the activities of the Black Forest band. Before considering developments there we must turn our attention to events in the neighbouring Black Forest region.

---

22   Elmar Kuhn, Der Seehaufen in Elmar L. Kuhn / Peter Blickle (Eds.): *Der Bauernkrieg in Oberschwaben*. (Tübingen: bibliotheca academica, 2000), pp.97–139.
23   In 1527 he was remanded by the League and imprisoned for a long time without a trial. He died in 1531, having entered French service in 1528. Cf. Kuhn, *Der Seehaufen*, p.25.

THE GERMAN PEASANTS' WAR 1524-26

The Black Forest and the Hegau – 1525

Chronology

30 January	The Swabian League strikes an agreement with the peasants of Villingen.
6 April	Renewed action by the peasants in Hegau and the Black Forest.
17 April	Revolt spreads through Klettgau, Hegau and the Black Forest.
2 May	Uprising in Baden.
7 May	Uprising in Kraichgau.
8 May	Peasant articles submitted to the town council of Villingen.
14 May	Peasant bands converge on Freiburg and lay siege.
24 May	Freiburg is occupied.
June	Siege of Radolfzell by Black Forest, Hegau and Klettgau peasants.
27 June	End of the siege of Radolfzell after the advance of Mark Sittich von Ems.
30 June	Hans Müller von Bulgenbach leaves Radolfzell.
2 July	Final defeat of the Hegau peasants near Radolfzell at the 'Laffensteige' and near Hilzingen,
12 July	The Black Forest contingents return home to escape the punishments meted out by von Ems.
14 July	Hans Müller is captured.
25 July	The Treaty of Hilzingen.

After Weingarten the Truchsess received reports of peasant activity in the Black Forest and the Hegau. The ongoing insurrection had flared up at the beginning of April with its epicentre around Löffingen and Bonndorf, where Hans Müller von Bulgenbach was camped. Together with the Hegauer Band he led the surrounding towns and communities in mobilising to join his cause by sealing off the access routes to Radolfzell. Radolfzell was a relatively small municipality but as the residence of a number of noble families including the Austrian officals Christian Fuchs von Fuchsberg and Jakob Stürzel von Buchheim, it functioned as an administrative capital.

The Truchsess was intent on crushing these two bands or neutralising them with a further treaty along the lines of Weingarten. On 25 April he met with the peasant leadership to negotiate terms but his demand that the peasants should disarm and hand over 20 hostages otherwise there would have to be bloodshed. The terms were of course unacceptable for the rebels. However, new orders had arrived from Ulm urging the Truchsess to move at all haste to Württemberg where the nobility was gravely concerned about developments. The League army thus began its march north towards Stuttgart leaving the Black Forest and Hegau bands free to continue their mobilisition throughout the territory. Initially the two bands united in pursuit of the League army at some distance for they were eager to assist

1525 THE RISE AND FALL OF THE REVOLT

their comrades in Württemberg in what they knew would ultimately be a major military confrontation. At the beginning of May, however, Hans Müller von Bulgenbach broke away to lead his Black Forest troop in a 10-day march towards Freiburg – the capital of Breisgau. Müller was convinced of the need for large scale cooperation between the bands and he unerringly took up the new ideas coming from Upper Swabia in also establishing a 'Christian Union' derived from the word of God.[24] As he moved through the Black Forest at the head of the train was a wagon decorated and bearing the flag with a 'herald' at the front urging villagers to join the union.[25] On 8 May he submitted a letter of articles to the city council of Villingen urging them to take up their cause or face a secular ban. The radical intent of the Black Forest band can be seen in the following extract from the letter:

> Whereas all treachery, coercion and depravity befalls us and stems from castles, convents and clerical institutions, they shall from this hour hence be placed under the ban. If, however, nobles, monks, or priests are willing to quit their castles, convents and foundations and take up residence in common houses, as other foreign persons and join this Christian Union, they shall be cordially and righteously admitted with all their goods and chattels. Thereafter everything which befits and belongs to them by godly law shall be accorded to them faithfully and honourably without let or hindrance.[26]

Villingen refused, however, to submit to the peasants' demands and began to organise a counter-offensive involving other resistant municialities which belonged to Outer Austria.

Müller continued his march westwards towards Freiburg where he was able to coordinate with other peasant troops which had assembled and were advancing on the city. By this time he had become somewhat of a charismatic leader clad in a red cloak and feathered beret and known for his eloquence.[27] He was readily acknowledged as the supreme commander of the Black Forest bands. Coordinating with the Ortenau band to the north of the city and the peasants of upper and lower Margraviate of Baden from the south and west respectively he laid siege on Freiburg in mid-May.

---

24 Horst Buszello, *Neue Deutsche Biographie* 18, 1997 pp.397–398 online version <https://www.deutsche-biographie.de/pnd119122723.html#ndbcontent> (accessed 13 July 2022).

25 Hans-Martin Maurer 1929 *Bauernkrieg als Massenerhebung* einer revolutionären Bewegung, in: *Bausteine zur geschichtlichen Landeskunde von Baden-Württemberg*, (die Kommission für geschichtliche Landeskunde), p.241.

26 Letter of articles of the Black Forest Peasants before May 8, 1525 – translation from Scott and Scribner p.137.

27 Christian Roder C.1883 *Heinrich Hugs Villinger Chronik von 1495 bis 1533* (Literarischer Verein in Stuttgart, 1883), p.105.

THE GERMAN PEASANTS' WAR 1524-26

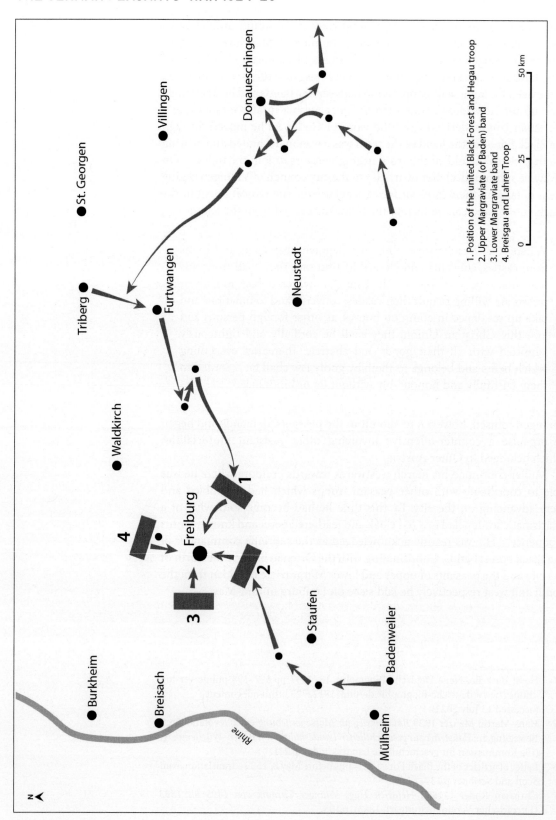

Map 4. The siege of Freiburg 24 May 1525

1525 THE RISE AND FALL OF THE REVOLT

Freiburg was a city with allegiance to the Habsburgs. Its gates remained closed to the peasants and already at the end of December 1524, its council had organised a meeting with other cities to coordinate joint action against the insurgency. However, by mid-May no help was forthcoming, since all those cities which had not joined the rebel cause were fully preoccupied with their own efforts to maintain internal stability. The converging peasant bands succeeded in encircling the city. A total of 12,000 insurgents, divided into 20 bands, are said to have gathered in the various camps around the city. Thanks to a well-organised intelligence service, the city was already aware of the peasants' advance on 9 May and tried in vain to obtain money and soldiers.[28] On 14 May, the Black Forest peasants were the first to call on Freiburg to open its gates and join their Christian Union. Negotiations dragged on for a number of days. On 21 May, all the peasant troops again wrote to the city, but again in vain.

Freiburg's garrison was depleted as numerous soldiers had been loaned out during the preceding months. The nobility, which had been brought into the city, was unable to bridge the gap, providing only a single troop of 50 men. The defence force was mainly made up of the city's watch recruited in 12 shifts primarily from the guilds. Even the university had provided a contingent of 60–70 men.

While negotiations were still in progress, the peasants succeeded in draining the city of water from its wells and mills around 21 May They also prepared to occupy the strategically important Schlossberg, secretly positioning field guns and firearms on the hill overlooking the city. A somewhat legendary report says that the watch had been had been resting at the square in front of the local hostelry when on the orders of Bulgenbach a hundred shots rained down on them from the rebels hook guns.[29]

The defence of the city became almost impossible after the capture of this strategic position and Freiburg opened its gates on 23 May and joined the Christian Union on the following day. Two days later Breisach, important because of the strategically important Rhine bridge to neighbouring Alsace,

The castle on the hill overlooking the city of Freiburg had been neglected and was easily occupied by the peasants who used this vantage point to fire upon the defensive forces below. (Photo: Joergens.mi, public domain).

---

28 Hoyer, *Militärwesen*, p.166.
29 Friedrich Schaub 1935 Der Bauernkrieg in Freiburg in *Zeitschrift des Freiburger Geschichtsvereins*, Vol. 46 quoted in Hoyer, *Militärwesen*, p167.

THE GERMAN PEASANTS' WAR 1524-26

was forced to take the same step. In the agreement drawn up with the city's council Breisach was instructed not to let anyone cross the Rhine bridge who was against the Christian Union. Four falconets were to be made available to protect the bridge and four companies of men were to be transferred to Freiburg along with ordnance and crews as and when needed. As the course of the war began to change by the end of May, these promises were never fulfilled.

After taking Freiburg the peasant troops from Breisgau and the Margraviate returned to their homelands. The Ortenauers succeeded in concluding a treaty with their lords in Renchen on 25 May according to which the parish priests were to be elected, the small tithe was to be abolished, along with the death penalty and obligatory services were to be limited to four days a year. While this treaty addressed some of the peasants' complaints, feudal rule remained intact since peasant assemblies were to be henceforth policed.[30] The city of Freiburg endeavoured to commit the Black Forest peasants and Hans Müller von Bulgenbach to an agreement along the lines of the Ortenau treaty, but Müller left with his troop along with those detachments of Hegau rebels to march on Radolfzell to aid the rebel siege of the city which clearly would have major strategic importance were it to finally fall. While Müller camped with his men in Hüfingen between 1 and 19 June, Heinz Maler, commander of the Hegau troop, endeavoured to strike an agreement with the authorities in Radolfzell in an exchange of correspondence on 9 and 10 June but the latter had already called on the Swabian League for assistance. On the 18 June the Austrian commander Mark Sittich von Ems had arrived at Überlingen with 2,000 men. At the age of 69 von Ems was a veteran who had served at Pavia and been awarded with a pension by the Archduke. His force was enhanced with a 400-strong contingent from the city under the command of Caspar Dornberger. With a further 2,000 men who had mustered at Sernatingen, von Ems could now confront the Hegauers.

When news arrived of the approach of an Austrian army, Müller broke camp at Hüfingen and joined the Hegau troop outside Radolfzell. Although the

An ambitious nobleman Marx Sittich I von Ems had already demonstrated his military skills as a 'war entrepreneur' in the service of Emperors Maximilian I and Charles V and was given the commission to mop up the remaining pockets of resistance in the Hegau area. An ardent advocate of the Counter-Reformation, and known and feared nationwide as a 'peasant butcher' his commitment extended to Tyrol where he unsuccessfully hunted the Tyrolean rebel leader Michael Gaismair. (Photo: Helmut Klapper, CC.BY.4.0 Vorarlberg State Library, with permission).

---

30 Cf. Scott and Scribner pp.284–288.

1525 THE RISE AND FALL OF THE REVOLT

combined band numbered between 10,000 and 14,000 men he sent word to his allies in Freiburg and the Swiss Confederation to come to their assistance but there was no response. In the meantime von Ems was on the move uniting with the contingents at Sernatingen. On 26 June he set fire to the village of Wahlwies and attacked an outpost manned by 200 peasants and situated on the road to the village of Möggingen which lies 4km north-east of Radolfzell. After a four hour exchange of fire between the respective squads of handgunners, with casualties on both sides, the peasants made off into the woods. Two rebels were taken prisoner and interrogated to determine the exact size of the combined peasant army. There were frantic efforts at mediation which proved futile as von Ems had orders to destroy the peasants.[31]

On 27 June the peasants abandoned their siege of Radolfzell and withdrew to their camp at Steisslingen where they could take up a more advantageous position against von Ems' horse. Their stock of artillery ammunition was low – they had to rely on stone and wooden shot and loaded even clubs into their cannon.[32] Despite their numerical superiority the situation did not look good. News would no doubt have reached the rebel camps of the defeats at Böblingen (12 May), Frankenhausen (15 May) and Saverne (18 May) and Königshofen (3 June). In the early hours of 1 July Hans Müller pulled his men out leaving the Hegauer to their fate. On 4 July after a two-hour skirmish with League troops under the command of Count Felix von Werdenburg the peasants retreated but regrouped and dug in on the so-called Laffensteig hill near Hilzingen. Here they were eventually defeated by the League army on 4 July.

This woodcut by Hans Tirol is one of the few contemporary images of a group of mounted peasants. Source unknown.

---

31 Casimir Bumiller, *Der Bauernkrieg im Hegau 1524/5 Rekonstruktion einer revolutionären Bewegung* in *Hilzingen Geschichte und Geschichten band 1* (Gemeinde Hilzingen,1998), pp.406–407.

32 Kasimir Walchner, *Geschichte Der Stadt Ratolphzell: Aus Handschriftlichen Und Anderen Zuverlässigen Quellen Bearbeitet, Nebst Erläuterungen Und Urkunden* (Radolfzell am Bodensee, 1825), pp.108–109.

On 16 July those pockets of peasants who had been holding out on the Laffensteig finally surrendered. In a symbolic move Mark Sittich set up camp at Hilzingen which some nine months earlier had been the place where the uprising had started. On 25 July Christoph Fuchs von Fuchsberg, captain and councillor in the Upper Austrian government in Ensisheim, oversaw the signing of the treaty of Hilzingen which brought the Hegau revolt to an end.

Württemberg and Franconia

Württemberg

Chronology

Feb 21	Duke Ulrich of Wurttemberg begins his march on Stuttgart to retake his Duchy
March 17	Ulrich fails and retreats to his fortress of Hohentwiel
	March/April Peasant uprising nearby Schwäbisch-Gmund
	Beginning of the uprising in the Nördlingen Ries area
April 12	The Ries troop disbands
April 17	Emergence of the Württemberg Band at Wunnerstein
	Uprising in Gaildorf
April 25	Württemberg Band occupies Stuttgart
May 8	The peasants of the Ries are defeated by the Margrave's army at Ostheim
May 12	Battle of Böblingen

Following Weingarten, the Truchsess had been given orders to suppress the uprising in the Duchy of Württemberg. This lay in the valley of the Neckar River, from Tübingen to Heilbronn, with its capital and largest city, Stuttgart, at its centre. The northern part of the Duchy was wide and open, with large rivers making for decent arable land, the southern part mountainous and wooded, with the Black Forest to the west and the Swabian Alb to the east. At the very south-eastern part of the Duchy, on the other side of the Swabian Alb, lay Ulm, the headquarters of the Swabian League and the Danube River basin. This territory presented a particular challenge for the League since, in addition to the rising discontent amongst the peasantry, the exiled Duke Ulrich was persistent in his attempt to retake his territory where possible using the peasants in his quest.

This was the second time the Truchsess had traversed these lands having pursued the Duke on his earlier attempt to take back Stuttgart. On March 13, 1525, the Duke was forced to turn back however as his Swiss mercenaries deserted him. On the same day the first riots broke out in the city. Stuttgart's population, which numbered barely more than 6,000, resembled a typical Swabian city: numerous respectable winegrowers,

1525 THE RISE AND FALL OF THE REVOLT

wealthy artisans, peasant farmers and an elite of merchants, princely officials, and servants. As news spread of the disturbances in the Hegau and Upper Swabia, the government of the Duchy which had been placed in the hands of Habsburg administrators following the exile of the Duke, put out a forlorn call to arms to the militias to defend the territory against the rebellious peasants. On March 27 about 1500 peasants had assembled near the village of Deiningen a town which is located approximately 70 miles east of Stuttgart and situated in a crater known as the (Nördlinger) Ries. A week later the number had already grown to 8000. Interestingly, the Ries or Deininger band raised a banner which showed a peasant and a Landsknecht with hands outstretched towards each other. On March 31 they decided, 'to attack all monasteries and priests' houses, to chase monks and priests out of the city to drive out all lords in the Ries, to annex the Ries to the city of Nördlingen and to become lords themselves.'

Anton Forner, the deputy mayor of the city and considered to be experienced in military matters, was elected leader and the popular uprising was declared on April 1st. Forner was briefly taken into custody but released 3 days later and elected as the first mayor. He now ruled almost without restriction and let the peasants share out money, grain and wood. Demands were submitted to the nobles of Öttingen to relieve the peasants of all their burdens and vestiges of serfdom. As compensation, the counts were to receive all the goods of the churches. During negotiations near Nördlingen on April 7th, 1525, the peasants agreed to a court of arbitration to be formed by both parties. However, when the Counts of Öttingen refused their consent, the Deininger (Ries) band dissolved on April 12.

In Bottwar to the north of Stuttgart, the citizens refused to sign up to a call by the authorities to provide men to quell the uprisings in the territory calling themselves on the villages in the area to meet on the hill at Wunnenstein where on April 16th they formed a band. They summoned and duly elected Matern Feuerbacher, a local inn keeper who as a known moderate had been encouraged by the local authorities to ride out to the assembly and infiltrate the peasant organisation. To the east of Stuttgart and in the surrounding area south of the free imperial city of Schwäbisch Hall a

Wunnenstein hill where the peasants of Grossbottwar (Württemberg) first rallied. (Photo: K. Jähne, public domain).

peasant troop assembled with its centre in the village of Gaildorf. Soon its members began wandering through the city with white crosses stitched on their hats openly expressing their rebellious views.

The council (of Hall) also asked the League council in Ulm to return those men in Upper Swabia as they had offered to the League army (for its campaign) in Upper Swabia; they needed them now for the city's own defence. The League refused. If, they wrote, they returned Hall's contingent of horse and infantry it could cause a rift among the other members of the League, and everything would fall apart. The city council gathered as much information as possible from the various peasant groups to be prepared for any assault on the city. In the event that a great army, including as expected the peasants of Hall, should march on the city, it was decided in advance to send a delegation to meet them and offer peace, with the request that they leave the city alone. While appeasement was underway the council was eagerly reinforcing its defences as this detailed account from the pastor Johannes Herolt describes:

This involved a continuous supplying of the city walls and towers with firearms powder, stones, lanterns, sulphur and pitch hoops, and devices for withstanding siege. Boards, nailed one on top of the other in lattice fashion, with the nails protruding were placed in those trenches where an assault would come first. The city trenches themselves were cleaned, the ramparts raised, palisades hammered in, gabions made, all supplies of timber outside the city walls were brought in and piles erected to ward off an assault; all gates, all important points of the inner city were manned with falconets mounted on wagons, cannon, culverins and other ordnance, sentries were doubled, and blockhouses erected at the gates which were reinforced with metal sheets. Guards were posted everywhere and each commanded by a council member .... large stocks of flour were purchased, the cattle were brought near the city, and grain was distributed among the inhabitants. The most skilful instructed the citizens in the new ordinance for dealing with a siege and in self-defence. In the event of a forced exit, a wagon full of pikes was kept ready so that, if required, the hand gunners could make use of them.

To the East of the Duchy about 600 peasants assembled on the 'Lange Wiese'- a field to the north of the town of Ellwangen. Reinforced by the peasants of Limpurg, the Ellwanger Band occupied the monastery of Mönchsroth, south of Dinkelsbühl, on April 28th, and razed it to the ground. By this time the Bottwar band had united with the Zabergäu troop under Hans Wunderer. To this steadily growing army came the discredited leader Jäcklein Rohrbach with an unspecified number of Franconian rebels. In addition, a band of Black Forest peasants under the command of Thomas Maier and a further troop from the Kraichgau under the command of the pastor Anton Eisenhut joined their ranks. Feuerbacher found himself at the head of an 12,000 strong troop which became known as the Heller Christlicher Haufen – (the bright Christian band). As it moved through the countryside it brought a number of towns into the fold.

1525 THE RISE AND FALL OF THE REVOLT

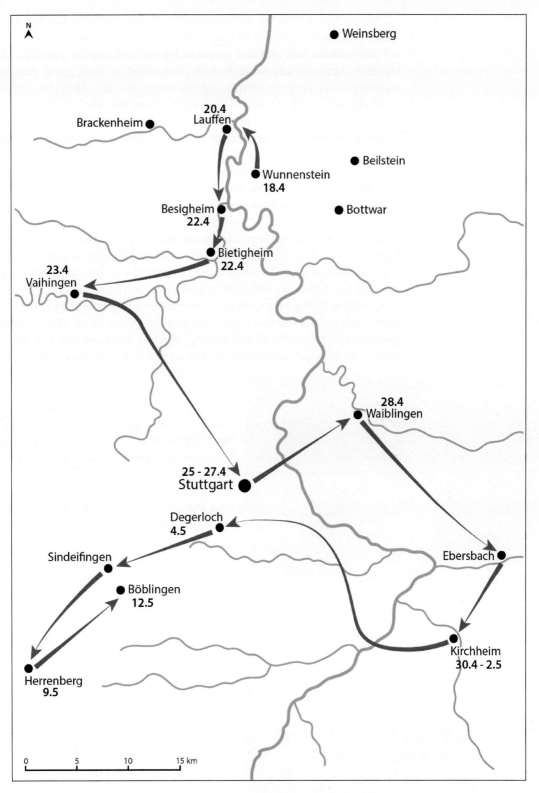

Map 5. Movements of the Württemberg Troop

THE GERMAN PEASANTS' WAR 1524-26

Meanwhile following the withdrawal of the Swabian League army which had been in pursuit of Duke Ulrich, the city of Stuttgart had been left unprotected and was not prepared for an onslaught of peasants. On the 25th April the city officials were confronted by some 6000 peasants standing before the gates demanding entrance to the city. At the head of the peasant band stood the artist Jörg Ratgeb whom the rebels had chosen as their commander and lead negotiator. Soon Stuttgart had become a major debating chamber for the combined peasant bands where the moderating influence of Feuerbacher, still holding the rank of supreme commander, held sway. Despite his protestations he could not, however, prevent rebel detachments from making forays into the outlying districts to plunder castles and monasteries. On May 7th, 1525, the rebels plundered the nearby Auhausen monastery and moved along the "High Street" – (Hohe Strasse)- via Ostheim in the direction of Heidenheim. With more than 200 wagons of booty they reached the Geilbuck to the south of Ostheim where they were confronted by 400 of the Margrave of Ansbach's heavily armed horsemen and 500 Landsknechts with light artillery in tow. The band drove back the margrave's infantry, wounding many of them, until the latter regrouped with their artillery on a rise and fired down into the village. Some 1000 peasants perished and 3000 surrendered seeking mercy. A good number were able to escape, while those Landsknechts in the service of the peasants were granted free withdrawal.

Having neutralised the upper Swabian peasants with a successful conclusion of the Treaty of Weingarten on the 17th of April, the Truchsess of Waldburg ordered the League army to push northwards to suppress the revolt in the Duchy. Having marched through Tuttlingen, Balingen and Tübingen the League army set up camp at Rottenburg on the Neckar. As reports came in of the League's movements, the Württemberg band marched towards Herrenberg and on the 10th May they stormed the town,

Casimir (or Kasimir) of Brandenburg-Bayreuth (27 December 1481–21 September 1527) was Margrave of Bayreuth from 1515 to 1527. Casimir opposed the Reformation, unlike his brother George. At considerable financial and personal expense, he hired mercenaries and organised the defence of his territory which included Rothenburg ob der Tauber and the districts of Crailsheim, Lobenhausen-Anhausen, Werdeck-Gerabronn and Bamberg-Wiesenbach. As the riots spread through Franconia into Casimir's territory, he withdrew to Ansbach and dug in having to rely on Bohemian mercenaries to defend the castles in his territory. Portrait by Hans von Kulmbach, (Alte Pinakothek.CC-BY-SA, 4.0 Creative Commons).

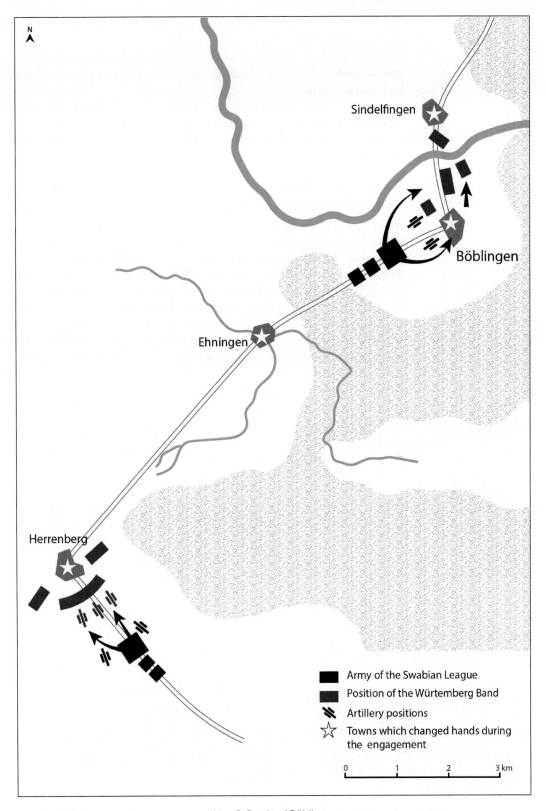

Map 6. Battle of Böblingen

THE GERMAN PEASANTS' WAR 1524-26

overpowered the garrison and set up three camps on the hills above with well dug in artillery. The Truchsess refrained from any frontal assault on what was clearly an advantageous peasant position since he was in any event preoccupied with stilling a mutiny within his ranks as his Landsknechts had not been paid.

Fortunately for the League, the Württemberger decided to withdraw under cover of darkness to what they considered to be a more favourable position between Sindelfingen and Böblingen. Between both towns the peasants set up a number of detachments and erected a wagonfort on what was known as the Galgenberg, positioning 18 cannons in the direction of the League advance. On May 12th the Truchsess ordered his men into battle formation but knew that a frontal attack would be foolhardy. He managed to persuade the Böblinger to come over to his side and they allowed him entry into the town whereupon a fresh supply of hook guns and culverins were trained upon the peasant positions below. Although he had managed to outflank the peasants the League commander was still unwilling to commit his mounted men at arms into a frontal attack on the peasant positions. He turned his attention on to the wagon fort which he took with some ease, dispatched the peasant vanguard from which position he was able to train his field artillery on to the peasant main 'battle'. As the vanguard broke ranks and retreated into the main battle column behind, the Truchsess ordered his squadrons of horse into the fray from both sides, Soon the main body of the peasant army was in retreat pursued up to some 10 kilometres by the League horse.

The forerunners of cavalry are likely to have been a mix of knights and vassals clad in their customary *Waffenrock* tunics and/or light armour. This image shows such a group assembling, possibly before going into action. Woodcut purportedly by Hans Tirol.

Out of a 12000 strong army, some 6000 peasant souls were lost. On the other hand, according to the victors, the losses on the side of the Swabian League were extraordinarily low – it is claimed only 25 horsemen and 15 footsoldiers . The war booty was considerable. 6 banners were taken along with 18 cannons and all the supplies within the wagon fort. Captured in Sindelfingen on the very evening of the battle was Melchior Nonnenmacher - one of the main culprits of the Weinsberg massacre (See next section). Along with Jäcklein Rohrbach who was captured on the same day with some other peasants between Markgröningen and Vaihingen, he was handed over to the Truchsess and roasted alive near Neckargartach on May 21st.

Böblingen marked the end of the Württemberg insurrection although elsewhere in the Duchy the authorities still needed to engage in a mopping up exercise. When, on May 17th a small force of 300 mounted men at arms and 300 Landsknechts sent by Ludwig, the Elector Palatine, razed the village of Dalkingen, the Ellwanger band were provoked into marching out to confront the elector's men at Aalen in what proved to be a resounding defeat for the rebels. According to one report, 436 peasants were left lying on the battlefield. The last remnants of the Württemberg rebels finally surrendered on this day.

Franconia

Chronology

March	22	The Rothenburg militia revolt
	26	Peasants storm the monastery in Mergentheim
		The Odenwald Peasant band is formed.
April	1	First uprising in the Bishopric of Würzburg
		In Franconia the peasants from Rothenburg, Würzburg and the Tauber valley form an alliance
	2	Bildhausen Band, the Neckar Valley and Odenwald Bands are formed.
	16	Peasant assault on the castle at Weinsberg. Duke Helfenstein is put to death.
	19	City of Heilbronn identifies with the peasant cause.
	27	Götz von Berlichingen joins the main Neckar Valley/ Odenwald band
May	7	Tauber Valley band arrives in Heidingsfeld. Start of siege of the Marienberg fortress in Würzburg
	21	Weinsberg is razed to the ground by the army of the Swabian League.
	23	Neckar Valley and Odenwald peasant bands give up their siege of Würzburg
	26	Götz von Berlichingen abandons peasants.
June	2	Battle of Königshofen
	4	Battle of Ingolstadt/Sulzdorf
	8	Retaking of Würzburg by the League army

THE GERMAN PEASANTS' WAR 1524–26

In Franconia, the state power was in the hands of several territorial rulers, namely the bishoprics of Würzburg and Bamberg, the Margrave of Ansbach Kulmbach and the Counts of Henneberg. In addition there were a number of imperial cities the most important of which were Nuremberg and Rothenburg (ob der Tauber). As the uprising spread three large bands formed between March and April: the Tauber Valley Band to the south and southeast of the prince-bishop's territory, the Odenwald/Neckar Valley band and the Bildhausen band to the north. See Plate C

The Tauber Valley Band

On 21st March 1525, a group of thirty peasants from the large village of Ohrenbach marched into the imperial city of Rothenburg ob der Tauber in protest at the high taxes they were forced to pay. The villagers had been in regular contact with a small group of burghers and innkeepers who shared their anger. Their protest was soon fronted by the nobleman Stephan von Menzingen. Menzingen who had his own agenda, orchestrated a coup against the city council and a new governing 'committee' was set up. On 22nd March, the day after their protest in Rothenburg, the village of Ohrenbach urged Brettheim to join their movement. Brettheim did not hesitate and began urging the surrounding villages in the southern part of Rothenburg's territory to join the rebellion, while Ohrenbach rallied to the north. As men from the villages assembled at the camp at Insingen a leadership council was elected and the so-called Tauber valley Band was formed. The troop moved north towards Rothenburg setting up camp at Gebsattel with the pastors Denner and Hollenpach serving as scribes and

Rothenburg ob der Tauber city hall (Photo: Berthold Werner).

secretaries for the peasants as they presented a list of grievances to the city council. The grievance letter incorporated the language of the 12 articles of the Swabian peasants. This approach proved fruitless and the sudden appearance of a troop of fifty horsemen dispatched by Margrave Casimir whose territory bordered on the city unsettled both town and peasantry. The Margrave's subjects were instructed not to join the band.

At the end of March the band moved southeast of Rothenburg to Oberstetten and with that outside of the city's jurisdiction. Here numbers of men flocked from the Tauber valley between Mergentheim and Tauberbischofsheim who were seeking concessions from Zeisolf von Rosenberg, a vassal of the bishop of Würzburg. Many of these toiled in the vineyards between Rothenburg and Wertheim and were particularly poor. At Schäftersheim. there were changes in leadership before the band marched up the Tauber valley to Gerlachsheim, where they camped for three days. It was here that a nobleman, Florian Geyer, volunteered his help. Geyer, an ardent Protestant who possessed considerable military and diplomatic experience was accepted by the council as their head. Geyer's admission into the band coincided with the onset of the bands campaign to destroy of all the castles in Franconia which was to mark a dramatic escalation of the rebellion. Around April 16 the band marched back up the Tauber valley to Mergentheim where they destroyed the Teutonic Order's castle, Neuburg. While the Tauber band camped at Aub, the leaders considered moving south to besiege Rothenburg to force the city to hand over two large siege cannons together with auxiliary equipment and gunpowder to assist them with their aim. However, their call to arms in the surrounding countryside produced such a response from Ochsenfurt, they pitched camp there on April 25. The arrival of so many men from the Main region necessitated a re-organization of the leadership council at Ochsenfurt. Jacob Kohl replaced Florian Geyer, who was away representing the peasants in negotiations with the surrounding governments. The new leadership established military-style regulations for daily life in camp in the form of a field ordinance (See Appendix I)

Via Iphofen the band moved to Schwarzach where they looted the abbey and then on to Gerolzhofen where they stormed the castle. All moveable goods were removed, divided, and sold. Other independent bands which had formed in the nearby Steigerwald forest destroyed castles at Zabelstein, Castell, and Speckfeld. However, a faction within the Tauber band began lobbying for a reversal of direction of their march towards the regional capital of Würzburg. Having convened a ring, however, the entire band decided to besiege the bishop's castle which overlooked the city. On Sunday, 7th May, they entered Heidingsfeld 5 km south of the city.

THE GERMAN PEASANTS' WAR 1524-26

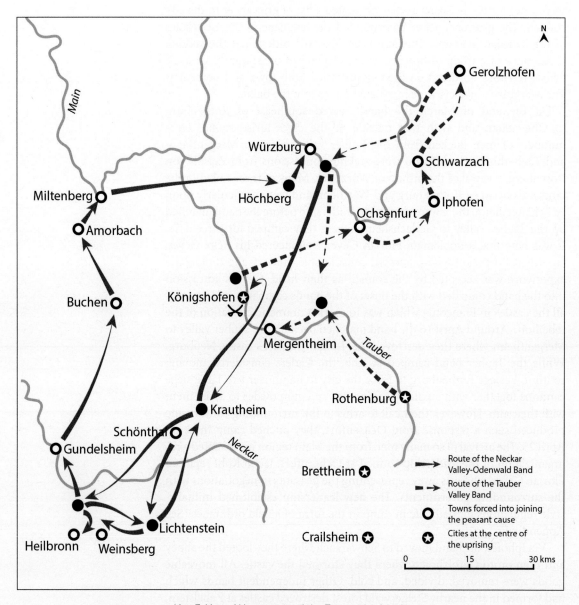

Map 7. Map of Movements of the Franconian bands

Neckar Valley/Odenwald band

The second band to organise emerged in the so-called Odenwald (a low forested mountain range which today straddles the German states of Hesse, Bavaria and Baden-Württemberg). Subjects of the territories of the Archbishop of Mainz, the count of Hohenlohe and the duchy of Württemberg began to spontaneously assemble in late March. Their leader, an innkeeper by the name of Georg Metzler, had placed a 'Bundschuh' on the end of a pole as a rallying point while others marched behind a crucifix. He was joined by Wendel Hipler, a nobleman from Öhringen who had served as secretary to Count Hohenlohe from 1490 to 1514 and had had cause for dispute with the counts during the preceding decade. On the 4th of April the peasants of the Odenwald occupied the convent of Schöntal on the river Jagst where they set up a temporary base. Here they were joined by a troop of some 1500 men from the Neckar valley under the command of a serf from Böckingen by the name of Jäcklein Rohrbach. Rohrbach had military experience but had served periods in gaol following a number of disputes with the authorities. His band consisted of disaffected peasants from villages and farmsteads surrounding the imperial city of Heilbronn and the Weinsberg valley who gathered in Flein on the outskirts of Heilbronn. On April 6th his band marched on Öhringen and from there to Schöntal where the united Neckartal-Odenwalder also called the 'Bright' Band (Heller Haufen) was formed. This joint band numbered about 8000 men and clearly posed a threat to the immediate nobility who were the counts of Hohenlohe.

On April 11 Counts Albrecht and Georg von Hohenlohe accepted the 12 Articles in an open field below their castle at Waldenburg and joined the band. The following day the monastery of Lichtenstein went up in flames. On Good Friday April 14, the peasants marched through the Sulm valley and occupied the Teutonic Order town of Neckarsulm. The governor of Weinsberg, Count Ludwig von Helfenstein, a son-in-law of Emperor Maximilian I, was asked to join the Christian Union but was in no mood for negotiation ordering his horsemen to repeatedly attack the rear-guard of the peasant train. He had already undertaken a number of raids on peasant farmsteads putting to the sword any peasants and threatened to take revenge on the wives and children of anyone identifying with the rebel cause.

In Neckarsulm, it was decided to march on the town of Weinsberg, Helfenstein's residence. From Neckarsulm the Bright Band sent an ultimatum to the council of Weinsberg and the Helfensteiner. On both sides, scouts probed each other. Some elements within the town council were prepared to open the gates to the rebels but Helfenstein had his spies everywhere. On Easter Sunday the peasants stormed his poorly defended castle and pursued the Count and his entourage of knights in the town where they fought a rear-guard action from the tower of St. John's Church. A number of knights perished in the ensuing melee and some 16 were taken prisoner including the Count.

THE GERMAN PEASANTS' WAR 1524–26

Contemporary image by Hans Baldung Grien of Castle Weibertreu in Weinsberg, residence of the count of Helfenstein. Signatur Cod. Karlsruhe 2476 (Kupferstichkabinett der Kunsthalle Karlsruhe, with permission).

A later image dated 1629 depicting the Countess of Helfenstein pleading with Jaeckleiin Rohrbach to spare her husband. In the background is the gauntlet of pike set up by the peasants. Artist: Mathaeus Merian the Elder, originally from Johann Ludwig Gottfried: *Historische Chronica der vier Monarchien* (1629–1632).

1525 THE RISE AND FALL OF THE REVOLT

The execution of Helfenstein and his entourage on Easter Monday – they were forced to run a gauntlet of pike - shocked the nobility since this was a punishment normally reserved for rank-and-file mercenaries. The more moderate peasant leaders who had hoped for a negotiated settlement with the princes saw their hopes dashed by this one act. Yet in the wider context the Weinsberg massacre was no more repulsive than the actions of the nobility following a military victory whereby peasant ringleaders would normally face a beheading . The authorities did not see things this way of course. Luther wrote his pamphlet "Wider die mörderischen Rotten der Bauern" (Against the murderous gangs of the peasants) in response to the events in which the most telling words were:

> Therefore, dear lords, here is a place where you can release, rescue, help. Have mercy on these poor people [whom the peasants have compelled to join them]. Stab, smite, slay, whoever can. If you die in doing it, well for you! A more blessed death can never be yours, for you die obeying the divine Word and commandment in Romans XIII, and in loving service of your neighbour, whom you are rescuing from the bonds of hell and of the devil……

From Weinsberg the Bright Band continued to Heilbronn, where they were able to march through open gates on April 17, as the city sided with the peasant cause, handing over 1,200 florins and providing a company of volunteers to reinforce the band. Rohrbach appears at this point to have become persona non grata and he left the band shortly after with 200 followers to join the Württemberg peasants under Matern Feuerbacher. Plans were hatched to convene a 'Peasants' Parliament' in the city. On the April 22 the Bright band marched onwards to Gundelsheim where they pressed the knight Götz von Berlichingen to join their cause. Fearful of damage to the Hornberg (his castle to the north of the town) he reluctantly became a member of their leadership council. He now moved with Metzler and the peasants via Buchen to Amorbach, where they stayed from April 30 to May 5. Throughout the surrounding countryside, the peasants provided the nobility with a dose of its own medicine - threatening to destroy their property unless they swore an oath to their cause. One such prize for the peasants was Count Georg von Wertheim whose territory lay to the west of Würzburg who joined the band on the May 5. While in Amorbach a Franconian version of the 12 articles, written by Hipler and the Heilbronn citizen Hans Berlin was published as the Amorbach Declaration. Invitations were sent out to the peasant bands active within Franconia, Swabia and on the Rhine to meet in Heilbronn in mid-May for a peasant parliament. In an important political development, a delegation from the Electorate of Mainz met with the leadership of the band at Miltenberg on May 7 and swore an oath to the Amorbach Declaration in the name of their archbishop effectively accepting the surrender of the most eminent ecclesiastical principality in Germany and acknowledging the importance of a reformation as a means of settling the dispute between the lords and the peasants.

The Gauntlet of Pike at Weinsberg

Before Weinsberg lies an open space ……. beneath the former lower gate, which leads to Heilbronn, where the peasants led the Count of Helfenstein with the rest of the nobility …….on Easter Monday at sunrise. A rough fellow, who had formerly served the count as a piper, walked in front of him with a pipe and said: 'I once played the whistle for you so often at the table, now I will play for you another dance for free'. …….. At …word of command, the peasants formed two lines; drums and whistles sounded, and Hans Konrad von Winterstetten – .was the first whom they chased through their pikes in front of the others. This was followed by his lord, Konrad Schenk von Winterstetten and the other knights, nobles and servants, as Count Ludwig Helferich von Helfenstein, Burkhard von Ehingen, Dietrich von Westerstetten, Friedrich von Neuhausen, Konrad von Ehingen, Georg Wolf von Neuhausen, Philipp von Bernhausen, Hans Späth von Höpfigheim, Pleickard von Ruchzingen, Rudolph von Hirnheim, Georg von Kaltenthal, and Weiler the Younger, soon to follow his father in death, also of the Count of Helfenstein ,court jester and several servants and priests. When the peasants stormed the castle, they also summoned the countess to the place of execution, ……. In vain the countess threw herself at the feet of the peasants ……… and begged in the name of the …child for the life of his father. The rebels were unmoved. The count fell pierced through. Andreas Rymy, a peasant from Zimmern, stuck the feathers from the count's helmet into his hat, while their leader Jäcklein Rohrbach, put on his armour. The countess was robbed of her jewellery and the child on her arm wounded. A manure wagon was brought up, on which they put the countess with her maid, and sent them off in the direction of Heilbronn: 'You may have entered Weinsberg on a golden carriage', they said mockingly, 'but you can (damn) well leave on a manure wagon!'[33]

The Bright band united with the Tauber Valley band at their camp at Heidingsfeld south of the city of Würzburg. Together they now numbered some 15,000 men. On 3 May the citizens of Würzburg declared their support for the peasant cause. The military objective was now the taking of the fortress of Marienberg – residence of Bishop Konrad von Thüngen – which towered over the city. However before describing the siege of the

---

33 Justinus Andreas Christian Kerner 1848 *Die Bestürmung der württembergischen Stadt Weinsberg im Jahr 1525, aus handschriftlichen Überlieferungen der damaligen Zeit dargestellt*; Heilbronn .Translation author.

Marienberg it is necessary to trace the movements of the third Franconian band which emerged from the territory surrounding Bildhausen to the north of the bishopric.

The Bildhausen Band

On 8 April, a gathering of concerned peasants and townsfolk in Munnerstadt heard of the news of developments further south in the prince-bishopric and decided on similar action. The abbot of the monastery at Bildhausen learned of their plans and requested armed assistance to protect his estate. Hans von Maßbach – the bailiff of Wildberg – sent a troop of 150 men but little response was forthcoming from elsewhere. On 12 April, about 300 peasants marched to the monastery of Bildhausen with drums and fifes playing. The gates were opened without further resistance. When the militia arrived, they joined the peasant ranks. Attempts to persuade the peasants to disband proved fruitless and a camp was established on the Petersberg Hill while access points into the monastery were fortified. The Bildhausen band elected Hans Schnabel and Hans Schaar as their captains and called on all towns, offices and villages to join them.[34]

Gottfried 'Götz' von Berlichingen (1480 – 23 July 1562), also known as Götz of the Iron Hand, was an imperial knight who reluctantly led the Odenwald peasant band abandoning them after four weeks of pressed service to sit out the rest of the rebellion in his castle at Burg Jagsthausen. This portrait shows him in Maximilian armour. (Museum Boijmans Van Beuningen, with permission).

The band was initially moderate in its aims, but tensions began to arise at the beginning of May when the leadership began to demand levies of men for the band, calling up a quarter of all adult males from the allied towns and a third from the rural communities. The farmworkers complained that the townsfolk were able to pay for mercenaries to join the ranks of the band

---

34 Michael Böckler, Der Bildhäuser Bauernhaufen im Bauernkrieg, *Heimatblätter für Kultur, Geschichte und Brauchtum im Grabfeld* (Verein für Heimatgeschichte im Grabfeld e.V. und Museumspädagogisches Zentrum Bad Königshofen 2011) No.19 p.12.

and thereby avoid conscription while they had to serve. They insisted that the levies should be raised more equitably from both groups. Complaints arose about the inadequate representation of the commons within the leadership resulting in the adoption of more radical articles. Nobles for example were to be allowed to join the band but were to march on foot like everyone else and not on horseback. Grain stores were to be seized from castles and monastic houses and nobles' castles were to be destroyed, although it was left to their owners' discretion whether they would do so or not. Moreover, four men were to be appointed by the commons as aides to the captains, two of whom were to act as co-captains, without whose advice and agreement the captains were to undertake nothing. These stipulations may have signalled division between townsfolk and peasants. and may have reflected a radicalisation under the influence of the Tauber Valley programme, which in certain respects they resembled.

The Bildhausen band served to distract Count Wilhelm von Henneberg from coming to the aid of the prince-bishop, but its military and strategic contribution was otherwise insignificant. The agreed strategy on 6–7 May was that the three Franconian bands would converge on Würzburg, but it was not until 10 May that the camp in Bildhausen was abandoned with the troop setting off in the direction of Schweinfurt with the intention of uniting with the other Franconian bands to besiege the Marienberg in the regional capital. However, a call for assistance from the peasants at Mellrichstadt caused the band to change direction. The Landgrave Philipp of Hesse was already in the vicinity of Meiningen and posing a threat to the rebels in the Franconian highlands. While the Bildhausen band lay in wait until 14 May for the Landgrave in Mellrichstadt, Philipp of Hesse had other plans having changed direction to march on Mühlhausen– the epicentre of the uprising in Thüringia – to deal with the radical cleric Thomas Müntzer. The rebels decided to split their army with contingents remaining in Meiningen under the command of its mayor while Schnabel and Schaar set off in the direction of Würzburg to link up with the other Franconian bands.

Table 1: The Franconian Bands

	Strength	Commanders
Tauber Valley Band	4,000	Jakob Kohl, Wendel Hipler
Neckar Valley/ Odenwald Band	8,000	Georg Metzler, Jäcklein Rohrbach Götz von Berlichingen
Bildhausen Band	7,000	Hans Schnabel, Hans Scharr

Source: Bensing & Hoyer op. cit.

1525 THE RISE AND FALL OF THE REVOLT

Born into a Franconian noble family about 1466 Konrad von Thüngen was appointed Prince-Bishop of Würzburg by Pope Leo X in 1519. His Prince-Bishopric was one of the main centres of the German Peasants' War, and he was forced to flee his residence in the Marienberg in the city. Engraving by Johann Salver, (Museum für Franken – Staatliches Museum für Kunst and Kulturgeschichte in Würzburg with permission).

The Defence of Würzburg

The four Franconian princes (the bishops of Würzburg, Bamberg and Eichstätt as well as the Margrave of Brandenburg-Ansbach) were on high alert as news reached them of the peasant uprisings in their territories. At a meeting in Neustadt an der Aisch they considered requesting the help of the Swabian League at an early stage, since the formation of a combined force had failed due to an absence of their own contingents and finances. Mainz, the Palatinate, Saxony, Bavaria and Hesse were also to be approached. Much time would elapse before the official application for League assistance let alone the arrival of troops would transpire. Since the neighbouring territories had to deal with their own uprisings, each would have to rely on their own means in the interim.

Konrad von Thüngen approached his ally the Palatine Elector Ludwig V on 15 April requesting a cannon and gunnery master. Additional requests for assistance further specified three more trained artillery specialists and a hundred assistants. From these requests the prince-bishop was clearly already anticipating an assault by the peasants on the Marienberg fortress. On 18 April, however, the Count Palatine rejected the request as news reached him about the bloodbath at Weinsberg. He offered instead 5,000 Dutch mercenaries who were sitting idly in Cologne. However, the prince-bishop did not have the financial means to recruit them. He turned to Wilhelm von Henneberg who agreed to provide mercenaries and ordnance but a delivery of some 4,000 florins to pay for this assistance could not proceed as news arrived that Henneberg was caught up in intensive negotiations with the peasants. Much to the disgust of the prince-bishop, Henneberg joined the peasant cause. By 20 April it was becoming clear to von Thüngen that using his own military resources to suppress the uprising in disparate parts of his territory was a drain on his capability to defend Würzburg, so he ordered his troops back to the city and prepared to reinforce the fortress Marienberg with provisions and ordnance.

The only noble who had the capacity to resist the peasants was the Margrave Casimir von Brandenburg-Kulmbach. However, he too was stretched militarily so opted to appease the rebels at the beginning granting them use of the commons and a reduction in the tax burden. On 3 May, the citizens of Würzburg had called on the Odenwald band, which was currently under the leadership of Götz von Berlichingen, to join them. From their camp outside Gerolzhofen the Odenwalders also called on the Bildhausen band to come to their assistance. Around 5 May, the first larger peasant groups arrived and camped before Würzburg, near Heidingsfeld and Höchberg. The prince-bishop in the meantime, had already fled to Heidelberg seeking the protection of Count Palatine Ludwig V. He left word with his castellan on the Marienberg to stall the peasants by offering negotiations. On 7 May, the city opened its gates to the peasant army. Both groups had a common goal – the taking and demolition of the fortress which was viewed as a symbol of the bishop's rule.

The Siege of the Marienberg

In negotiations the hardliners amongst the peasants demanded the surrender of the castle and a free passage for the garrison on payment of 100,000 florins. When this was refused, a decision was taken to storm the fortress. Götz von Berlichingen, who was not entirely committed to the peasant cause, advised against the action but was unable to prevail. On 11 May the final decision to attack was made. Three weeks had lapsed between the prince-bishop's decision to reinforce the Marienberg and the peasant decision to commence an assault. This would prove to be crucial in determining the outcome of the siege, but much would depend on the ability of the defenders to hold out until relief came – something which was still unclear.

Thanks to the meticulous reports by Lorenz Fries[35] and the castellan Sebastian Rotenhan it is possible to reconstruct precisely what measures were

---

35 Lorenz Fries, *Geschichte, Namen, Geschlecht, Leben, Thaten und Absterben der Bischöfe von Würzburg und Herzoge von Franken, auch was während der Regierung jedes Einzelnen derselben Merkwürdiges sich ereignet*. 1546 (Verlag Bonitas-Bauer, 1924).

taken to defend the fortress.[36] Sebastian Rotenhan felt ill-equipped as a military commander to deal with the siege and tried to find a replacement but proved ultimately to be up to the task. He had the trees in the surrounding area cut down for a clear field of fire and the outer walls around the moat and the rubble removed so that no cover would be provided to the attackers. Spikes were erected in the moat, a high light fence around the castle itself, bastions, gates, towers and ramparts were strengthened and repaired and embrasures were broken into the walls. Stockpiling of provisions included water, wine, wood, coal, bacon, eggs, butter, dried fish, etcetera. A mill was built for grinding flour as was a powder mill. Supplies of coal, sulphur and saltpetre were procured. The horses of the occupying troops, which were useless for a siege, were stabled away from the fortress.

Marienberg Fortress – the residence of Konrad von Thüngen. (Photo: Christian Horvat, public domain).

Compared to the peasant army, the garrison was ridiculously small. Rotenhan reports of just 350 men. Fifteen percent of the garrison were noblemen. In addition, there were two barbers, six millers, 12 carpenters, four innkeepers, two laundresses, 12 gunsmiths, three stonemasons, seven blacksmiths, eight bakers, 12 cooks and scullions, three butchers and two servants in charge of the well. Even the city executioner had sought refuge in the fortress.

Only a small number had actual military experience. Dietrich von Thüngen was master of the fortress artillery and Philipp von Bernheim captained some 30 men who were tasked with defending the outer bailey. Two further men were positioned on lookout in each of the two towers. On the other side, the defences to the south, towards the Nikolausberg were

---

36   I am grateful to Rainer Leng for his assistance with material on the siege. cf. Leng, *Bauern vor den Mauern*.

THE GERMAN PEASANTS' WAR 1524–26

Sebastian Rotenhan, the castellan of the Marienberg responsible for the successful defence of the siege during the Franconian uprising. Medallion designed by Hans Schwarz (Dresden, Staatliche Kunstsammlungen Dresden (SKD), Münzkabinett, Signatur/Inventar-Nr: 1752, SLUB Dresden / Deutsche Fotothek / Irene Godenschweg).

covered by five squads of men under the military command of Frederick of Brandenburg. They numbered approximately 40. These men together with the service personnel of the fortress were all housed in the main hall.

The main task of this group was to defend the so-called '*Schütt*', a defensive outerwork of rubble on the side of the fortress facing the city. It was here that a central attack was expected. It was manned by a further three squads numbering 39 men. The main inner gate, today called Scherenbergtor, was occupied by a separate squad under the command of Sigmund Fuchs. Here the garrison was comparatively weak, but it was protected to some degree by the outer bailey. A whole number of other defensive points were manned by between two and six defenders.

The watch was very precisely regulated as a precaution against any surprise attacks. The middle tower became the communication centre and office of the day watch. Twelve permanent guards were assigned to the outer walls, four each on the *Schütt* and in the bastions facing the valley and the Glesberg hill opposite. The outer castle had its own guards. They worked twelve-hour shifts changing at midnight. Inside the castle, two guards alternated between the armoury, two at the 'Wede', two guards at the 'new hall', two guards at the governor's residence and two guards at the council chamber. The outer guards communicated with the central office via a simple but effective system involving bells and whistles.

The siege began with an artillery duel. The peasants had erected a makeshift redoubt with some bulwarks. The exact location cannot be verified. If it was positioned on the ridge of the Glesberg as contemporary accounts would have us believe, the range was indeed great. If on the other hand the redoubt was located at the height of the church known as the Käppele, the range was indeed shorter, but the peasants' artillery would have been more exposed to counterfire here. Either way the peasant's cannon was no match for the fortress walls and return fire was deemed to be pointless. Instead, the fortress ordnance was trained on the city below and after several salvoes, panic broke out amongst the population.

The city arsenal did possess several culverins and these were trained by the peasants on the fortress and at one point four different artillery positions were trained on the Marienberg on three of its sides. However, this effort was all to no avail. Frustrated, the leadership of the peasants sent a letter to the peasant camp at Tauberbischofsheim lamenting the lack of effective shot and requesting three siege guns and heavier artillery pieces. This heavy ordnance was duly despatched but arrived too late for the first bombardment.

A. Imperial circles and the Holy Roman Empire
See Colour Plate Commentaries for further information.

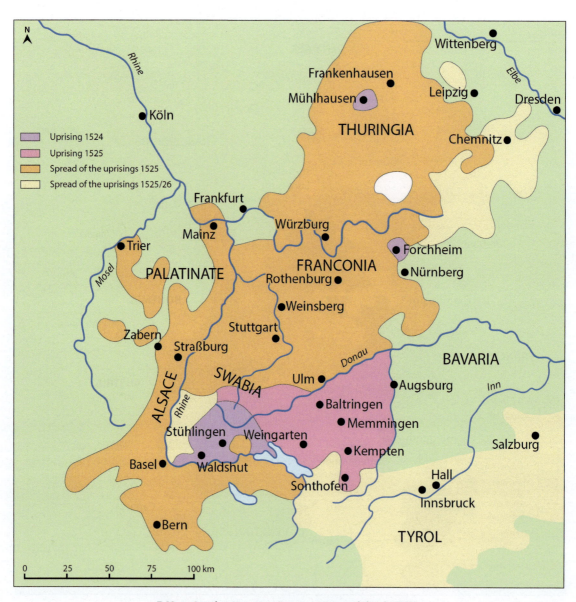

B. Map showing the overall area of the uprising in 1525.
See Colour Plate Commentaries for further information.

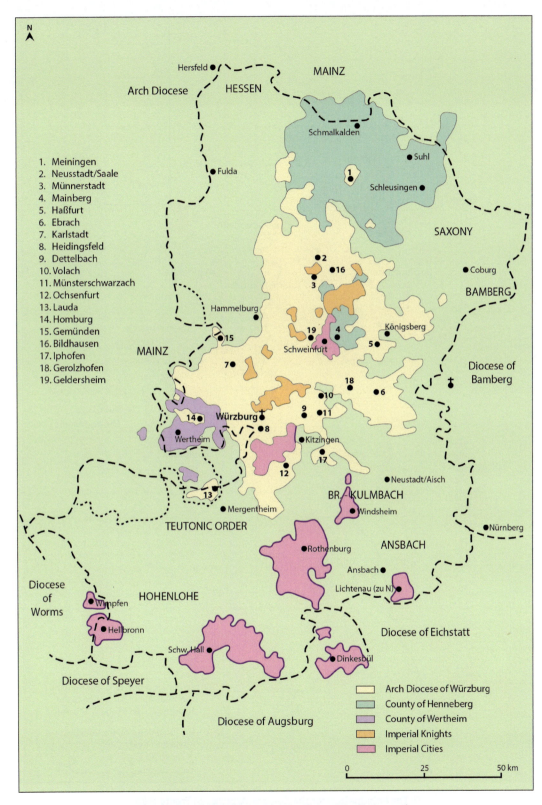

C. The Bishopric of Würzburg at the time of the Reformation.
See Colour Plate Commentaries for further information.

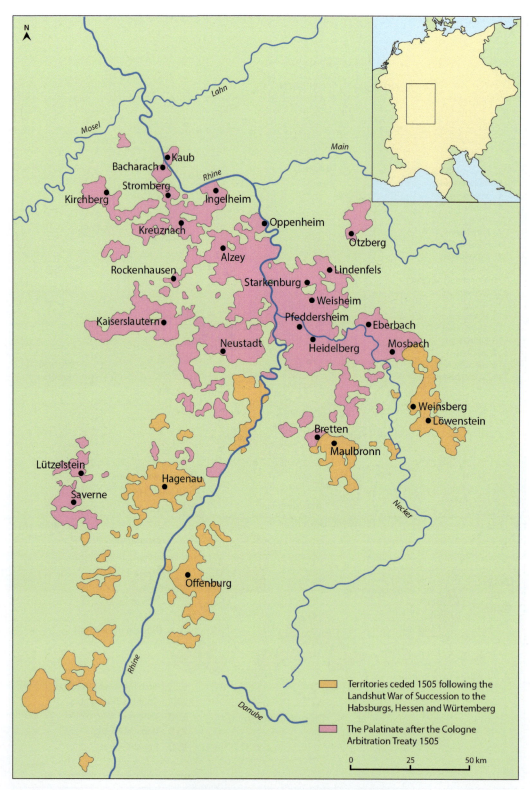

D. The Palatinate after the Cologne Arbitration Treaty 1505
See Colour Plate Commentaries for further information.

E. Peasant Banners
1 Bundschuh banner, 2 Upper Swabian Peasants, 3 Hegau band
(Illustration by Anderson Subtil, © Helion & Company)
See Colour Plate Commentaries for further information.

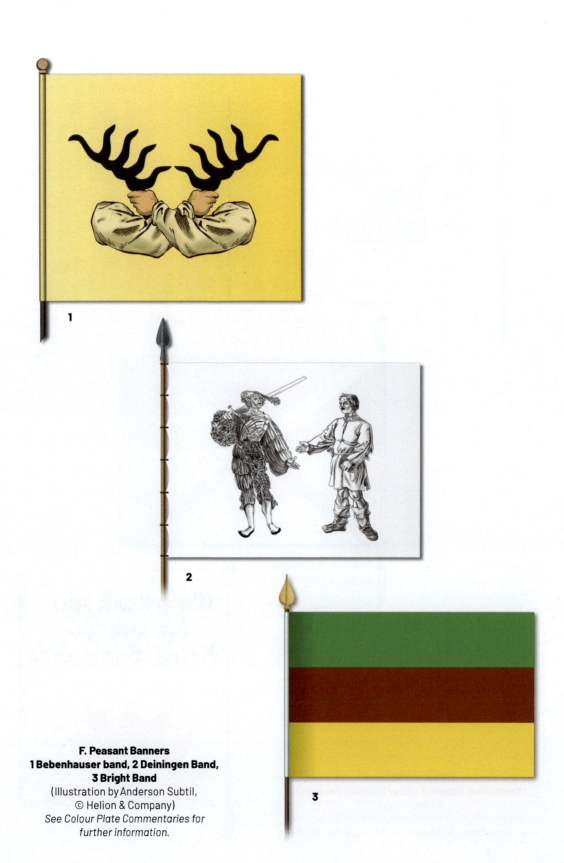

F. Peasant Banners
1 Bebenhauser band, 2 Deiningen Band, 3 Bright Band
(Illustration by Anderson Subtil, © Helion & Company)
See Colour Plate Commentaries for further information.

G. Peasant Banners
1 Odenwald band, 2 Eichsfelder band, 3 Gerstungen band
(Illustration by Giorgio Albertini, © Helion & Company)
See Colour Plate Commentaries for further information.

H. Peasant Banners
1 Mühlhausen band, 2 Sundgau band, 3 Ebersheimmünsterer Band
(Illustration by Giorgio Albertini,
© Helion & Company)
See Colour Plate Commentaries for further information.

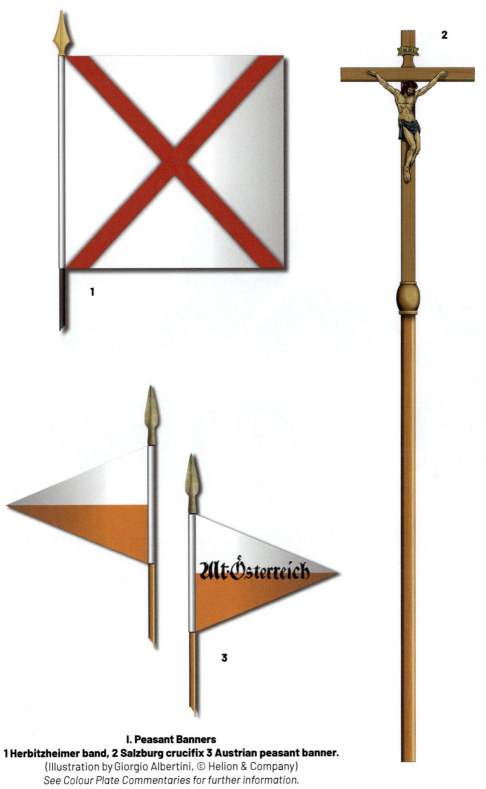

I. Peasant Banners
1 Herbitzheimer band, **2** Salzburg crucifix **3** Austrian peasant banner.
(Illustration by Giorgio Albertini, © Helion & Company)
See Colour Plate Commentaries for further information.

J. Demi Lancer attacking a Peasant
(Illustration by Giorgio Albertini, © Helion & Company)
See Colour Plate Commentaries for further information.

K. Peasant Drummer and Landsknecht Standard Bearer
(Illustration by Giorgio Albertini, © Helion & Company)
See Colour Plate Commentaries for further information.

L. Italian Handgunner and Stradiot
(Illustration by Giorgio Albertini, © Helion & Company)
See Colour Plate Commentaries for further information.

M. People on the Move

See Colour Plate Commentaries for further information.

Trier

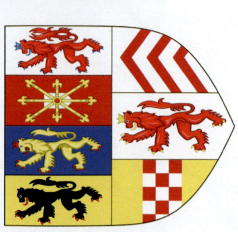

Cleves Julich Berg

N. Banners of Palatinate

See Colour Plate Commentaries for further information.

Mainz

O. Banner of Lorraine.
See Colour Plate Commentaries for further information.

**P. 1. Stained Glass Window Überlingen
2. Coat of Arms of the Elector Palatine. 1500**
See Colour Plate Commentaries for further information.

1525 THE RISE AND FALL OF THE REVOLT

The First Peasant Assault

After two days of bombardment the fortress defenders felt relatively safe behind the walls but the attack at dusk on the evening of the 15 May, may have come as a surprise. As darkness fell the garrison would have had some difficulty in finding targets. The peasants crept up the hill to the front of the ditch at the corner of the *Schütt* facing the narrow set of access steps from the city. With ladders and brandishing axes, they made their assault with flags, fifes and trumpets. The defenders remained disciplined, firing only when the enemy could be hit with some certainty. In the outer bailey, the reserves from the main hall lined up, to reinforce the crew of the *Schütt* if necessary. With small arms and the usual arsenal of weaponry for warding off siege attempts (such as thrown incendiary and explosive devices) the first wave was beaten back.

A second assault had some limited success. Some of the attackers made it through the earthworks via ladders they had brought with them to the outer bailey. A parallel attack was made against the other corner of the *Schütt* towards the Glesberg. Here, some were even able to penetrate the walls but by two o'clock in the morning this assault had also been repulsed. As an act of defiance, the garrison commander ordered a major artillery bombardment of the city to show that that they were still alive in the fortress. These assaults had drained the supply of shot for the arquebuses. Fires had to be lit to melt the lead and the casting of fresh shot took all night.

On Tuesday 16 May the artillery was rested. Sebastian von Rotenhan summoned the crew, thanked them for their efforts and had 100 florins distributed to the mercenaries as a reward from the fortress treasury. In the meantime, the peasants approached, requesting a truce so that the dead could be given a Christian burial. A truce was promised until midnight and the peasants were allowed to recover their dead in front of the earthworks. One estimate puts the number of casualties at 400.[37]

There were various devices used by defenders to resist assaults: forked poles for pushing away siege ladders, in some cases quite sophisticated exploding grenades and pitched wreaths. The latter consisted of a braided ring of string or twine, usually treated with saltpetre beforehand. The wreath was dipped in various mixtures of liquid pitch and gunpowder, which burnt explosively or slowly and could not be extinguished. From Ludwig Eyb, *Kriegsbuch* (University Library Erlangen-Nürnberg, MS.B 26, fol. 298v, with permission).

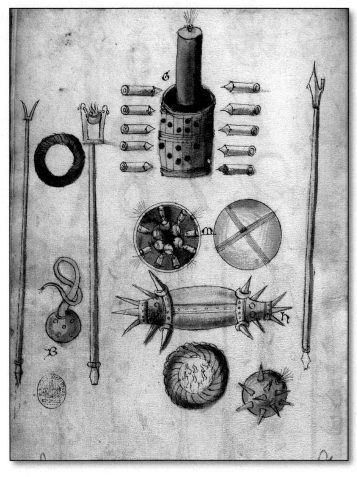

---

37 Martin Cronthal, *Die Stadt Würzburg Im Bauernkriege. Geschichte Des Kitzinger*

On 17 May the peasants erected two new redoubts. Both were located on the north side of the valley, one at the lower end near the city, the other above the path leading to the vineyards. From both sets of earthworks, the section above the Lustgarten bastion (*Zwinger*) was targeted, the aim being to generate sufficient rubble below for the peasants to be able traverse the moat. The peasant earthworks had been constructed as if from an artillery textbook. By now the heavy siege guns which the peasants had requested had arrived from Rothenburg. Each gun emplacement was protected by a wooden shield on a pivot and to each side were earthworks constructed of boards reinforced with metal which were backfilled with earth to provide protection during loading and firing.

Sebastian von Rothenhan later wrote to his student friend in Nuremberg, that over the course of eight days between 600 and 1,000 cannonballs per day were used. On the side of the peasants, according to his estimate, the peasants had approximately 40 larger hookguns mounted on wheels, but the assault parties would have also carried arquebuses. Against the now much more professional approach of the peasants, the defenders needed to step up their efforts on the artillery front. The fortress arsenal was opened up and three much larger cannon rolled out on to the battlements. They reinforced the artillery on the battlements to the east and fired into the town and the two redoubts. The new peasant earthworks proved to be completely inadequate against the heavy stone and iron shot from these larger cannons. Those salvoes which hit home were so devastating that even during the artillery exchange the peasant master gunners stood well away from their exposed position.[38]

It is difficult to assess whether a prolonged bombardment by the peasants would have penetrated the walls of the fortress sufficiently to allow a breakthrough. Rotenhan reported that a hole some 'three wagons wide' had been created two to three floors up on the northern side.[39] Despite this, efforts to hasten relief were intercepted by the peasants. Meanwhile, in the city, after successive attempts with heavy siege cannon had failed, the bombardment was halted. The peasant leadership calling on the fortress commander to surrender and discuss terms. The peasant council of war discussed how to proceed. One option was to mount a further assault, but Götz von Berlichingen advised against this and sought further negotiations.

The Odenwald peasants were not in favour of further casualties and argued for continued bombardment. However, heavier cannon would be required and an unsuccessful approach to the Count of Wertheim was made for artillery reinforcement. As new plans were discussed to tunnel under the fortress and miners had been recruited, news kept arriving daily of the extent of the peasant defeat in Württemberg (Böblingen) at the hands

---

Bauernkrieges 1881 Kessinger Publishing (10 Sept. 2010), p.65.
38   After the peasants abandoned their siege, an inspection of their gun emplacements found body parts strewn all over Fries, 246 in Leng, *Bauern vor den Mauern*, p.161.
39   Ibid.

1525 THE RISE AND FALL OF THE REVOLT

Contemporary image of the siege showing the damage created by peasant artillery: die Eroberung von Würzburg durch den Schwäbischen Bund RB.H.bell.f.1. fol 67 (Photo: Gerald Raab, Staatsbibliothek Bamberg, with permission).

of the Truchsess von Waldburg and that the League army was marching on Würzburg. On 23 May the Neckar Valley/Odenwald band abandoned its part in the siege with Hipler leading the peasants retreat to Krautheim. Several days later Götz von Berlichingen left the troop. The fact that the peasants heard that several of their villages had already surrendered to the authorities caused many of them to disperse.

After razing Weinsberg, as punishment for the execution of Helfenstein and his entourage, the main force of the Swabian League Army had united with troops of the Elector Prince Ludwig of the Palatinate at Neckarsulm on 26 May. In total the combined armies now numbered 3,200 horsemen and 9,000 infantry. In the army of the alliance alongside Ludwig and the Truchsess, rode Prince Ottheinrich, as well as the Bishops of Würzburg, Trier and Strasbourg. The Odenwälder had advanced as far as Neckarsulm and on 27 May they sent a call for help to Duke Ulrich of Württemberg, saying that they were now in the field with 20,000 to 30,000 men. However, he did not respond. To make matters worse Götz von Berlichingen declared that the agreed time of tenure of his office had expired and, as his relationship with the peasants had become fractious since the siege of the Marienberg, he abandoned the band on 28 May fearing an impending apocalypse and a need to reconcile with the oncoming princes. At Neckarsulm the rebel units in the city were besieged by the League army and capitulated after a short bombardment. Those peasant detachments which were still able retreated in the direction of Königshofen where they united with the Tauber Valley band and the main Franconian band at Heidingsfeld which had marched south from Würzburg to head off the oncoming relief army of the League.

They found themselves caught up in the carnage of 2 June there, with 4,000 dead and then subsequent fighting at Sulzdorf and Giebelstadt

103

THE GERMAN PEASANTS' WAR 1524-26

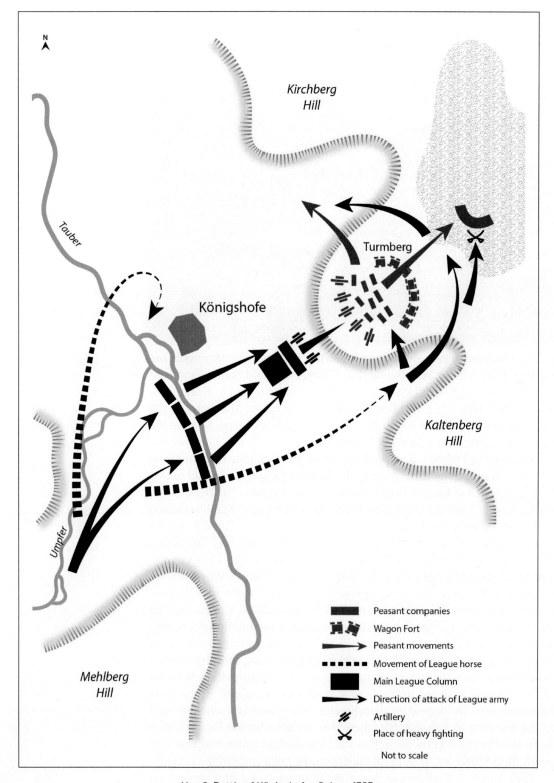

Map 8. Battle of Königshofen 2 June 1525

(Ingolstadt) on 4 June, where as many as 5,000 perished in the fields.[40] In the aftermath the Truchsess occupied Würzburg where he showed no mercy in dealing with the rebel ringleaders.[41]

Central Germany: Thüringia and Saxony

Chronology

1524	
July	Authorities begin search for the attackers of the Mellenbach Chapel at Allstedt.
24 August	Thomas Müntzer attracts support in Sangershausen and Allstedt.
8 September	Müntzer is forced to leave his post as pastor of Allstedt and moves to Mühlhausen.
2 October	Müntzer and Heinrich Pfeiffer establish the Everlasting covenant with God in Mühlhausen.

1525	
2–3 April	Müntzer displays his rainbow flag in Mühlhausen and organises for military action.
18 April	Uprising in Fulda in Hesse. Formation of a peasant band in the Werra valley.
26 April	The uprising spreads in the north of Thüringia.
30 April	Rebels assemble at Frankenhausen.
1 May	Combined Mühlhausen and Thuringian bands march through the Eichsfeld region.
3 May	Philipp of Hesse occupies Fulda.
10/11 May	Müntzer marches to Frankenhausen with 300 men.
12 May	Breakdown in negotiations between the Frankenhausen rebels and the Earl of Mansfeld.
14 May	Frankenhausen rebels initially repel the vanguard of Philipp of Hesse's army as it arrives before the town. Rebels set up a wagon fort on the hill overlooking the town.
15 May	Battle of Frankenhausen ends in a massacre.
20 May	Saxon silver miners' uprising in Joachimstal.
25 May	Mühlhausen surrenders to George of Saxony and Philipp of Hesse.
	Treaty between Saxon miners and Count von Schlick.
27 May	Execution of Müntzer and Pfeiffer outside Mühlhausen.
4 June	Defeat of the Bildhäuser band at Meiningen. End of the uprising in central Germany.

---

40 Cf. Miller, *The Army*, pp.75–79.
41 Miller, *The Army*, pp.80–81.

THE GERMAN PEASANTS' WAR 1524–26

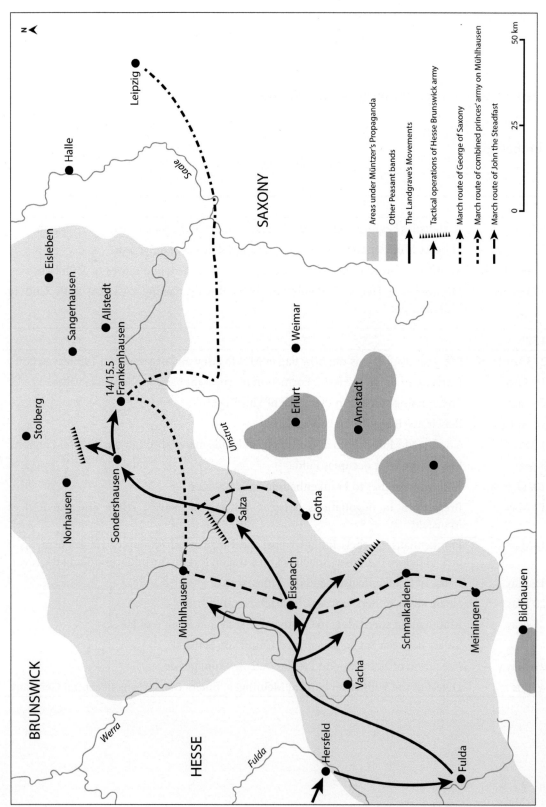

Map 9. The Uprising in Thuringia

Meanwhile in Thüringia, the region of east-central Germany between the Harz mountains and the Thuringian Forest, there was similar unrest. It borders today the neighbouring states of Lower Saxony to the northwest, Saxony-Anhalt to the northeast, Saxony to the southeast, Bavaria to the south and Hesse to the west which are not identical with those states of the Reformation period. The region at this time was ruled by the Ernestine and Albertine houses of the Wettin dynasty which ruled Saxony based on an agreed territorial partition in 1485. The greater southern part of the Duchy of Thüringia between the Werra, Unstrut, Weiss and Elster rivers and the Thuringian Forest lay under the control of the Ernestine Elector Prince, Frederick the Wise, who lay on his death bed at the height of the uprising. On 5 May he was succeeded by his brother John the Steadfast. The northern area between Langensalza, Weissensee and Eckartsberga were governed by the Duchies of Albertine in the person of Duke George of Saxony.

Within these principalities, however, was a myriad of smaller largely subordinate territories, counties, free imperial cities and other domains. The Earls of Henneberg-Schleusingen and Schwarzburg for example, retained a political independence but most nobles were vassals to the Ernestine and Albertine duchies. The district of Eichsfeld and the city of Erfurt and its environs remained under the rule of Albrecht, Margrave of Brandenburg who had obtained the Electorate of Mainz in 1514 and become cardinal in 1518. While the imperial cities of Mühlhausen and Nordhausen retained their autonomy under the terms of their status, other municipalities – some 62 in total – remained under the control of the nobility. Some functioned as administrative centres, others as residences of the nobility.

Thüringia and Saxony constituted the epicentre of the German Reformation – it was in Wittenberg that Luther had nailed his 95 Theses critique of the Catholic church and by the onset of the peasant war, reformist preachers were calling for the removal of any hierarchy within the clergy and the undoing of such dogmas as purgatory (*Fegefeuer*) and the sale of indulgences and new sacraments such as ordination and the veneration of saints. Two of Luther's original followers – Andreas Bodenstein von Karlstadt (Andreas Karlstadt) and Thomas Müntzer had become much more radical in their interpretation of Protestantism. Karlstadt, for example, worked towards reforming the church service during Luther's forced absence and wore secular clothing, removing all references to sacrifice and successfully requesting the removal of all imagery from churches (iconoclasm) in Wittenberg. Thomas Müntzer, who eventually would play an important role in the Thuringian insurgency, did not place the Bible at the centre of his teachings on faith and revelation. Instead, he emphasised the need to experience inner suffering to attain God's will. In this way a pure and spiritual church would materialise paving the way for the second coming of Christ. To this end, of course, the orthodox clergy, the monks and the scholastics had to be removed by the people of God.[42] It was

---

42   Mathias Riedl. 2013 The Charismatic Sword – Thomas Müntzer's Theology of

THE GERMAN PEASANTS' WAR 1524-26

Thomas Müntzer 1489-27 May 1525 as imagined in a 1608 engraving by Christoph von Sichem. Unfortunately, no contemporary portrait exists of the reformer who was born in late 1489 in the small town of Stolberg in the Harz Mountains of Germany. Müntzer's theological idea and organising principal was that God was looking for his chosen ones as society approached the end of days and that he saw himself as chosen to lead this movement. He was clearly an agitator being expelled from Aschersleben in 1516, Brunswick in 1517, Jüterbog in 1519, Zwickau in 1521, Prague in 1521, Nordhausen in 1522, Halle in 1523, Allstedt in 1524, Mühlhausen in 1524, and Fulda in 1525. His sermons were not Lutheran; he had not only become a full-fledged chiliast, but his language had grown extraordinarily violent, abusive, and gross, and his claim to be appointed by God to gather in the elect for the final armed struggle before the millennium was presented in terms outrageous even for those days. In Allstedt he began the secret organisation of the 'League of the Elect' which was responsible for the attack on the priory of Mallenberg. Within a short time, he was recruiting for his League in an ever-widening circle of communities in Thuringia. Müntzer was foremost amongst those reformers who took issue with Luther's compromises with feudal authority. In his sermon to the Princes at Allstedt in 1524 he gave the secular authorities only one choice: either to contribute to the establishment of the kingdom of God or to lose their government to the people who were zealously fighting for the cause of Christ. (Public Domain).

his period of service as pastor in Allstedt which brought him into conflict with the authorities. His delivery of the mass became a success throughout the region. Allstedt was a town of some 900 inhabitants, centre of a small Ernestinian enclave, governed by the relatively reform-friendly princes of Electoral Saxony. However, it was surrounded by orthodox Catholic areas, such as the county of Mansfeld. Its ruler, Count Ernst, was strictly opposed to any innovation in church affairs. In this respect he felt confirmed by a recent anti-reformatory mandate, issued by the emperor on 6 March 1523.

Accordingly, he prohibited the people in his county to attend the service in Allstedt. Müntzer was outraged and insulted the count in public. The count demanded satisfaction and requested permission to arrest the preacher. The Elector Frederick refused the request. Because of earlier experiences with Müntzer he probably feared a rebellion of his followers. Müntzer himself sent a letter to Frederick on 4 October, protesting Count Ernst's measures. Müntzer's activities in Allstedt had allegedly been responsible for an attack

---

Violence (handout & lecture manuscript) – Cambridge University. https://www.academia.edu/4482154/The_Charismatic_Sword_Thomas_M%C3%BCntzers_Theology_of_Violence_handout_and_lecture_manuscript_Cambridge_2013> accessed 28 Sept. 2022.

by his supporters on the Chapel of our Lady in Mallerbach in March 1524 and his practices as a priest gave cause for the authorities to expel him. He moved to the imperial city of Mühlhausen where together with the former monk Heinrich Pfeifer, he agitated for the establishment in the city of a new Eternal Council of God.

In 1523, Thomas Müntzer became pastor in Allstedt's St Johannis Church. A year later, he delivered his famous sermon to the princes (*Fürstenpredigt*) to Duke John the Steadfast and his son at Allstedt Castle. The sermon focuses on a chapter in the Book of Daniel in which he becomes an adviser to the king because of his ability to interpret dreams. In the sermon, Müntzer presented himself as a new Daniel interpreting the passage in the bible as speaking of the kingdom of God that would consume all earthly kingdoms. (Photo Erwin Meier, Creative Commons).

As the political message of the 12 Articles of Memmingen began to gain traction in other parts of Germany – within two months of their publication, they were printed over an unprecedented 25,000 times[43] – central Germany soon was caught up in this fervour. On 18 April 1525, there was an uprising in Fulda. Here the coadjutor (administrator) of the imperial abbey, Count Johann von Henneberg, was forced to accept the 13 Articles of Fulda, which had been influenced by the Memmingen declaration.[44] The peasants of Fulda had sent word to all corners of the region immediately following their uprising to support them in their demands. One district which responded in a determined manner was the upper Werra valley where the peasants formed an 1,800 strong band on 18 April in the area around the town of Vacha. Within days they had elected a commander in the person of Hans Sippel, a known Landsknecht and follower of Thomas Müntzer. Some 20 nobles who inhabited the district surrounding Vacha were forced to march dismounted with the peasants as a sign of equality with those who had assembled. As the band marched on Salzungen it soon swelled in numbers to an estimated 8,000 men. In Salzungen a decision was taken to head south towards Schmalkalden and Meiningen where the authorities had little military presence. En route the army camped outside the gates of Lengsfeld on 23 April 1525. Here the governor Ludwig I von Boyneburg, was forced to

---

43 Peter Blickle, *Die Geschichte der Stadt Memmingen, von den Anfängen bis zum Ende der Reichsstadtzeit* (Stuttgart, 1997), p.393.
44 Scott & Scribner, pp.181–182.

sign the peasants' demands, pay them 500 Meissen florins and accompany the band as a hostage as it marched onwards to Meiningen.

On 27 April, the Werra band reached Schmalkalden having left a trail of plundered monasteries and destroyed castles in its wake. The city had readied itself for a siege but in the end after a one-day inner city revolt, the council was forced to step down and accept the 12 Articles. The mayor Christoph Müller joined the peasant army as a captain and strengthened the force with firearms and ammunition from the municipal armoury. By the end of April, the revolt in Thüringia was in its ascendancy with bands forming in a number of districts. In the territories surrounding Wangenheim and Gleichen, in Salza, in Arnstadt in the Erfurt area, all the way to Lobeda (Jena), Kahla and Gera, there were local sporadic uprisings. In early May Luther was invited by the authorities to make a journey into the region but his efforts to appease the peasants came to nought.

Table 2: Peasant Bands in Thuringia

	Strength	**Commanders**
Fulda Band	6,000	Hans Dalhopf Preacher of Dipperz
Hersfeld Band	4,000	
Werra Band	Approx. 8,000	Hans Sippel
United Mühlhausen/ Thuringian Band	Approx 10,000	Jost and Volkmar Homrich Claus Pfannenschmidt Thomas Müntzer/Heinrich Pfeiffer
Frankenhausen Band	Approx 8,000	Bonaventura Kürschner
Combined Salza and Wangenheim Band	Approx. 5,500	Albrecht Menge, Jakob Krause, Melchior Wiegand
Erfurt Band	10,000	Hans Tunge and Hans Becke
Arnstädter Band	8,000	Hans Bauer
Saalfeld Band	4,000	?

Source: Bensing & Hoyer p.154

On 1 May the Werra band then moved further upstream towards the town of Meiningen which lay under the control of Würzburg. A day later the army stood before the town gates, where the band was informed of the alliance which had been forged between the city and the Bildhausen band thus rendering their planned occupation superfluous. After Count Wilhelm IV of Henneberg-Schleusingen recognised the 12 Articles the Werra band dissolved. One section of the band, disenchanted by the concessions granted to the nobility by its commanding officers, took to marauding. Soon they had taken a number of monasteries and residences belonging to the nobility. Of the original 8,000 strong band, a force of only 2,000 men appeared before the gates of Eisenach where the council declined the request to join the peasant cause. Hans Sippel and his immediate entourage were keen to acquire cannon and shot and naively entered the town in an attempt to negotiate its acquisition with their war chest. However, upon entering the gates they were arrested by officers of the council, tried and beheaded on 11 May.

Elsewhere in the region revolutionary fervour continued, particularly in the surrounding areas of the imperial city of Mühlhausen. The uprising there began amongst the citizenry but, had already taken on a military form at an early stage in the autumn of 1524 when the city council was replaced following agitation by Müntzer and Pfeiffer who called for the appointment of a captain, an ensign, a field surgeon and quartermaster. In mid-September they took advantage of long-standing tensions between the guilds and the city council to produce the city's own '11 Articles', which called for, inter alia, the dissolution of the existing ruling body and the formation of an 'eternal council' based on divine justice and the word of God. Copies of this were sent to the peasantry in the surrounding villages, but support failed to materialise, apparently because the articles expressed predominantly urban grievances which did not address the peasants' needs. On 27 September 1524, Müntzer and Pfeiffer were expelled from Mühlhausen.

Müntzer spent late 1524 in Nuremberg, then moved on to Hegau and Klettgau, centres of the Peasants' War in the Black Forest. In mid-February he and Pfeiffer were able to return to Mühlhausen where in the following month, the citizenry voted out the old council and a new 'Eternal League of God' was formed, composed of a cross-section of the male population and some former councillors. In March 1525 the city arsenal was reinforced with weapons and gunpowder following a threat from Duke George of Saxony to revoke the protections and privileges it enjoyed as an imperial city and to impose a blockade. Heavy cannon and handguns were cast and 225 pikes were ordered from a manufacturer in Eisenach and sold on to some members of the city defence. Supplies of gunpowder were stored in the Dominican monastery in the city.

Only Müntzer and Pfeifer's 'Eternal League of God' appeared to have more radical regional intentions seeking to build an alliance with the miners in the county of Mansfeld. First, however, they would need to take the fortress at Heldrungen – residence of Ernst von Mansfeld. However, there appeared to be more pressing matters for some of the peasant contingents

In the first quarter of the sixteenth century, the imperial city of Mühlhausen was the third biggest municipality in the region. Most of its inhabitants worked in agriculture and its offshoots tanning, cloth making and the production of natural dyestuffs. Despite this, only a fraction of the population had any electoral rights as far as the city council was concerned. This had already fomented political unrest in 1523 before Müntzer and Pfeifer began their agitation. Copper Engraving from Matthäus Merian the Elder (1593-1650). 1650 Topographia Superioris Saxoniae Thuringiae Misniae Lusatiae. Frankfurt, (Bavarian State Library, with permission).

who had allied to their cause. At the end of April, having been joined by a troop of peasants from the Eichsfeld[45] the Mühlhausen band plundered the nunnery at Marksrussa and a number of castles en route to Ebeleben where they held counsel. Here Müntzer declared before the ring that they should unite with the Frankenhausen Band (having promised them reinforcements) and march on the fortress of Heldrungen in the county of Mansfeld. However, they met with resistance:

> At this point, however, several Eichsfelders – Hans Gehausen, Hans Stein and Hans Kirchworbis and others – stepped forward to plead that they join them in a march on Eichsfeld for the lords had already attacked Dingelstädt and intended to kill all the common folk. If the band moved on Heldrungen, all would be lost before they returned. They succeeded in persuading the Mühlhausen leaders to direct their thrust towards the Eichsfeld where several noblemen, who had leased property and land from Cardinal Albrecht, were responsible for their continuing oppression.[46]

For seven days (29 April to 6 May) Müntzer and Pfeifer led a troop through the Eichsfeld which looted and burned a number of castles and priories using the booty to sustain themselves during the march before returning to Mühlhausen with a considerable haul. On returning Müntzer was still intent on coming to the aid of the rebels at Frankenhausen who now numbered some 8,000. On 10 May he set off with just 300 men and a modest eight cart guns (*Karrenbüchsen*) which the city had approved for release from its arsenal.

The Reaction of the Princes

The premature dispersal of the Werra band changed the balance of power in favour of the nobility which had been thrown into turmoil by events yet a substantial number had already sworn allegiance to the peasants – most notably Günther von Schwartzburg the Younger, Count Ernst von Hohnstein, the three Counts of Gleichen and Count Bodo von Stolberg and his son Wolfgang. A number had sought refuge in the Ernst von Mansfeld's fortress at Heldrungen from where urgent messages were being sent to Duke George of Saxony to provide troops to suppress the activities of the rebels who were amassing at Frankenhausen.

Duke George's son-in-law, the Landgrave Philipp of Hesse had been largely focusing his attention on events in the south of Germany, specifically

---

45 Eichsfeld, which translates as field of oaks, is a region in the centre of modern-day Germany, lying east of Göttingen and Kassel.
46 Mühlhausen Chronicle quoted in Scott and Scribner p.147.

the operational area of the Swabian League of which he was a member. It was not until 23 April that he turned his attention nearer home when the insurgency in Thüringia threatened his territory. In a letter to his father-in-law he wrote:

> We cannot keep from your grace (the news) that such a band of peasants is assembled in great numbers in the vicinity of our upper county and is daily growing in number: they are forming bands and have already seized many important towns and markets.... In recent days...the peasants have treacherously conquered the market town of Weinsberg and dealt so unchristianly and evilly with Count Ludwig of Helfenstein...that it is piteous and hard to relate..(If the peasants are not offered timely opposition, all authority is in danger) They have been heard to say in public which can also be seen in their written declarations, that they want to punish all princes, counts, lords and nobles at their pleasure...We will march in person with all our forces into our upper county and it is our renewed request to the your grace that you will appoint and send us five hundred well-armed horse, to help us and other lords and friends resist such evil deeds, which cannot be done without a bold force of cavalry; and they should arrive here at Marburg by next Sunday Cantate. (14 May)

The former Franciscan church of St Crucius today known as the Cornmarket church became a focal point within the city of Mühlhausen for the insurgents. Meetings were held here, and the building was also used to cast cannon barrels for their struggle. Today the church building houses a museum which commemorates the insurgency in Thuringia. Photo: Author.

He hurriedly mustered troops in Marburg and asked the Swabian League to return those contingents which he had despatched a month earlier. On 24 April he left Marburg in an easterly direction with a small but well-equipped army to suppress the uprisings first in Fulda and then Hersfeld. After taking both towns on 28 April and 3 May, the Landgrave turned against the Werra peasants, whom he feared might march on Eschwege and thereby carry the insurgency into Hesse.

As news reached him of the significance which Müntzer was bringing to bear on events, he began some correspondence with the Saxon princes itemising plans for the force which would be necessary to move on him at Mühlhausen: 6,000 foot, 6,000 horse, 15 medium and light guns, 400 hundredweight of powder and 600 sappers for the siege of the city. His plan was that George of Saxony should occupy the town of Salza, John the

THE GERMAN PEASANTS' WAR 1524–26

Heldrungen fortress was an impressive stronghold which had only recently been completed at the time before the battle of Frankenhausen. Count Ernst of Mansfeld had used his right to forced labour to enlist his subjects to construct a four-winged Renaissance residence between 1512 and 1518 then in the years from 1519 the residence had been converted into a fortress with 12 rondelles each with a cannon and a double moat. It is here in the tower shown that Thomas Müntzer was tortured before being moved to his place of execution at Mühlhausen. Little is left of the fortress as it was back then. (Photo: Author).

Steadfast Eisenach, and he himself would take Vacha. Operating individually or, if necessary, jointly, they could strike at the main rebel force. The Landgrave's initial focus was on the Werra band which his scouts overestimated to be 18,000 strong on 5 May. Philipp's own contingent, however numbered a mere 350 mounted men-at-arms and 1,500 Landsknechts. Therefore, on the same day, a request for military assistance was sent to the Dukes of Brunswick.

Duke Henry the Younger of Brunswick-Wolfenbüttel duly obliged. On 10 May Henry's contingents met up with Philipp's at Berka, northwest of Eisenach. It is unclear what the full strength was at this point. One estimate has a combined force of 2,000 mounted men-at-arms and 5,000 footsoldiers, which entered Salza on 12 May. From here the original plan was to proceed against Mühlhausen. When news arrived of Müntzer's move to Frankenhausen the princes changed their plan. They saw the greatest danger coming not from the imperial city per se, but from Müntzer and his followers. The key driver of the revolution had to be defeated to crush the movement at its most pivotal point.

While the combined Hesse-Brunswick army marched on Frankenhausen from (Langen)Salza to the south, an army was being hurriedly assembled to advance on Frankenhausen from the east under Duke George of Saxony. George (the Bearded) was a committed Catholic and head of government of those parts of Saxony which belonged to the Albertine line of the Wettin dynasty. In the second half of April, signs that the Peasants' War was threatening to overspill into the Duchy of Saxony began to alarm the duke at his court in Dresden. Although Philipp had urgently pressed George for military action, the contingents of mounted men-at-arms he had requested in earlier correspondence initially failed to materialise, primarily because the duke was unable to recruit the necessary troops. His efforts were not helped by financial weakness largely caused by his father's disastrous efforts to keep Friesland under his control. Thanks to revenues from silver mining in his territory, the duke had been able to restore a degree of solvency. On 24 April the insurrection in the neighbouring county of Schwarzburg and in Salza prompted him to act. Four days later he issued an order to his nobility and municipal officials to arm and be ready, and appointed Apel von Ebeleben and Sittich von Berlepsch as his commanders-in-chief.[47]

---

47 Both became targets of the insurrection with the castle at Ebeleben plundered and von Berlepsch taken prisoner at Mühlhausen having travelled there to negotiate the release of his kidnapped wife and child. Cf. <https://www.wikiwand.com/de/Hans_Sittich_von_Berlepsch> (accessed 11 August 2022).

Philip the Magnanimous, Landgrave of Hesse, 1504–1567 was a leading champion of the Protestant Reformation in Germany. Philipp was declared of age to rule at 14 and was 21 when he engaged in battle with the insurgents in Thuringia. The year before he converted to Protestantism but was acutely aware of the political threat posed by the radical theology of Thomas Müntzer and his followers – hence his military expedition into Thuringia to join forces with his father-in-law Duke George of Saxony. Woodcut Erhard Schön, public domain.

George let it be known that he requested help from a number of allies. On 30 April he notified Philipp that he would assist him in a campaign to crush the insurgency in Thüringia. He also approached his brother Frederick the Wise and his nephew Johann (the Ernestine line of the Wettin dynasty). Frederick, however, was on his deathbed and Johann had little appetite to engage in military action preferring a peaceful resolution of the peasants' grievances. Unlike the agreement requiring knights to provide a number of mounted men-at-arms, the position regarding a levy of peasants and townsfolk was risky. Duke George needed to recruit Landsknechts which would be costly. Moreover recruitment would need to be undertaken in those pockets of his territory as yet untouched by the disturbance where allegiance particularly among some of the younger men was questionable. Both George and his son Johann the Younger tried to recruit in the county of Meissen but this proved difficult. Johann appointed four recruiting officers but on 5 May informed his father not to expect a muster for another 12–

THE GERMAN PEASANTS' WAR 1524-26

George the Bearded, Duke of Saxony (1471-1539), was Duke of Saxony from 1500 to 1539. From the beginning of the Reformation in 1517, he became an ardent defender of the Catholic faith which brought him into conflict with Luther and later Müntzer. However, George felt compelled to join forces with his Protestant son in law, Philipp the Landgrave of Hesse, to smash the peasants at Frankenhausen. Portrait by Lucas Cranach the Elder 1534 (Creative Commons).

13 days. Given the rate at which events were unfolding this was an unrealistic timescale.

Duke George left Dresden on 1 May in the hope that he would recruit the necessary contingents on his march into Thüringia. On 3 May he arrived in Leipzig from where he ordered his nobility to muster with mounted men-at-arms at Heldrungen – the fortress of Ernst von Mansfeld. News would have reached him that some 1,500 men from Sangerhausen had joined the Frankenhausen band. Promises of contingents from Freiberg, Wolbert and Weissenfels failed to materialise as did commitments made by the Ernestines who now required troops to deal with their own disturbances. On 7 May Wolf von Schönburg acting on behalf of Cardinal Albrecht of Mainz informed George that he would send mounted men-at-arms within five days. In Leipzig, a highly populated city in which the townsfolk had strong reformist leanings, the city council nevertheless supported George with an authorisation to finance 300 Landsknechts for two months. These were to be recruited within Leipzig and its suburbs.

George's son Johann responded on 9 May with precise details of his recruitment efforts. If the municipalities met their promised commitments then the duke could count on between 1,000 and 1,250 men. Moreover the Bishopric of Meissen promised financial assistance in the recruitment. On May George 13 left Leipzig for Heldrungen writing to his brother Heinrich that he had not been able to raise the contingents he had hoped for but that he could wait no longer. From Leipzig to Eckartsberga is a 13 hour march as the crow flies. Duke George's troops would have camped late in the day. From here he informed the earls of Mansfeld that he would arrive on 14 May at 1:00 p.m. in Heldrungen. He requested that they despatch the contingents of Magdeburg auxiliaries under the command of Wolf Freiherr von Schönburg. In a letter to Philipp he reported that he would arrive with 800 mounted men-at-arms, 1,000 Landsknechts and 14 cannon. He also reported that he was waiting for three companies of foot and expected a full complement of 2,000 mounted men-at-arms and 1,500 foot. Duke George's army arrived at Heldrungen around midday on 14 May – just over a two-hour march south-east of Frankenhausen.

1525 THE RISE AND FALL OF THE REVOLT

Eight cart guns (*Karrenbüchsen*) which may have looked like this were supplied by the city arsenal at Muehlhausen to Thomas Muenzer's troop which set off for Frankenhausen on the 10 May 1525. from Philipp Mönch's *Kriegsbuch* 1496. (Universitätsbibliothek Heidelberg, Cod. Pal. germ. 126, with permission).

The Massacre at Frankenhausen 14–15 May 1525

On 14 May around eight o'clock in the morning, a scouting troop sent ahead by the Landgrave in advance of the main Hesse-Brunswick column appeared before the western approach to the salt town of Frankenhausen. They were soon repulsed by watchful peasant sentries camped outside the walls of the town. Peasant wagons were drawn together to provide a defensive shield. As the scouts reported back to the Landgrave, reinforcements, most probably in the form of mounted arquebusiers, were sent back to determine the extent of the peasant defences and numbers. When the main column of infantry and artillery arrived around midday, they remained at some distance from the town in the hamlet of Bendeleben where a decision was taken to camp overnight. A stream of mounted messengers would have been the main means of communication between the two converging armies which did

Peasants pushing a wagon uphill. Woodcut by Hans Weiditz aka the Petrarca Meister. (The Rijksmuseum, with permission).

THE GERMAN PEASANTS' WAR 1524–26

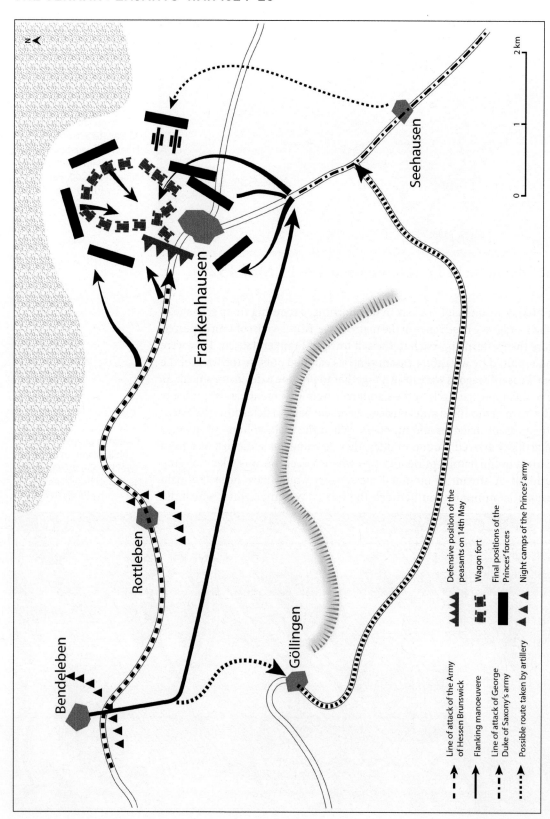

Map 10. Battle of Frankenhausen

not meet up until following morning south of the town. Following a council of war between the Landgrave, Duke George and Henry the Younger a decision was taken to arrange a parley to buy sufficient time to encircle the town. Overnight the rebels had moved their wagons and carts from the area in front of the town up on to the Hausberg – the hill which overlooked Frankenhausen – known today as 'battle hill' (*Schlachtberg*).

Henry the Younger was to mount an assault from the western approach while the Landgrave moved his artillery, light horsemen and infantry up the hill to the east where he erected a battery which could fire into the wagon fort from an elevated position. Duke George's troops remained on the plain in front of the town. The parley dragged on for some three hours as the rebels argued internally over the princes' demand to hand over Müntzer.

This photograph taken in the 1950s from the southwest point from which the barren chalk gully descends, shows the hill on which the wagon fort was erected later in the evening. (Regionalmuseum Bad Frankenhausen, with permission).

Sometime around midday when it became clear that the radical cleric was not going to be surrendered, the Hessian artillery opened fire causing panic within the wagon fort. The princes' light horse and forlorn hopes attacked from both sides and in the ensuing melee, there were heavy peasant casualties. Many sought refuge in the town below but were cut down in the narrow channels running off the hill – the so-called barren chalk (wüstes Kalktal) and blood gullies (Blutrinne).[48] Müntzer escaped but was discovered hiding in one of the gatehouses at the west end of the town. He was carted off to Heldrungen where he was tortured for his confession.[49]

---

48 For a detailed account of the battle cf. Miller, *Frankenhausen 1525*.
49 Wu Ming, *Thomas Müntzer Sermon to the Princes* (London: Verso, 2010) pp.93–97

Following the victory at Frankenhausen the princes' armies moved on to take Mühlhausen. Here, on 27 May, they executed Müntzer along with Heinrich Pfeiffer. At the camp at Schlotheim they were joined by troops led by Count Wilhelm von Henneburg and Elector Johann the Steadfast who had left his base in Weimar some days earlier. In the days at Schlotheim they drew up plans to create a troop to patrol the region in the wake of their victory. As they broke camp a combined new force numbering 4,000 mounted men and 8,000 Landsknechts moved south via Eisenach and Meiningen, aiming for Coburg, in order to protect the nobles who had fled there as well as to put down the uprisings in the Franconian territories. Meanwhile Archduke George returned to Saxony where news would reach him of serious disturbances in the mining industry on his border with Bohemia.

The Miners' Uprisings in Saxony

In Saxony there had been growing discontent amongst the miners of Mansfeld, Annaberg and Joachimstal (on the border with Bohemia).[50] In the Mansfeld mining, smelting and distribution industries, merchants from Nuremberg and Augsburg as well as local dignitaries had increasingly bought into the business, thus gaining a say. In the Joachimstal valley, where silver had been discovered in 1512, the mines and the town were owned by the Counts Schlick, one of the richest families in Bohemia. The miners had developed their own forms of organisation which were independent of traditional guild structures and tended to be both geographically and socially highly mobile given the possibility to buy shares in a mining enterprise. Despite this, working conditions were harsh and since the market for copper, silver and iron as well as other mining products at that time was no longer local with prices being determined by the big trading houses, especially from Southern Germany, wages in the industry had been suppressed. This only added to the prevailing grievances identified in the 12 Articles which by now were circulating through the countryside. The increasing discontent was exploited by Thomas Müntzer who made a passionate appeal to the miners and smelters of the southern Harz to unite with his cause.[51] Those individual miners who had been receptive to his ideas had joined the band which assembled at Frankenhausen. However, there was no formal organised response on the part of the Mansfeld miners to Müntzer's request to unite.

In Joachimsthal, following the discovery of silver in 1512, thousands had arrived to extract the deposits and other metals and the Schlick family began minting the famous silver Thalers from 1520 onwards, which were shipped

---

50 Joachimstal today goes by the Czech name Jáchymov.
51 Thomas Müntzer, Letter to the Mansfeld miners <https://www.harz-geschichte.de/page-band04/thomas-muentzer-brief.htm> (accessed 22 August 2022).

1525 THE RISE AND FALL OF THE REVOLT

to Leipzig and became accepted currency throughout Europe. An enormous worker camp sprawled along the valley and it became a hotbed of unrest. Archduke George of Saxony was on campaign at Frankenhausen when the Joachimstal uprising broke out on 20 May when miners and members of the community gathered at the bread market, stormed the town hall and ransacked the house of the mine agent. The Schlicks' castle Freudenstein was also stormed, with supplies, food, drinks and clothing carried away. In the house of the captain the plunderers took 3,000 guilders with them. The mine agent was able to escape to join the Schlicks at their residence in Schlackenwerth where he informed them that the miners of Annaberg and Schneeberg were mobilising and would be joining the Joachimstalers. Thomas Seidel, a miners' leader, requested assistance from the Annaberg miners' guild, in the form of 500 pikes, two hundredweight of gunpowder and cannon and reached out to disaffected peasants near Leipzig. In the valley, miners went from house to house to commit the occupants to support the insurgents and soon two camps had set up. On the one side – allegedly

Stephan Schlick 1487–1526) was a Bohemian nobleman and mining entrepreneur. In the few years of his rule, there were troubled times in the burgeoning metropolis of Joachimstal, which with 18,000 inhabitants soon became the second largest city in Bohemia. He was able to settle uprisings in 1517, 1522/1523 and 1525 again through negotiations and concessions. Attributed to David Frumerie, (Nationalmuseum of Fine Arts Sweden, public domain).

10,000 men strong and organised into six companies and equipped with armour, a field gun, hackbuts and pike behaving in an organised manner with its men under strict orders to refrain from further acts of looting.[52] The other was described as a 'rabble', nevertheless 8,000 strong and armed mainly with axes and intent on plunder.

Stephan Schlick had originally wanted to intervene with a troop of 300 men but had returned to Schlackenwerth because of the large number of insurgents. With the help of local nobles, he was able to muster 1,000 mounted men-at-arms and 2,000 Landsknechts. All efforts, however, appear to have been geared towards a negotiated settlement.[53] Although the 12 Articles of Memmingen had been circulating in the Erzgebirge for some time, the structures of the mining industry shaped the agenda of the miners going into the negotiations. The Joachimsthal articles drawn up late in May consisted of 17 provisions.[54]

On 25 May, a treaty was drawn up between Stephan Schlick and the miners' association including the council. Given the recent defeat of the peasants at Frankenhausen, Schlick and those vassals of Archduke George who had returned from Thüringia had cause to approach the negotiations in a bullish manner as far as punishment was concerned. However, in the preamble to the treaty any punishment to those miners and members of the community who had engaged in the storming of the castle and the town hall and the agent's office was to be waived. Mindful of the emigration of his miners and the damage which any reprisals would have inflicted on the industry in the valley, the treaty incorporating a new mining ordinance[55] was particularly lenient, unlike the settlements of the conflict elsewhere in Central and Southern Germany.[56]

The Battle of Meiningen

Meanwhile following the execution of Müntzer and Pfeiffer, Elector John the Steadfast and the Count von Henneberg led their combined force south, reaching Walldorf north of Meiningen, a town in the Prince-Bishopric of Würzburg on the river Werra on 2 June. Due to this threatening situation, the people of Meiningen had called for help from the 7,000 strong peasant army camped near Mellrichstadt. As the peasant vanguard which included numerous wagons approached Dreißigacker west of the town, it was attacked by units of Count Wilhelm IV of Henneberg on 3 June. They sped off in the direction of Walldorf leaving over 40 peasant casualties. As reports were fed back to the main column about the skirmish and the size of the

---

52   Sieber, *Der Joachimstaler Aufstand*, pp.46–47.
53   Sieber, p.50.
54   Cf. Scott and Scribner, pp.221–222.
55   Scott and Scribner, pp.223–224.
56   Sieber, p.51.

1525 THE RISE AND FALL OF THE REVOLT

Johann I (1468-1532), the Steadfast, Elector of Saxony 1532-1533 Lucas Cranach the Elder and Workshop. (Metropolitan Museum of Art, with permission).

elector's army, a decision was taken to dig in behind a wagon fort on the 'Bielstein' hill near Meiningen.

Before the wagon fort could be completed the elector's army had commenced its assault across the plateau, along an old trade route to the west of Meiningen. The Bildhausen troop had only 17 light guns at its disposal, but with their help the peasants nevertheless withstood the enemy superiority with its cavalry and heavy guns for a long time. In the process, a number of elector's mounted men-at-arms and the commander of the artillery were killed. By evening, however, the peasant army had to retreat behind the protective walls of the town after the loss of more than 240 men and many hundreds of wounded. The elector's heavy artillery had caused damage and the peasants had to abandon their artillery. Hans Schnabel the commander of the Bildhausen band argued for his men to leave the city under cover of darkness but was persuaded by his comrades-in-arms to stay. Two days later on 5 June, faced with a numerically superior army before the gates and the hopeless situation, the town of Meiningen was forced to capitulate.

A delegation of town councillors and representatives of the peasant army asked Elector John to spare the townsfolk and peasants, which he granted. But the price was the surrender of the ringleaders including Hans Schnabel as well as Hans Scharr. On 30 June, 14 members of the leadership council including the Meiningen pastor, were executed in the town on the orders of the prince-bishop Konrad von Thüngen. Schnabel and Scharr, who were handed over to Wilhelm von Henneberg were executed in Mellrichstadt on 3 July. The Bildhausen band then dispersed in haste. As an act of punishment, the Meiningen municipal council was stood down by the prince with the result that the town lost its independence. High demands for damages and punishments were issued to the towns and peasantry involved in the uprising.

THE GERMAN PEASANTS' WAR 1524-26

The Peasant War in Alsace and the Middle Rhine (Palatinate)

Chronology

1524 December	Artisans' uprising in Colmar
1525 February	Opposition to council emerges in Zabern (Saverne)
2 April	Peasants free the Strasburg preacher Clemens Ziegler from custody
14 April	Formation of first peasant bands in Alsace
End of April	Insurgents lay siege to Weissenburg
May	Peasant troops march through central Alsace
	Beginning of uprisings in the Sundgau
11 May	Molsheim assembly draws up field ordinance
12 May	Rebels occupy Zabern (Saverne)
16 May	Victory of Antoine Duke of Lorraine over rebels at Battle of Saverne
20 May	Battle of Scherwiller
24 May	Duke Antoine returns to Lorraine
25 May	Sundgau peasants seek peace terms with Basle
26 May	Battle of Pfeddersheim
5 June	Armistice declared in Sundgau
8 July	Electors of Palatine and Trier lay siege to Weissenburg
13 July	Triumphant return of Electors' army to Heidelberg

Alsace

In Alsace, peasant unrest had already occurred at the end of 1524 and during the winter months. The region, like Franconia, had shown great resistance against feudalism in the past. The two great trading cities of Strasbourg and Basle had spread their tentacles out into the Alsace and the Sundgau region to its south. Basle had belonged to the Swiss Confederation since 1501 and was considered a stronghold of Reformation thinking. The border between Upper and Lower Alsace, the so-called *Landgraben* which ran south of Schlettstadt[57] played a significant role during the Peasants' War. The Sundgau was ruled by the Habsburgs. In its territory was the independent abbey of Murbach. To the west of Alsace, geographically separated by the Vosges Mountains, lay the powerful Catholic bastion of Lorraine, headed by Duke Anton and stretching far to the north. In the years 1439 to 1445,

---

57 An old Roman provincial border (Gaul in the south – Germania in the north) and medieval border between the Nordgau and Südgau.

1525 THE RISE AND FALL OF THE REVOLT

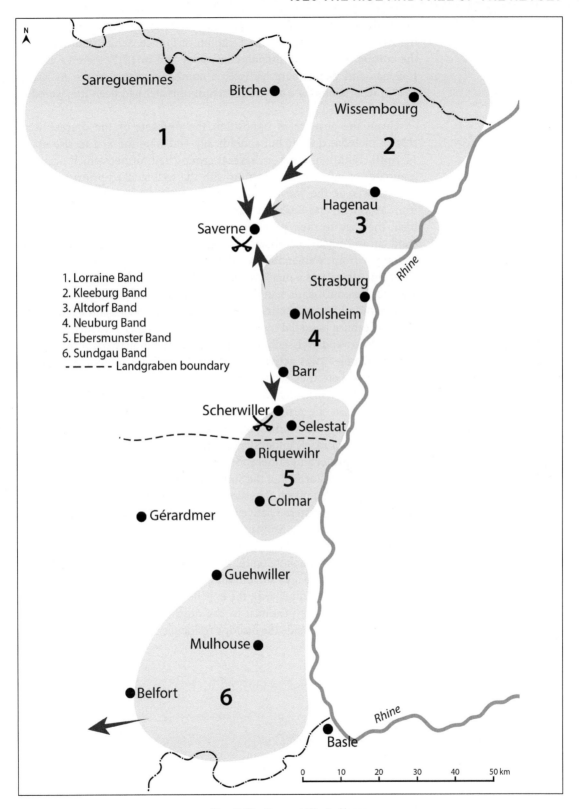

Map 11. The Peasant War in Alsace

under the Bundschuh banner, the peasants of Upper Alsace had resisted the Armagnac army led by the Dauphin of France. Schlettstadt had been the epicentre of the Bundschuh conspiracy and in 1517, the area around Hagenau and Weißenburg had seen a number of disturbances. As late as 1519, preparations for a new Bundschuh uprising had been uncovered in Dangolsheim.

Given the absence of opposition the peasants of the diocese were able to mobilise quickly but sporadically and were the first to rise up on 14 April. Within a few days, several groups had formed which occupied a number of monasteries, starting with the well-stocked priory at Altorf. The leaders of the movement were Erasmus Gerber and Georg Ittel, from Molsheim and Rosheim respectively. At the head of a troop of 1,500 men, they set up their initial headquarters at the priory. From here the band moved on to the abbey at Mauermünster. In another part of the country – from Weißenburg on the Palatine border in the north to the Sundgau – there was a major rebel mobilisation. By the end of April 1525, six large peasant bands had formed, a Lorraine band with its epicentres in Saargmünd (Sarreguemines) and Bitsch (Bitche); a second band known as the Kleeburg band led by the Weissenburg burgher Bacchus Fischbach and based around Weissenburg and the Kleeburg monastery. A third troop – 8,000 strong – was active around the Neuenburg monastery north of Strasbourg where they were joined by the peasants of the Hagenau and Bitsch areas. Their leader was Hans Küfer. South of Strasbourg, peasants joined forces at the priories of Altorf and Mauermünster with Erasmus Gerber as their commanding officer. This was known as the Molsheimer band. A band of rebels under the command of Wolf Wagner gathered near Ebersheimmünster and Mittelweiler covering the central part of Alsace. The largest rebel band formed in the Sundgau. Several small and medium-sized towns (Zabern, Dambach, Kaysersberg) were persuaded to lend military assistance but these were relatively insignificant compared the major cities of Colmar, Strasbourg, Mülhausen and Hagenau whose gates remained closed to the rebels. By early April, the insurrection had spread far beyond the Sundgau into Franche-Comté. The city of Belfort opened its gates to the peasants. Even in the area surrounding Besançon there were disturbances. In Mömpelgard (Montbéliard), the expelled Duke Ulrich of Württemberg tried to ally with the peasants. In the north, the Kleeburg-Weissenburg band set up camp outside the bishop's residence.

1525 THE RISE AND FALL OF THE REVOLT

The Spread of the Uprising: The Peasants' Assembly at Molsheim

On 11 May representatives of the various troops met for a general peasant assembly at Molsheim. They elected Erasmus Gerber as their leader and adopted the 11 Articles for restoring justice, which derived from the Gospel and laid down a set of principles for maintaining discipline within each band. (see Appendix III) Thus, Northern Alsace became the epicentre of the uprising which included the entire Alsace itself, Eastern Lorraine as well as parts of the Palatinate and territory belonging to Baden.

Under Gerber's leadership, the Molsheim band developed a system of rotation. At the end of April, he had the men of the Alsatian villages and farmsteads who were fit to fight divided into four groups. Everyone had to serve in the band for eight days and do field work for the remaining three weeks. Only in the case of acute danger would all four groups called to arms. Thus, during the uprising, all men of military age could belong to their band for a single or several periods of duty. This seems to have been a unique form of peasant organisation with no such reports being known for other theatres of the Peasants' War. Here the large rebel bands gradually came together from small companies and detachments of men who would stay together until the decisive battle. Gerber divided his rapidly formed band into small units and had them operate in different areas of the country.

The Battle of Saverne (Zabern) 15 May 1525

As disturbances broke out, the authorities were at pains to mount an effective opposition. Alsace was Habsburg territory, but Archduke Ferdinand had his hands full with the uprisings in Styria and the Tyrol. The Bishop of Strasbourg who administered his diocese from Mainz felt compelled to sue for peace particularly as the powerful city of Strasbourg maintained a strict policy of neutrality.

Watching from the wings in France was the arch-catholic Duke of Lorraine who viewed the uprising in the north of his territory as an act of Lutheran heresy and pledged to cross the border from France in a holy crusade against the rebels. The local Alsatian nobility was fragmented but placed their faith in the duke, especially since the lower nobility to the east of the Rhine was also bound by the uprising. Basel and Strasbourg, as well as a number of other key cities in the region remained neutral during the revolt although some leading figures such as Martin Bucer (aka Butzer) and Mathäus Zell, the Protestant reformer based in Strasbourg, tried to dissuade the peasants of the surrounding villages from joining the uprising.

THE GERMAN PEASANTS' WAR 1524-26

Table 3: Order of Battle at Zabern/Saverne

	Mounted horse	Infantry	Weaponry
Army of Duke of Lorraine	6,000	5,000	12 Field guns Large arquebuses
Lower Alsace band	?	c.18,000	Artillery, hook guns
Lupstein relief column	?	6,000	Field guns, hook guns
Second rebel relief column	?	c.3,000	?

Source: Bensing & Hoyer op. cit. p.117

On 12 May the Lower Alsatians had moved from Mauermünster to occupy Zabern (today known as Saverne). More than 18,000 strong, the band was one of the largest of the Peasants' War. News arrived that Duke Anton of Lorraine was approaching from the west with a large army of mercenaries. The duke's movements have been described in detail by his scribe Nicolaus Vollcyr de Séronville.[58] According to this account his army comprised some 6,000 heavy horsemen, 5,000 Landsknechts and at least 12 field guns. The duke had cast his net wide to recruit his foot soldiers who included a motley crew of Spaniards, Flemish, Italian handgunners and Albanian stradiots, alongside German mercenaries. On arriving before Saverne, Duke Antoine sent his herald, the poet Pierre Grégoire and a trumpeter to the city gates to demand that 'the peasants accept combat or surrender'. But, according to Volcyr, the messenger was greeted by a volley of arquebuses and culverins. The herald managed to get to safety, but the trumpeter was killed. The duke ordered his artillery to open fire which was returned by the rebel guns on the ramparts. During the exchange, a larger fieldpiece belonging to the

Antoine (4 June 1489 –14 June 1544), known as the Good, was Duke of Lorraine from 1508 until his death. A staunch Catholic he had to face the spreading of Protestant Reformation, against which he published an edict on 26 December 1523. When the reformist inspired peasant uprising broke out in the neighbouring Alsace, he launched an expedition in which he massacred a peasant army at Saverne on 16 May and 4 days later he decisively defeated another peasant army at Schwerwiller near Sélestat. Artist: Hans Holbein the Younger. (Photo: Jörg P. Anders, Gemäldegalerie der Staatlichen Museen zu Berlin, with permission).

---

58   Cf. de Sérouville, *The History*.

1525 THE RISE AND FALL OF THE REVOLT

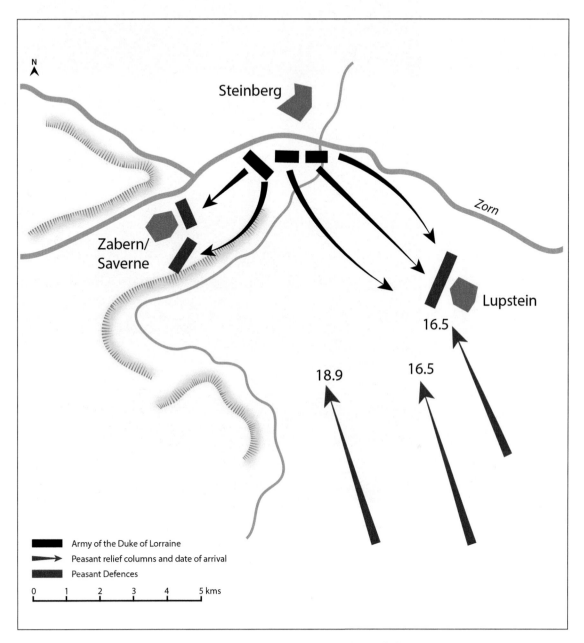

Map 12. Battle of Zabern/Saverne 15 May 1525

THE GERMAN PEASANTS' WAR 1524-26

Woodcut by Gabrielle Salmon from Nicole Volcyr de Serouville – 1526: *The History and Collection of the Triumphant and Glorious Victory Won Against the Seduced, and Abused Lutheran Miscreants of the Land of Daulsays and Others* (Bibliothèques de Nancy, Rés. 4228, public domain).

duke exploded having been overloaded with too much gunpowder. There is no detail concerning the peasant ordnance and state of weaponry, but the duke's scribe reports that his army was forced to pull back because the rebel artillery fire proved to be very accurate. Surprised by this fierce resistance, the duke's army redeployed on higher ground by the villages of St. John and Steinburg which overlooked the town. Setting up a perimeter guard and sealing off all possible routes in and out of the town, his troops camped there until the following day.

Erasmus Gerber, assessing the situation, had called out for reinforcements from the surrounding areas. Some units received the call too late, nevertheless, two relief armies advanced on Saverne on 16 May. A troop of about 6,000 men approached but was still eight kilometres southeast of the town when a well-armed second troop advanced in the direction of the village of Lupstein, to the east of Saverne. One of the duke's captains, Claudius of Lorraine, the Duke of Guise, spotted this troop of peasants and took a detachment of his best troops along with field artillery to defend this flank. The peasants hastily deployed their supply wagons into an impromptu wagon fort with the village to their rear and fired upon the duke's men with their culverins, falconets and hook guns.

However, the first attack of the duke's men proved to be so effective that the rebels were forced to pull back into defensive positions within the village. Those units of the duke's horse which were able to penetrate the rebels' defences were swiftly beaten back. The duke needed to have some covering fire and despatched his heavy horse with Italian arquebusiers riding with them to take up positions close to the village where they would be able to provide suppressing fire as cover for the infantry to mount their assault. However, the rebels steadfastly repulsed the duke's efforts, refusing to surrender while hoping for reinforcements from the town. When many of them took refuge in a church, it was set on fire, giving what they declared an appropriate end for these 'Lutheran heretics with their hardened hearts'. Then they set fire to the whole village and 5,000–6,000 peasants lost their lives, many of them burning in the flames. The ensuing 'slaughter was so

This depiction of the massacre at Zabern/Saverne is the only contemporary woodcut of a particular battle of the war and shows the banner of Alsace: a yellow double cross on a white and red horizontally divided field. Woodcut by Gabrielle Salmon 1526, (Libraries of Nancy, with permission).

terrible', wrote the duke's scribe, 'that the blood, mixed with rainwater, ran in streams down the village alleyways'.

It is unclear why the mass of rebels inside the town walls did not seek to break out in support of their comrades. One must surmise that the duke's remaining troops presented a formidable bloc in front of the town gates or that the rebels wished to sue for peace. Erasmus Gerber had sought assistance from the council of the city of Strasbourg in a letter sent on 15 May but this was to no avail. Negotiations continued between Duke Anton and Erasmus Gerber and the city council. Duke Anton demanded the unconditional surrender of the town and one hundred hostages. They agreed that the city would surrender to the duke unconditionally, but that the peasants were to be given safe conduct to leave the city for their homes, providing they undertook to pay no heed to the preaching of Martin Luther and his cohorts.

While the column of peasants was passing unarmed through the army of Duke Anton, on a hill outside the walls known as Martyrberg (Montmartre), they shouted: 'Long live the excellent Luther', prompting the duke's mercenaries to turn on them forcing the rebels to run back into the town. There then followed an orgy of uninhibited bloodletting in which some 20,000 rebels and townsfolk were slaughtered. It is said that the dead lay so thickly in the streets that it was difficult to find a way through the mounds of bodies. Duke Anton ordered Gerber to be hanged on the trees outside the town along with other peasant leaders. The slaughter did not stop there:

> Today the Lorraine cavalry and foot have attacked Dossenheim (sur Insel), where they smashed open the gates of the churchyard, broke open all the chests in the church and the powder tower, burned the powder therein and caused much distress in the village, ran after the womenfolk and struck some of them. so that whatever man. woman, or child could escape from Dossenheim is now lodged with me in the castle. Things are indeed in a sorry state in these parts.
>
> At 4:00 p.m today I saw Lupstein go up in flames. but I do not know who were the perpetrators. The poor people of Dossenheim do not know how to act or react Moreover, if they have to remain much longer up here they are afraid that the food will run out. May your graces please instruct me what I am henceforth to do'.[59]

Early in the morning of Thursday, 18 May, the princes gathered their council of war and the captains of their army to decide whether to continue the campaign. The council was divided. Some asked that the army return to Nancy now that all danger was over. They feared that a new victory against

---

59   Wolf Full from Geispolsheim, Bailiff of Herrenstein Castle, to the Strasbourg Council, 16 May 1525 translation from Scott and Scribner, p.308.

the peasant bands was not as certain as the one easily won at Saverne. The duke's commanders argued for pushing south towards Sundgau in the Upper Alsace. In the mid-morning of the 18 May, the army set off towards Marmoutier, followed by carriages full of booty and women and young girls captured in Saverne.

On Friday, 19 May, the duke summoned the entire population of Marmoutier and ordered them to renew their oath of allegiance to him. He had two men accused of sympathising with the rebels hanged from a window of the town hall. His army then set out for Molsheim, the town where Gerber's wife and children had taken refuge and which refused to open its gates to the Lorraine nobility. Following a night march in the direction of Schlettstadt (Sélestat) the Lorraine army encountered 8,000 peasants at Scherwiller who were determined to fight.[60]

The peasant band of Ébersmunster commanded by Wolf Wagner was relatively well-equipped with arquebuses and ordnance plundered en route. The band had detachments of Swiss mercenaries and had deployed in a favourable position in the valley at Scherwiller situated right on the border of Upper and Lower Alsace. The village lay in the district of Schlettstadt where a Bundschuh had been fought in 1493. The peasant force was protected from the front by vineyards, from behind by the river Willer. In order to take Scherwiller the enemy had to pass a narrow gap, fortified by the peasants. But here the peasants were betrayed by a town bailiff, who by creating a distracting noise, made them leave their position in the direction of Kestenholz (Chatenois). At seven o'clock in the evening the duke's Italian vanguard, launched the first assault. They set fire to the village to light up the battlefield. Behind the village, however, the peasants defended themselves resolutely but during this fight, as had occurred at Leipheim and Böblingen, the duke's cavalry had ridden around the vineyard and broke through the defile that the peasants had abandoned in the confusion caused by the bailiff. A group of them swung around and commenced firing on their own. By this time, it had become very dark and events were only partially lit by the flames. Knowledgeable of the terrain, the peasants retreated behind their wagons; but a squad of Italian mercenaries had slipped under the wagons and pushed a number aside to pave a way for the duke's cavalry. It was ten o'clock at night. With 3,000 dead and reduced to 1,000 able-bodied men, the peasants held their ground on a hill where they made their last stand. The victory came at a price for the Duke of Lorraine. In one of the few records of casualties on the princes' side during the war, Vollcyr noted the loss of the

---

60 There had however been discord in the ranks of the rebels which had restricted the northward march of this troop. The captains of the Lower and Upper Alsatian troops had disagreed over crossing the fosse (Landgraben) which marked the boundary between two regions. Some leaders of the Upper Alsatians refused to cross arguing that the dispute with the bishop of Strasbourg was none of their business, since they belonged to the diocese of Basle. However, those elements within the rebel band who had been moved by news of the slaughter at Zabern forced the captains to march north to engage with the duke.

commander of the duke's horse – a Lord von Isenburg, a Welsh nobleman and about 500 Dutch Landsknechts.[61] Furious at the loss of so many men the duke ordered the execution of 300 prisoners.[62] These losses prompted Duke Anton to return to his duchy spurning requests for help from the Upper Alsatian and Sundgau nobility.

Defeated in Lower and Middle Alsace, the rebels still held part of the south. The German princes and the authorities of Alsace (Strasbourg, imperial city remains neutral) asked Antoine to continue the expedition. Probably affected by the extent of the killings, he refused and preferred to return to Nancy via the Val de Villé. The expeditionary force continued to face attacks from peasant bands in the Vosges passes. Finally, the regiments regrouped in Lunéville and Saint-Nicolas-de-Port, where they could sell the products of their booty. In a letter to Bernhard Clesius, Bishop of Trent, written on 30 May Dr. Johann Zasius, assessor in the imperial chancellery in Esslingen felt compelled to write:

> After he had slain up to thirty thousand men at Saverne and in those parts and plundered towns and villages, the Duke of Lorraine has left German territory with his entire army and has headed back to Lorraine with fifteen hundred wagonsful of booty.[63]

The end of the duke's expedition did not, however, end the war. In the region of Wissembourg, the insurgents were ruthlessly hunted down. The peasant struggle continued for several months in Upper Alsace, especially in Sundgau as well as in Franche-Comté around Belfort and Montbéliard. Notwithstanding these ongoing military actions, the back of the peasant revolt in Alsace was broken. Duke Anton made a speedy march back to Lorraine to lick his wounds. He was suddenly deaf to the other requests from Sundgau that he also come there and punish the peasants. On 24 May, the duke and his retinue were received triumphantly in the capital of Lorraine. On 25 May, the 'all-Christian prince' ended his bloody performance with a pilgrimage.

A note about casualties: the disparity of the estimates of the number of peasants killed in Alsace makes real accuracy difficult. Some record as few as 7,000 peasants killed in all three battles, whereas others report the number at 38,000. The most widely accepted number of peasants who lost their lives in the Alsatian region is 25,000. On the other hand, many more losses were inflicted on the Ducal forces in Alsace than in the battles of Swabia, Franconia and Thüringia.

---

61 As reported in Heinrich Schreiber 1863 *Urkundenbuch der Stadt Freiburg im Breisgau: Der deutsche Bauernkrieg...Januar bis Juli, 1525.*< http://dl.ub.uni-freiburg.de/diglit/schreiber_urkundenbuch_ga> (accessed 29 June 2022).
62 Alexandre Weill, *Der Bauernkrieg* (Darmstadt: Leske, 1847), pp.352–354.
63 Written 30 May 1525 – translation in Scott & Scribner p.308.

The Peasants' War in the Electoral Palatinate

Rebellion broke out in the Electoral Palatinate (*Kurpfalz*) at the same time as the revolt in Alsace. The Palatinate was a state of the Holy Roman Empire and the counts palatine of the Rhine had served as prince-electors (*Kurfürsten*) since their confirmation as electors by the Golden Bull of 1356. They ranked among the most significant secular figures in the Empire holding the office of imperial vicars in the territories under Frankish law (Franconia, Swabia and the Rhineland). Ludwig V, the Elector Palatine, thus had a vested interest in ensuring that the rebellion in other parts of the empire was crushed.

The Palatinate was administered from Heidelberg but, as was the case in other parts of the empire, it was territorially fragmented (see Plate D). From the middle of April, disparate uprisings occurred on the right and left banks of the river Rhine in what today is the eastern reach of the state of Rhineland Palatinate and the western reach of Baden-Württemberg. The first was in Durlach in the district of the city of Speyer on 19 April. Upon the formation of a peasant band, the city of Bruchsal was occupied along with the bishop's residence at Udenheim. The prelate was forced to agree to the 12 Articles while all rents and dues paid to the clergy were to be suspended until the church had been reformed. Having secured a promise from the elector as well as the Margrave Philip of Baden, the Bruchsal peasants stood down but on 7 May a new peasant troop emerged in the Kraichgau region under the command of Anton Eisenhut, a chaplain at Eppingen. Eisenhut had already been involved with the rebel commanders Hans Wunderer and Matern Feuerbacher of the Neckar and Württemberg bands but had left them to organise the peasants in the Kraichgau, a strategic area through which the armies of the princes would pass.[64] From Gochsheim near Eppingen, he appealed to the peasants in the surrounding villages to assemble there on 7 May, so that the Gospel and righteousness would overcome the conditions of feudalism. Ludwig's secretary, Peter Haarer, describes what followed:

> in a short time he raised almost twelve hundred, formed a band and called it the 'Bright band'. Last Sunday evening Christoph Haffner, mayor of the Palatinate market of Hilsbach, marched out of the gate with thirteen or fourteen companions and forced all they met to take an oath to be Christian brothers and so joined Eisenhut. Among other things, those from Gochsheim attacked the lords of

---

64 A hilly region in Baden-Württemberg, bordered by the Odenwald and the Neckar to the North, the Black Forest to the South and the Upper Rhine Plain to the West. On the western end of the Kraichgau is the town of Bruchsal centre of the activities of the Bundschuh leader Joss Fritz. Cf. Michael Klebon, *Im Taumel des Evangeliums: Anton Eisenhut und der Kraichgauer Haufen im Bauernkrieg* (Verlag Regionalkultur, 2020), p.73.

THE GERMAN PEASANTS' WAR 1524-26

Menzingen and plundered their castle and the aforesaid Eisenhut marched with his folk, with their ragged banners flying, to the village of Eppingen. …. He then marched to the town of Heidelsheim, which lies between Bretten and Bruchsal, which he also conquered in the same fashion. …. likewise, the village of Hilsbach, in which the Elector [Palatine] had built a new warehouse. There they seized the cellarer and plundered the cellars and the houses of priests and nobility. From here they marched with the band, which increased continually, to the village of Sinsheim, where there was a fine ecclesiastical foundation. They were admitted by the citizens there in the same way, without opposition, attacked the canons in their houses, smashed their windows, stripping some of them out, devastated the houses, seized and plundered what they found inside and remained encamped there for some days, for they had adequate food and drink in the canons' houses. En route, they burnt to the ground the castle of Hans Hyppolitus von Venningen, called the Steinsberg, lying between Hilsbach and Sinsheim, creating such a bonfire that it could be seen everywhere in the region, for this castle 'lay upon a hill visible from far away.[65]

Louis V, Count Palatine of the Rhine (German: Ludwig V. von der Pfalz) (2 July 1478, in Heidelberg – 16 March 1544, in Heidelberg), also known as Louis the Pacific, was a member of the Wittelsbach dynasty. Despite appearing to accede to a number of peasants' demands in the Treaty of Neustadt, he was far from 'pacific' in his suppression of the rebel army which had occupied Pfeddersheim. (Unknown artist: public domain).

On 14 May negotiations took place between the peasants and a delegation of officials from Heidelberg. A day later – after news reached the peasants of the crushing defeat of the Württemberg peasant army on 12 May near Böblingen – Eisenhut was ready to dissolve the Kraichgau band. On 18 May a treaty was signed in Hilsbach and the band dissolved. Eisenhut went back to Eppingen but was captured there, a few days later, together with the priest and two comrades-in-arms by troops of the Swabian League.

Further to the north, in a separate uprising in the district of Landau, a group of peasants assembled at the church festival at Nussdorf on 23 April. Some 200 strong, they marched on to the estate of Geilweiler belonging to the Cistercian monastery Eußerthal and camped nearby. This alarmed Jakob von Fleckenstein, the Elector Palatine's bailiff in Germersheim, who succeeded in dispersing the peasants without any violence. On 28 April, the council of Landau warned its citizens not to join the peasants. On 30 April, however, disturbances broke out again involving Landau citizenry, with attacks occurring on the monasteries at Clingenmunster, Herde, Heynbach and Mechtersheim where food supplies were plundered.

---

65   Translation of Peter Haarer in Scott and Scribner, p.236.

1525 THE RISE AND FALL OF THE REVOLT

Three bands from the Geilweiler, Kleeburg (23 April) and Kolben districts (30 April) were particularly active. On 29 April, a further peasant troop mobilised in the north at Böchingen. While at the outset the peasants' ire was directed against church property, by the beginning of May castles had become their target.[66] Böchingen was the first castle to fall victim to an expanded Geilweiler band which moved further north and also destroyed the Kropsburg and the castles of Edesheim, Kästenburg and Kirrweil. Continuing their march northward, the band which had first formed in Nußdorf on 23 April, besieged Neustadt.[67]

On 10 May Ludwig met with Geilweiler and the Bockenheim bands in the village of Forst.[68] The peasants used the opportunity to demonstrate their intent. Some 8,000 men, with flags and weapons, are alleged to have assembled before the elector. In addition to their demand for doctrine according to the Gospel, the peasants demanded the election of pastors, rejected the introduction of Roman law, and called for a withdrawal or reduction of taxes and services (*Frondienste*) and demanded the old peasant rights again to fish and hunt along with the reinstatement of common land (*Allmendrechte*).[69]

No written version of the treaty exists but on the promise of organising a diet to consider the peasants grievances which bore close resemblance to the 12 Memmingen Articles, Ludwig agreed to obtain the opinions of two eminent theologians, Philip Melanchthon and Johannes Brenz, by way of preparing for the diet. In return the bands agreed to disperse with the Bockenheim and Geilweiler troops separating and moving north and south

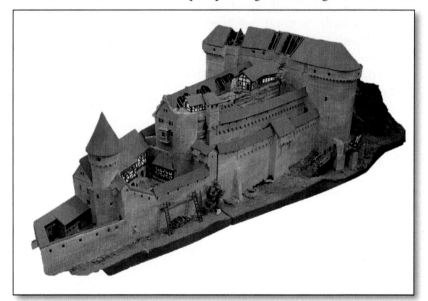

The fortress at Neuscharfeneck Castle was owned by Count Friedrich von Löwenstein (1502–1541) who preferred the safety of the city of Landau during the unrest. He had placed the fortress in the care of his son in law castellan Gibelin. In mid-April 1525, four weeks before the castle was taken by the peasants, the latter had ordered two tonnes of powder. Neuscharfeneck was one of the strongholds in the region with a massive curtain wall, 10 cannon and 50 hook guns. These were not used against the peasants on their arrival before the gates on 14 May. It has been argued that the fortress had a depleted gun crew – gunners came at a premium. Anticipating a siege, Gibelin hurried to the peasant camp at Frankweiler and offered the peasants to surrender the fortress in exchange for being allowed to leave freely with his family and his personal belongings, on the promise that the fortress would be spared. The peasants agreed but once the castellan and his family and garrison had left, they set fire to the castle despite their promise.[69] Model by Erich Merz, Photo: H. Schreiber.

---

66 Cf. Rolf Übel < https://www.landau-nussdorf.de/mains/geschichte.html#bauernkrieg > (accessed 10 May 2022).
67 Today – Neustadt an der Weinstrasse.
68 Now Forst an der Weinstrasse.
69 Heuser, Emil: 1925 *Der Bauernkrieg 1525 in der Pfalz, rechts und links des Rheines.* Neustadt a. d. Haardt, Marnet., 1925.

respectively. However, they did not fully disband. On 14 May the fortress at Neuscharfeneck was occupied by the peasants with no resistance being offered. The same occurred on 17 May at Madenburg castle, the Bishop of Speyer's residence.[70] Both fortresses were set alight.

Without waiting for the opinions of his theologians, Ludwig marched against the peasants having grown impatient at the slow nature of their dispersal. On 13 May he set out with the Archbishop of Trier, the Prince-Bishop of Würzburg and Count Palatine Otto Heinrich, from Heidelberg with 1,000 horsemen and 2,000 infantry to put an end to the peasants' uprising in his territory. On 23 May, a larger army consisting of 4,500 Landsknechts, 1,800 horsemen and an artillery train arrived in Bruchsal via Malsch and Kislau. On 25 May, Bruchsal surrendered to the Elector Ludwig V. After a wave of arrests, numerous peasants and four known ringleaders, including the captured priest Eisenhut, were beheaded on the castle bridge at Kislau. The city elders pleaded for mercy and Ludwig handed it over to his brother Georg, the Bishop of Speyer. In the submission treaty, Bruchsal had to pay 40,000 gold florins as penance.

The Elector Ludwig's March Formation

The vanguard of 150 horse under commander Wilhelm von Habern. Nine horses to a line with the Rennfahne in the fifth line/ Standard bearer Peter von Ehrenberg. 14 lines.

Main body of horse commanded by Eberhard Schenck von Erbach with 15 horses to a line. Johann Wild was the red ensign and Palatinate colours were in the seventh line.

Followed by 300 horse of the Archbishop of Trier, 11 horses to a line with a sixth line carrying the banner.

The United Duchies of Jülich-Cleves-Berg contingent followed with 250 horse in blue and white livery and ensigns(?).

A further 200 Cleves mounted troops from the Alzey district under the command of Dietrich von Schönberg 11 men per line with Friedrich von Flersheim ensign. (See Plate N)

Rotation

3,000 Landsknecht infantry under the command of Leonhard von Schwarzenberg.
Georg Nippenberg Commander of the Ordnance.
Friedrich Halbgewachten Master of the Train.
1,500 Trier Landsknechts to bring up the rear of the column.

---

70   <https://burgen-pfalz.com/burgenkatalog/madenburg/geschichte/madenburg-im-bauernkrieg–1525/> (last accessed 10 May 2022).

1525 THE RISE AND FALL OF THE REVOLT

Having secured what he thought was peace in the area, the elector and the other princes left for Neckarsulm to unite with the army of the Swabian League in order to suppress the insurgency to the east in Franconia. The two armies met at Fürfeld (Bad Rappenau), west of Neckarsulm – a three-hour march away – on 27 May. Neckarsulm capitulated a day later paving the way for the combined army to surge north, where following the peasant defeats at Königshofen and Ingolstadt the city of Würzburg could be retaken. Ludwig could now return to his territory where a 7,000–8,000 strong peasant army had assembled at Dalheim and was cutting a swathe through the elector's estates destroying properties on their way. On his route back the elector was reinforced with 300 horse from the governor of Mainz. Having crossed the river Main, Ludwig despatched his *Rennfahne* under the command of Wilhelm von Habern to ascertain the rebels' whereabouts. Von Habern reported back that they were an hour ahead of them and heading for the free imperial city of Pfeddersheim.

Situated in the Pfrimm valley the walled city lay in the centre of winegrowing country, a good third of which was owned by the clergy, nobility and the monasteries. In particular, the clergy held the most valuable cultivable land known for winegrowing. This fact met with little approval from the population. Although there had been no direct contact between the townsfolk and the peasants during April and May 1525 because the council had forbidden it, both groups had been kept informed. When the peasant army arrived, the gates were opened and the rebels occupied the city.

The Battle of Pfeddersheim 23–24 June 1525

The following is based on the contemporary account of Peter Haarer, secretary in the Electoral Palatine chancellery in Heidelberg who took part in Elector Ludwig V's campaign in Franconia and in the Palatinate, and penned the official report of the war.[71]

Wilhelm von Habern reported back to Schenck Ebert von Erbach, Ludwig's son-in-law and supreme commander, who immediately drew up battle plans. Units of horse and infantry were deployed along with artillery within range of the northern city walls beside the Georgenberg monastery. The lighter field pieces were drawn up closer to the walls and began volleying. The rebels returned fire and this exchange lasted for about an hour with had little effect on either side. At this point orders were given for a detachment of horse to cross the Pfrimm and seek out a position from where the peasant movements could be better observed. Some 150 horse under the command of Dietrich von Schönberg positioned themselves on a rise beside a church to the southwest of the city. They were joined by a

---

71   Peter Haarer 1531 *Wahrhafte u. gründliche Beschreibung d. Bauernkriegs* (Kessinger Legacy Reprints, 2010).

THE GERMAN PEASANTS' WAR 1524-26

The former free imperial city Pfeddersheim located in the valley of the river Pfrimm showed solidarity with the peasants of the Palatinate for which thousands of citizens and occupying rebels perished at the hands of the army of Ludwig V. Engraving by Matthias Merian Topographia Palatinatus Rheni, 1645 (Bavarian State Library, with permission).

detachment of horse from Cologne. Their task was to sound the alert if the peasants were to break out of the city.

Further units of horse and infantry were deployed to the west from the north, which essentially meant an encirclement of the city since there was no gate to the eastern side. Nevertheless, orders were given to set up a camp here for the supply train. Frowen von Hutten and Wilhelm von Habern were tasked with organising this. This eventually became the command centre. While these deployments were occurring, no further bombardment of the walls was undertaken. Once the defenders had satisfied themselves that the elector's army had taken up its final positions, the gates opened and a small troop of peasants came out of the west gate. It was suspected that they wanted to run over the artillery positions on the Georgenberg but also the mounted horse to the southwest were also a target. However, neither ploy materialised as suddenly the entire peasant troop stormed out of the gate and attacked the horse which was encamped there. Their tactics were ill judged as the horse of the Electors of Mainz, Trier and Jülich proved too much of a match.

The rebels began to retreat into the vineyards where some defence was provided by the rows of vines which hindered the elector's men as they pursued the peasants. The rebels had brought out light field pieces which they turned to fire on to the main 'battle' of the elector's mercenaries. There were casualties amongst the elector's men. It would have been difficult to assess the movements of the peasants as they dodged in and out of the vines, but the rebels regrouped to charge into the elector's main column of infantry whereupon by a clever stroke Friederich Halbgewachsen, master of the train, had repositioned three falconets which volleyed into their ranks. The ensuing carnage caused panic and numbers of rebels ran back towards the northern gates where they caught by the Mainz horse and pursued by the elector's mercenaries. There was carnage as some 4,000 souls were slain in the so-called '*Bluthohl*' on the Morstädter road which has been commemorated by the city. Some peasants were able to flee in the direction of Worms.

Since it was already nightfall by the time the remaining peasants were either in the city or had been killed, three companies of the elector's mercenaries and a troop of 1,000 mounted men were posted around the city for the rest of the night. The following morning the elector ordered the

1525 THE RISE AND FALL OF THE REVOLT

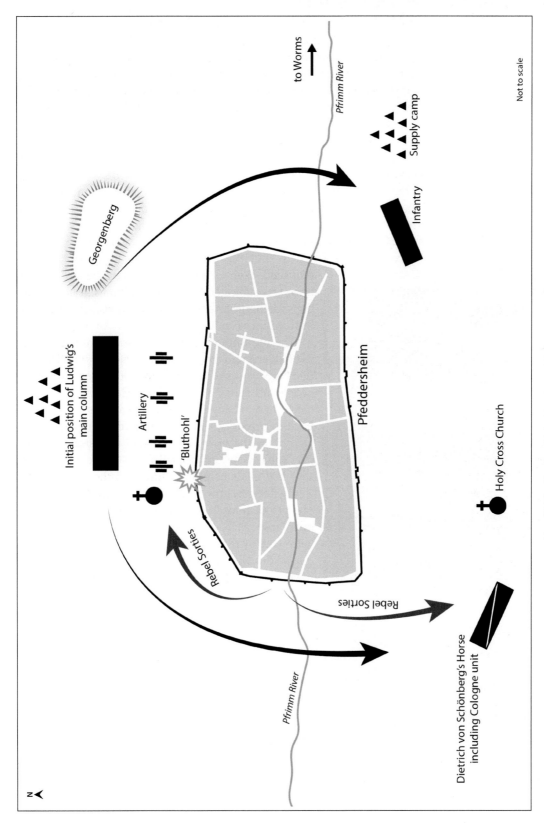

Map 13. The Battle of Pfeddersheim 23–24 June 1525

THE GERMAN PEASANTS' WAR 1524-26

artillery barrage to recommence and after three hours and 262 cannonballs fired, the peasants finally surrendered. On 25 June, all peasants who were not Palatine subjects were ordered to leave the city unarmed. About 3,000 obeyed the order. Although they had been warned not to attempt escape, many peasants, fearing punishment, seized the first opportunity they could. They were caught by the elector's men and the ensuing bloodbath cost the lives of 800 rebels. Thirty ringleaders were immediately beheaded, while the other peasants were released to their homes with harsh conditions.

After the bloodbath, the troops occupied the town. The remaining peasants had to gather in the churchyard, 180 ringleaders were locked up in the church. The citizens of Pfeddersheim had to guard them. For every peasant who escaped, they were warned, a citizen would have to give his life. The inhabitants had to hand over all those in hiding by the next morning and 24 leaders were executed. All the remaining peasants were released in exchange for payment. But the Pfeddersheimers were also severely punished. Four of their leaders were beheaded. The town was subjected to severe conditions: it had to pay high surcharges, hand over all weapons, and renounce its freedom as an imperial city.

The Memorial at the site of the Bluthohl at Pfeddersheim (Author)

The punishment of the Electoral Palatinate towns of Pfeddersheim, Freinsheim and Neustadt had shown that Ludwig was serious about his punitive action. Now people in Landau feared that the elector might accuse the town of having participated in attacks on Electoral Palatine property, which had indeed taken place in the vicinity of the town. The Landau magistrate handed over subjects just as he acted against citizens of the city who had made common cause with the peasants. On 2 July, the elector's army arrived in front of the city. The prince himself took up quarters in Godramstein, but placed his troops in the villages who were supplied with wine by the Landauers. On 4 July, Ludwig's army moved on. The elector had taken no action against the town, probably because he considered its participation in the Peasants' War to be marginal. The defeat of the peasants at Pfeddersheim did not quite end the war in the Palatinate. The Electors of the Palatinate and Trier saw in the city of Weissenburg (today Wissembourg) some 80 kilometres south of Pfeddersheim 'the poison pit, from which the peasants drew all their poison and had to be punished'.[72] On 8 July the electors began their siege.

---

72   Balthasar Boell, *Der Bauernkrieg um Weißenburg Anno 1525* (Johann Ohleyer, Weißenburg 1873) p.45.

1525 THE RISE AND FALL OF THE REVOLT

Otto-Henry (*Ottheinrich*), 1502–1559 was Count Palatine of Palatinate-Neuburg from 1505 to 1559. The young noble accompanied Ludwig V on his campaign and was entrusted with commanding the siege of Weissenburg which brought the peasant uprising on the left bank of the Rhine to an end. Portrait by Barthel Beham 1535, Staatsgalerie Neuburg (Creative Commons, CC BY-SA 4.0).

Count Palatine Ottheinrich, who reportedly took overall command of the siege, ordered his infantry and artillery to take up position at Haselbach in the valley opposite the castle of St. Paul while the Electorate of Trier's men were stationed at Rechtenbach. On the following day, according to Peter Harer's report, after four days of heavy bombardment, the city was ready for surrender negotiations.[73] Prior to the siege, the Palatinate and Electorate of Trier had demanded the extradition of 10 rebels for execution. When they finally entered the city on 12 July, eight individuals were delivered up, three of whom were beheaded, the others had their fingers cut off. With reparations extracted from the city, the electors' army returned in triumph to Heidelberg where on 19 July the end of the Peasants' War in the Palatinate was celebrated with a solemn service of thanksgiving.[74]

---

73   Haarer, pp.108–109.
74   Haarer, p.111.

THE GERMAN PEASANTS' WAR 1524–26

The Peasant War in the Alpine Lands

Chronology

1525	
22 January	Beginning of the Schwaz miner's uprising against the Fuggers.
21 January	Archduke Ferdinand of Austria prevents the Schwaz miners from marching on Innsbruck.
9 May	Start of the Uprising in the Tyrol.
10 May	Brixen in the Tyrol is occupied by the rebels.
11 May	Michael Gaißmair is appointed supreme commander of the Tyrolean rebels.
3 July	Schladming is occupied by the peasants.
16 August	Frundsberg arrives at Salzburg with his relief force.
31 August	Peace treaty is negotiated in Salzburg.
1526	
February	Drafting of Tyrolean Constitution.
March	Second rebellion breaks out in Pinzgau in the archbishopric of Salzburg.
21 June	Gaißmair joins the rebels. Fighting around Radstadt in the Enns valley.
1 July	Pinzgau rebels are defeated.
2 July	Siege of Radstadt is lifted.
6 July	Gaißmair escapes to Southern Tyrol.
12 July	Gaißmair finds asylum in Venice. Alpine revolt collapses.

From the second half of the fifteenth century onwards those circumstances prevailing in Southern and Central Germany had triggered peasant uprisings in several Austrian provinces. These were usually prompted by local grievances and were directed against the local lord, never against the emperor. The unrest was given fresh impetus via the religious teachings of Luther and other reformers and by events to the north. The Tyrol, the Archbishopric of Salzburg as well as parts of Styria, Lower Austria, Upper Austria, and Carinthia, were all affected. A key feature of the uprisings in these areas was the involvement of miners predominantly from the silver and gold mineworks at Schwaz and Bad Gastein. Silver mining provided huge profits for both the Fugger banking family while gold had been a source of wealth for the lesser known Weitmoser and Strasser families. These workings were lucrative for the Habsburgs. Grievances amongst the miners who toiled under hazardous working conditions had grown. Irregular wage payments, overpriced foodstuffs and high tax burdens fomented existing discontent and when proposals were tabled to abolish a

1525 THE RISE AND FALL OF THE REVOLT

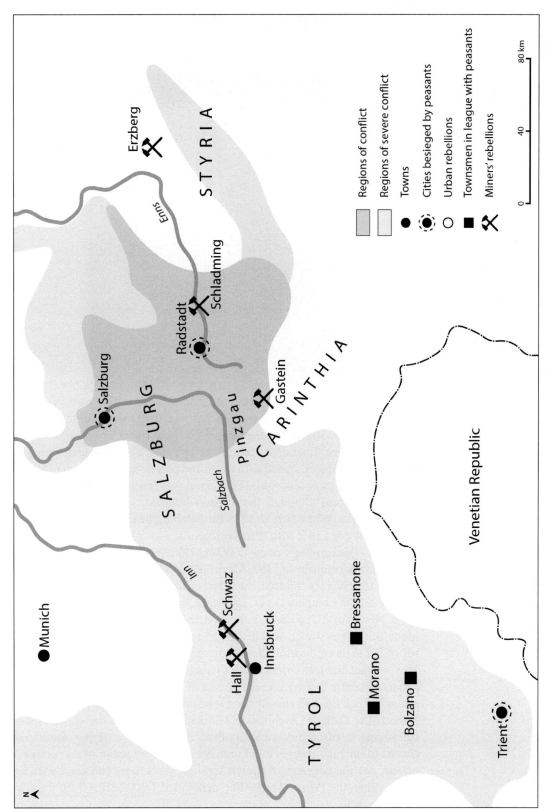

Map 14. The War in the Alpine Lands

THE GERMAN PEASANTS' WAR 1524–26

Jakob Fugger 1459-1525 was a major German merchant, mining entrepreneur, and banker and a descendant of a family of Augsburg based merchants. At the time of his death in 1525, Fugger's personal wealth was equivalent to two percent of the gross domestic product of Europe having built his fortune through the acquisition of silver mines. With his support of the Habsburg dynasty as a banker he had a decisive influence on European politics at the time. He financed the rise of Maximilian I and made considerable contributions to secure the election of the Spanish king Charles I to become Holy Roman Emperor Charles V. Jakob Fugger also funded the marriages which later resulted in the House of Habsburg gaining the kingdoms of Bohemia and Hungary. Portrait by Albrecht Dürer 1519, Staatsgalerie Altdeutsche Meister, (Creative Commons).

number of public holidays the discontent boiled over and the miners sought not only the reinstatement of the holidays and the payment of their wages on time but demanded that the Fugger's mining rights be revoked. When the Archduke Ferdinand reacted to the uprising by threatening punitive measures, the miners, armed with sticks and poles, seized the town of Halle, and blockaded its access roads. Ferdinand was forced to climb down and make concessions although the Fuggers hold on the industry remained firmly in place. When later in 1525 the Salzburg peasants rose, the miners sought common cause with their brethren.

During Maximilian's reign (1493–1519) the House of Habsburg had expanded enormously. In 1497, Maximilian's son Philip, married Joanna of Castile. They had six children, the eldest of whom became Emperor Charles V and ruled the kingdoms of Castile and Aragon (including their colonies in the New World), Southern Italy, Austria and the Low Countries in 1516. Much of Charles's reign was dedicated to the fight against Protestantism, which led to its eradication throughout vast areas under Habsburg control. This brought him into conflict with a rising wave of Lutheran support which had its epicentre in Zurich in the person of Ulrich Zwingli. In Salzburg, for example, criticism had already been levelled at the provincial synod of 1522 towards the Catholic Archbishop Matthäus Lang about the ecclesiastical conditions in his prince-archbishopric. A year later a review found no change in the high charges for church events, the behaviour of journeymen priests, nor the language of church services which were still conducted in Latin. When the Prince-Archbishop demanded 1,000 florins from the city

1525 THE RISE AND FALL OF THE REVOLT

The Hohensalzburg fortress residence of Archbishop Lang. During the siege of the fortress the rebels' intention was to starve the archbishop's men into surrender. As legend has it as provisions began to run low the defenders produced a ruse to deceive the rebels. Down to their last bull they swung it out over the castle walls on a hoist each time changing its colour by rubbing it with mud then washing him down and covering him with soot. This way they looked as though they were well supplied and would be able to withstand a prolonged siege. When the siege had been lifted, they took the bull down to the river Salzach and washed it, hence the nickname 'bull washers' which Salzburgers bear to this day. (Photo: Leonard Niederwimmer).

of Salzburg as a contribution to the consecration tax and, in addition, an amount to cover his travel costs to the coronation of Charles V in Aachen and the Diet in Regensburg, there were citizens' rallies and Lang feared an outbreak of open hostilities.

The discontent increased in the city again when Lang issued a mandate in religious matters on 5 October with the aim of finally eradicating protestant doctrine from his archdiocese. Lutheran thinking had spread widely in the Alpine region and to counter it the archbishop had threatened all such religious offences with severe punishment (for example, imprisonment or exile). The death penalty was threatened to all those who denied the virginity of Mary or rejected the doctrine of purgatory. As late as March 1525, Lang tried to persuade the priests to 'mend their ways' but it was too late to prevent the already fermenting religious unrest. He ordered the fortress of Hohensalzburg to be put in a state of alert and recruited a force of 1,000 mercenaries in the Tyrol. The city mayors were forced to beg forgiveness before the prince-archbishop while the city was stripped of its rights and privileges and taxed to pay for the cost of his hastily recruited troop of Landsknechts.

Outbreak of the Revolt in 1525

When a group of opponents succeeded in freeing a Tyrolean priest by the name of Eustachius von Heiterwang, who had been served a life sentence for his reformist preaching, two of his liberators were arrested and summarily executed without trial at the foot of the Hohensalzburg. News of Lang's deed spread fast within the archdiocese. In addition, the miners of Gastein and Rauris seeking redress for their own grievances began to place themselves at the head of steadily growing movement. On 25 May, miners and tradesmen's representatives met in the Gastein Valley to discuss how they would move against the archbishop. Meanwhile a group of dissatisfied peasants also formed in Zell am See and drew up a set of demands including the free preaching of the Gospel, the free election of pastors and the abolition of serfdom, but retention of the tithe. In line with the 12 Articles drawn up by the Swabian peasants they called for the recognition of common land and free hunting and fishing rights.

The newly assembled bands decided to move against the city of Salzburg and occupied the fortress of Hohenwerfen en route. The citizens of Salzburg were favourably disposed to the insurgency although the council unsuccessfully offered to support the archbishop in return for the restoration of the city's rights and privileges. In no mood to compromise and feeling increasingly threatened, the archbishop withdrew to the fortress of Hohensalzburg.

Matthäus Lang von Wellenburg (1468–1540), was the archbishop of Salzburg In the course of the Protestant Reformation, Lang's adherence to the older faith together with his pride and arrogance, made him very unpopular in his Salzburg diocese. As early as in 1523 he was involved in a serious struggle with his subjects in the City of Salzburg, which erupted in 1525. Engraving by Hieronymus Hopfer, (Yale University Art Gallery with permission).

By the end of May the rebellion spread from Salzburg into the Austrian Alpine lands (Styria and Carinthia) and to Upper Austria. On Whit Monday, 5 June, the citizens of Salzburg opened the gates to the peasants and miners who promptly plundered the archbishop's residence. Lang's response was to bombard the rebels from the fortress above, forcing them to retreat into the Nonn Valley and up the Rainberg hill. From June through to the end of August his fortress lay under siege. At the beginning of July 1525, 1,200 men from the Salzburg siege force, 1,000 from the Pinzgau region and a further 1,150 from the Pongau and the Rauris district assembled at a field camp at the Mandling Pass along the Enns valley between Radstadt and Schladming. The force stood under the command of Michael Gruber, a well-respected mine owner with military experience. They had, however, little in the way of cannon or mounted troops. This would be more than compensated by their knowledge of the local terrain.

1525 THE RISE AND FALL OF THE REVOLT

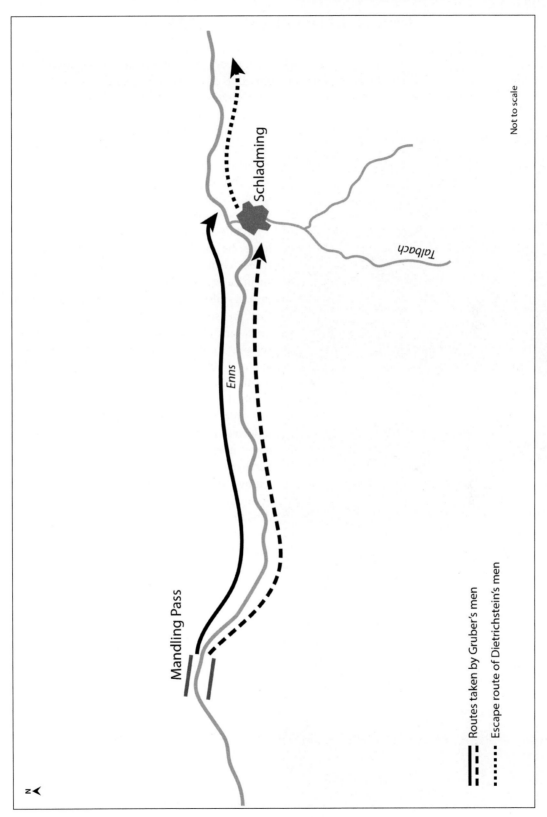

Map 15. Battle of Schladming 3 July 1525

THE GERMAN PEASANTS' WAR 1524–26

Battle of Schladming 4 June 1525

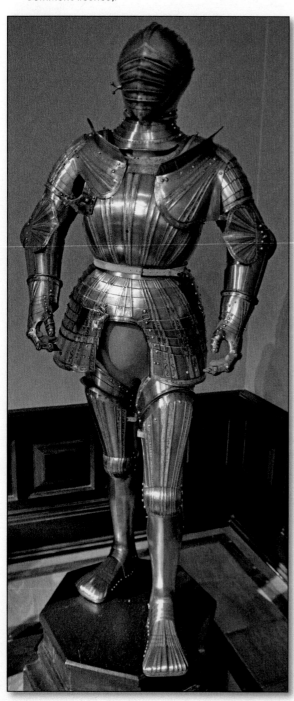

Archbishop Lang's suit of armour dating from 1511. (Photo: Sandstein, Kunsthistorisches Museum Vienna – Creative Commons licence).

A troop of some 4,000 men under the command of Siegmund von Dietrichstein had been mobilised to deal with the rebellion with a strategic aim to retake the fortress at Hohenwerfen but this had failed due to a mutiny within the ranks as his Landsknechts had not been paid. With some difficulty he managed to occupy the town of Schladming. Archduke Ferdinand, aware of the situation, had commissioned his supreme commander Count Niklas von Salm to come to the aid of von Dietrichstein.

While he awaited the arrival of this relief force, he tried to gain time by negotiating a truce. Gruber, however, decided to mount a surprise strike. Dietrichstein had lulled itself into a false sense of security in assuming that the surrounding valley slopes would be untraversable. On the evening of 2 July Gruber set out from Mandling for Schladming with about 3,500 men and marched most of the night. In Pichl he divided his men: one troop climbed the steep slope in a north-easterly direction into the Ramsauer Leiten, which it followed, past the farmsteads, to the east until it was north above Schladming. Now they only had to descend into the valley. The main column led by local scouts had the more difficult route. They climbed from Preunegg in a south easterly direction descended into the valley and climbed the Fastenberg. The main force now also only had to push straight downhill. The coordination of this twin night march on bad roads, over steep slopes, through forests and streams was a masterstroke. In the absence of watches, maps, or compasses, accurate local knowledge, sure sense of time and exact agreements among the division leaders were necessary. Lanterns or torches as path-lighting or signalling devices were only to be used, if at all, when they were not visible from the valley. Any unforeseen event, such as harsh weather, would have severely compromised Gruber's plan.

This planned pincer movement more than made up for the lack of horsemen and ordnance. Dietrichstein's army had camped in front of Schladming while his knights had

1525 THE RISE AND FALL OF THE REVOLT

Nicholas, Count of Salm 1459–1530 was a German soldier and an imperial senior military commander. His greatest achievement was the defence of Vienna during the first siege by the Turks in 1529 but he was called upon to relieve the beleaguered count von Dietrichstein following the defeat at Schladming. Unknown artist.

billeted in the town. On the morning of 3 July they were taken by surprise. On Dietrichstein's orders the mounted contingents had left the town on a sortie leaving the gates open and poorly guarded. A troop of 130 Salzburg rebels soon took control of the town gate allowing Gruber's main column to enter the town and overpower Dietrichstein and his entourage. Everyone in front of the city who did not escape was slain or thrown into the Enns and all the Austrian artillery was captured. Some 3,000 were slain in the attack.

Dietrichstein was woken by shouts of 'The enemy is here!'. He threw on his armour but as he opened the window, he was stabbed in the neck. He was nevertheless able to mount his horse and marshal some 200 of his men on the town square who had been caught up in the melee. His horse was stabbed five times and he himself received a hard blow to his head. Kuendorf, one of his officers was shot beside him. Christoph Welser was stabbed and hung from his saddle.[75] Dietrichstein made for the upper

---

75 Cf.<https://www.ennstalwiki.at/wiki/index.php/Schladminger_Bauern-_und_

gatehouse with a group of other knights but there they found the rebels and a number of their own mercenaries blocking their way. Two knights – Koenigsfelder and Ruprecht von Welser – tried to force their way through but were slain. The commander and his remaining nobility sought refuge in the church tower but were eventually forced to surrender.

Eighteen nobles were brought down from the tower and taken with other prisoners into the rebel ring to be addressed by Gruber and his provost marshal. The consensus in the ring was that they should meet the same fate as the nobles in Weinsberg – to run a gauntlet of pike, such was the hatred of von Dietrichstein who had brutally suppressed an uprising 10 years earlier in Steiermark. All hands were raised. However, Dietrichstein stepped forward and reminded those Landsknechts in the ring that they had sworn an oath to honour knightly imprisonment over execution. As a former mercenary himself Gruber found himself torn and a quarrel broke out between those mercenaries present and the rebels. Dietrichstein's argument prevailed and he was put in irons along with a number of other nobles. Before they were led off ignominiously in peasant smocks on oxen to be imprisoned in the Castle at Hohenwerfen, they were made to watch the beheading of 32 of their Bohemian horsemen in the ring. In Schladming, the peasants found all the money that Dietrichstein had previously extorted by plundering and much property of the nobility and the army.[76]

Siegmund von Dietrichstein (1484-1533) An Austrian nobleman, officer, imperial councillor, in the Duchy of Carinthia, Governor of the Duchy of Styria and Governor of the inner-Austrian lands. Siegmund was a son in law of Emperor Maximilian I, and enjoyed the trust of Archduke Ferdinand I. Photo: Michael Sander, Schlossmuseum in Weimar, with permission.

Schladming was a high point for the rebels – the nobility had been put on the defensive, but a counter-offensive had to be undertaken. As unrest spread up the Enns valley Archduke Ferdinand requested his supreme commander Count Niklas von Salm to take the offensive but the imprisoned nobles at Hohenwerfen Castle protested vehemently because they saw their lives threatened by such an action. Orders were issued instead to concentrate on the relief of Schladming. At Rottenmann the Count was informed of Dietrichstein's defeat, however the small force at his disposal was too weak to undertake such a mission so Salm set up camp near Leoben to secure the Innerberg area. He had only 120 Landsknechts and 300 light cavalry at his disposal. At Rottenmann his mounted troop was reinforced with the remnants of Dietrichstein's horsemen. Out of a troop of 500 horsemen who had initially escaped Schladming he was allowed to retain 200 and the rest had to be discharged.

Knappenaufstand_1525> (accessed 7 May 2022).
76   Ibid.

Count Salm was informed of Dietrichstein's defeat at Rottenmann. The small force at his disposal was too weak for a relief of Schladming. Salm set up camp near Leoben to secure the Innerberg area. Archduke Ferdinand of Austria issued a strict mandate on 10 July, warning against any connection with the rebels who had invaded from Salzburg. Anyone who did not obey Salm's orders was to be 'burnt to the ground'. Fearing this retribution, the citizens of Schladming and the 'community' of the Enns Valley sent a letter of apology to Archduke Ferdinand. In this letter they asked to be spared explaining that they had only gathered to defend the land when Dietrichstein had occupied the town with his Bohemian and Hungarian mercenaries and caused them a lot of damage.

However, some 2,000 rebels were still gathered in the upper Enns Valley around Radstadt. The peasants continued to erect new defences while the vice governor and the court council gave instructions to Count Salm to destroy the 'rebellious village' of Schladming on the Enns. But Salm still remained in Leoben due to lack of forces. It was not until 30 August that a new call to muster was issued for all of Styria with Leoben the rally point. After sufficient mercenaries had reported for duty in the first days of September, Salm carried out his order to take Schladming and punish its inhabitants on 14 September. However, it was not until the end of September that von Salm finally received the final order to burn Schladming to the ground and confiscate all mining and smelting works and supplies owned by the citizens. While von Salm was advancing against the town in the last days of September, he was told that the rebels had built a bastion nearby and that about 4,000 men were gathered there. His vanguard found a unit of 300 miners gathered outside the gates who retreated into the town once they caught sight of the enemy. The vanguard horse pursued them and put some 50 to the sword. The rebels and townsfolk fled the town into the mountains from the upper city gate. Since there was no fear of an attack by the miners, von Salm forbade any plundering. Acting on orders he set fire to the town and razed it to the ground at the beginning of October.[77]

During this time Archbishop Lang, still under siege in the Hohensalzburg fortress, desperately sought help but was not a member of the Swabian League. The League however understood the gravity of the situation and offered assistance through Duke Wilhelm of Bavaria. While the Salzburg insurgency was reinforced by refugees from the Upper Styrian regions, the Archduke sought to stall through mediation and a one-week truce was reached in early July. In the secret negotiations that followed, Lang agreed to the demand that Ernst Duke of Bavaria be recognised as his coadjutor.

The siege of the fortress continued. Lang rejected a new truce and on 4 August recommenced his bombardment of the rebel positions in the city below. This did not deter the insurgents who stood firm even on the arrival of an army under the joint command of Duke Ludwig of Bavaria and

---

77   <https://www.ennstalwiki.at/wiki/index.php/Schladminger_Bauern-_und_Knappenaufstand_1525#September_1525> (accessed 17 August 2022).

Georg von Frundsberg on 16 August.[78] Although this relief force attacked the peasants from both sides of the Salzach river, they could not get them to withdraw. Gruber proved to be a shrewd tactician. Realising that victory could only be achieved militarily with extremely high sacrifices, negotiations began afresh, ending the uprising with a treaty on 31 August. In the first days of September, Cardinal Lang rode side by side with Ludwig and Frundsberg through the streets of Salzburg. In return for the promise of a diet to address the rebel's grievances, Gruber laid the rebels' banner at the feet of the nobles. Extracting such a peace came at a price for the prince-archbishop however, who now had to pay the Swabian League 45,000 florins for their services. The diet did not meet until January 1526 but produced no agreement and was adjourned to an unspecified date.

East-southeast view of Hohenwerfen Castle, also known as Hohenwerfen Fortress, in the Salzburg market town of Werfen. Built from the eleventh century, the castle was a strategic bulwark between the Tennen and Hagen mountains on a 155-metre-high prominent rock cone in the Salzach valley. Photo: Arne Müseler / arne-mueseler.com / CC-BY-SA-3.0.

The situation in northern Tyrol enabled some units of mercenaries to be stood down as Archduke Ferdinand convened a special diet in June at Innsbruck attended by a peasants' delegation. This was unprecedented. At its head was Michael Gaißmair, the son of a mining entrepreneur, who had become secretary of the powerful Bishop of Brixen (Bresannone). Gaißmair along with Peter Pässler had led peasant uprisings along the Eisack and Puster valleys. Influenced by Anabaptist ideas he framed his political thinking around the abolition of the Catholic Church and its rituals, replacing it by a faith based on a direct contact with God, through the personal interpretation of Scripture. He also envisioned a democracy in which titles of nobility were eliminated and land and mineworks nationalised. This was of course anathema to the Habsburgs and Ferdinand succeeded in politically isolating Gaißmair at the diet. When he was invited

---

78   Cf. Miller, *The Army*, pp.92–93.

back to Innsbruck for further talks in August this became an interrogation and he was jailed for treason. After two months, he managed to escape, travelling to Graubünden, Switzerland. In Switzerland Gaißmair met the reformer Ulrich Zwingli and began to develop a draft for a new territorial constitution to establish an egalitarian, democratic, Christian state. It was published in the spring of 1526 as trouble began to flare up again in the Archbishopric of Salzburg.

1526: Second and Last Year of Revolts

After Lang convened a diet on 11 March 1526, at which the deputies authorised him to pay 100,000 florins in compensation and to raise 2,000 Landsknechts (who were to enforce peace in the archdiocese), the radical peasants in the Pinzgau refused to give their consent and there were disturbances in Saalfelden. In April Mittersill was occupied and the insurgents succeeded in repulsing a night raid by Lang's troops on 20 April. The following day the pass at Lueg fell under the control of Pinzgau insurgents. Gaißmair had learned of the unrest in Salzburg and organised a troop of 700 men from the Tyrol. In May he joined forces with an old acquaintance, Peter Päßler who was commander of the Pinzgauer band. As the unrest spread, peasants in the Pongau region also rose up. The two peasant troops split up with Päßler's troop heading to assist the uprising in the Pinzgau. Archbishop Lang had only two strongholds – the fortress of Hohenwerfen and the walled town of Radstadt. The latter was defended by the local keeper Christoph Schernberg with a garrison of 150 Landsknechts.

The Siege of Radstadt 24 June–3. July 1526

The discontented Pongau peasants and miners appeared before the walls of Radstadt as their first target on 14 April 1526. The peasants were initially commanded by Christoph Setzenwein, then by Marx Neufang in rotation with his lieutenant Matthäus von Oberschwarzach. Taking Radstadt was of the utmost importance because it would give the insurgents the ordnance which they badly lacked and it was this shortcoming which was making an assault on the town almost impossible.

Trusting in the strength of the town's fortress walls, Christoph Count von Schernberg, keeper of Radstadt, refused to comply with the insurgents' demands. With his small garrison of 150 Landsknechts, von Schernberg was still confident of withstanding any siege. During a stand-off, several attempts were made by units funded by the Swabian League to come to the relief of von Schernberg. On 20 May, the peasants defeated the Salzburg deputy, Franz von Tannhausen, on the heights of the Radstädter pass. Then some four days later around 24 May, Marx Neufang succeeded in turning back Michael Gruber, the former peasant leader turned officer in the pay of the archbishop who had taken two companies of Landsknechts into the

THE GERMAN PEASANTS' WAR 1524-26

Georg von Frundsberg (1473-1528) replaced Georg Truchsess of Waldburg in June 1525 as commander-in-chief of the League army and was tasked with coming to the aid of Archbishop Lang in Salzburg. Woodcut from the *Kriegsbuch des Grafen Reinhard zu Solms* in Ernst Heinrich Ehlers 1919 *Hans Döring – ein hessischer Maler des 16. Jahrhunderts*, Frankfurt am Main (Heidelberg University Library, with permission).

Upper Pinzgau as a diversionary manoeuvre. Finally, on 30 May, the bulk of the League army under the command of Burkhart von Ems (Hohenems) was pushed back at St Martin as they sought to approach Radstadt down the Lammer Valley.[79]

---

[79] The following account is from an analysis by Herbert Klein of three contemporary sources: the diary of the Radstadt citizen Leonhard Dürrnbacher; the letters of the Augsburg accountant Haug Zoll responsible for the supply of provisions to Radstadt from Salzburg to his hometown and the chronicle of an unknown Gastein peasant who took part in the siege army. Cf. Klein H. 1952 Die Kämpfe um Radstadt am 24. Juni 1526 und daß Ende des Salzburger Bauernkriegs in *Gesellschaft für Salzburger Landeskunde, Salzburg, Austria* available at <www.zobodat.at> as <Radstadt%20 MGSL_92_0124-0129.pdf> (accessed 15 August 2022).

1525 THE RISE AND FALL OF THE REVOLT

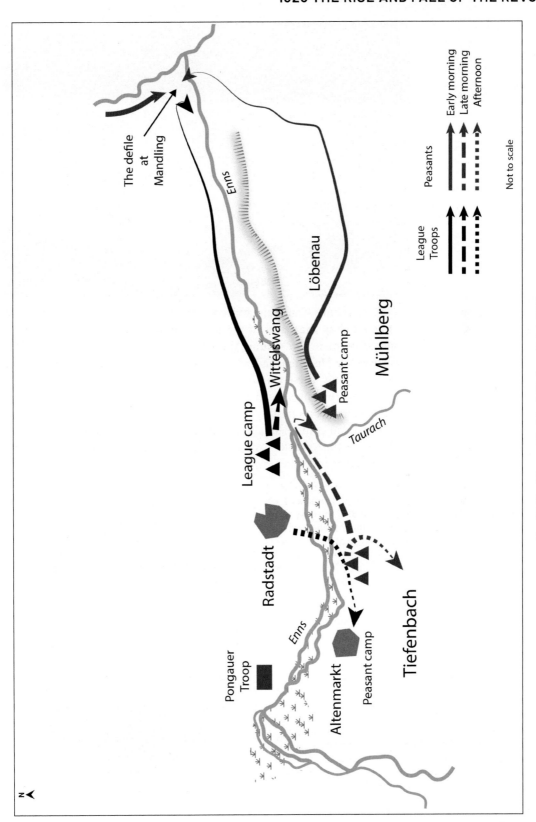

Map 16. The Siege of Radstadt 24 June–3 July 1526

THE GERMAN PEASANTS' WAR 1524–26

Bastion and part of city walls at Radstadt. Photo: Alois Oppeneiger, Creative Commons.3.0.

In early June Gaißmair arrived with three companies of men 1,200 strong, swelling the ranks of the besieging army to a combined force of some 5,000 men. On 4 June, the first assault was launched, but it was unsuccessful. His men had attacked the city with home-made, already tested cannons. These cannons were made of hard wood and were held together by iron rings. Such artillery could only take a weak charge likely to only damage a monastery or castle gate. The walls of Radstadt remained unscathed and combined with a wide ditch made an assault very difficult. In addition, the townsfolk were willingly deployed to man the battlements with hot pitch and water.

Born in 1490 into a wealthy farming and mining family in Tschöfs near Sterzing, Michael Gaismair graduated as a clerk in mining and later served in the office of the governor Leonhard von Völs in the provincial administration of Tyrol. While working as a clerk to the archbishop of Brixen – he was confronted with the case of Peter Pässler, who had been sentenced to death for violently defending his fishing rights. Pässler was freed by a group of armed peasants who went on to loot the houses of a number of wealthy Brixen nobles and storm the Hofburg castle and the Neustift monastery. In Zurich Gaismair met the reformer Ulrich Zwingli. Disappointed by Archduke Ferdinand I's reaction to the emerging demands of the peasants, he became a radical thinker. Gaismair is one of the few peasant leaders with a political concept. In his draft for a free peasant republic, he called for a society without privileges, the abolition of nobility and the clergy. His programme brought him into conflict with the authorities and he was forced to flee with 1500 and seek asylum in the Republic of Venice, from where he continued his fight for freedom. Archduke Ferdinand placed a bounty on his head and on April 15, 1532, he was stabbed to death by three men in his apartments in Padua. No surviving image of Gaismair exists. This medal by Othmar Winkler was struck in 1975 on the occasion of the 450th anniversary of the war. (Auction House Rauch, Vienna, with permission).

1525 THE RISE AND FALL OF THE REVOLT

These setbacks prompted Burkhart von Ems to convene a council of war (Hallein, 3 June) to revise the plan of attack. The main army would no longer make a direct assault on the rebel army at Radstadt but would approach the town via the pass at Mandling where the peasant siege army would be weakened having sent detachments of men to parts of the Pinzgau. This force would consist of six companies: two Austrian, two Salzburg, a detachment each from Augsburg and Nuremberg. Philipp Stumpf was given overall command of this troop. It was reinforced in the Enns Valley by a further two companies which had previously been stationed in Rottenmann under the respective command of Andreas Hoffmann and Stephan Graswein.

On 19 June, this force, now consisting of eight companies took the defile at the Mandling Pass on the border between the Archbishopric and Styria without meeting any resistance. The rebels had cleared their two camps either side of the town and retreated to Altenmarkt. The relief force left the baggage train at the pass to hastily move down the valley towards the town. Here they were met with cheering and the ringing of the church bell by the defenders and set up camp to the northeast of the town. Any hopes of lifting the siege soon evaporated as the rebels moved back into a camp closer to the town, near the hamlet of Tiefenbach. To the southeast there was a further peasant camp located on the Mühlberg – a hill which provided a good vantage point across and along the valley. Soon a shortage of supplies quickly made itself felt among the League troops and the order was given for two companies – Stumpf's own and a Salzburg company under the command of Melchior Lamberg to clear the way for these to arrive from Rottenmann. Some 1,000 men marched off in the direction of the Mandling Pass.

Michel Gaißmair, who had observed this march from the Mühlberg took three companies over the mountains – at any rate through the Löbenau – and dropped down near Mandling and together with a unit of peasants which had been hiding in the woods, crashed into the League column which was unable in the narrow confines of the pass to adopt a battle formation. Only a few escaped leaving weapons and clothing strewn across the ground. The League train which had been left at the pass made off swiftly in the direction of Salzburg arriving, it is reported, in a pitiful condition.[80]

While the League troops were being cut down at Mandling, the peasant units[81] at Tiefenbach began to march across the meadows towards the south of Radstadt towards the hamlet, which at that time was still called Wittlswang, but today is called Dörfl, one and a half kilometres to the east of the town. Their intention was to attack the remaining League troops stationed there. They were met by detachments of League horse and Landsknecht handgunners supported by light artillery. A fierce skirmish

---

80 Klein, *Die Kämpfe*, p.127.
81 Differing accounts estimate this to have been between three and five companies strong.

ensued in the village, which went up in flames. Two hundred rebel peasants fell and 40 alone burnt to death in a house. The rest fled into the woods.

By the afternoon, the scattered peasant army had not yet regrouped. Stumpf himself had returned to Radstadt and ordered the whole relief force to sweep across to the peasant camp at Tiefenbach which lay deserted but for a few rebels and women belonging to the peasants' train. They hastily tried to take up a defensive formation but were soon outnumbered and fled into the woods once it became clear that the Pongau band would not be able to come to their aid. The camp fell into the hands of the enemy. A detachment of the same threw itself upon Altenmarkt and burnt the village to the ground. Towards evening the League force withdrew to Radstadt.

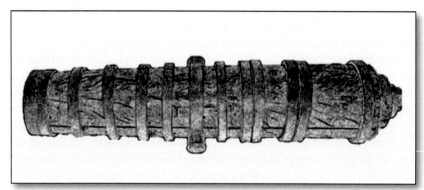

Contemporary images of wooden cannon fabricated by the peasants are remarkably similar to this later piece on display at the Musee de l'armee in Paris. The barrel was drilled out of a tree trunk and reinforced with iron rings rendering it a dangerous piece of ordnance for the user. Image: Geoff Laws.

The following day, the peasants regrouped back in the Tiefenbach and Mühlberg camps. Stumpf still remained surrounded and cut off from any supplies. His men therefore sought to raid nearby farmsteads to capture livestock (30 June–1 July). Since no funds could get through, his Landsknechts became unruly. In Salzburg, where news came from those on both sides who had escaped a contradictory picture was beginning to emerge of a victory to both the League and the rebels. Gaißmair's troop cleared the positions around Radstadt a full seven days after hostilities began but on 2 July his army withdrew from Radstadt. News had reached the peasant camp that events had turned for the worse for the rebel band in the Pinzgau. Here Burkhart von Ems had moved with the main League army and encountered a large rebel force under Peter Päßler – Gaißmair's close friend. He had taken up a strong entrenched position at Frohnwies, south of Oberweißbach in the pass there, blocking the route into the central Pinzgau.

Aware of this disadvantage von Ems took his army on a circuitous route in a bid to come up at the rear of Pässler's troop. The rebels, however, took up a new blocking position on both sides of the lake at what is now the town of Zell am See. On 1 July he ordered an assault on the rebel entrenchments to the west of the lake and south of the town. Some 400 rebels were slain and a number taken prisoner. The rest dispersed. When news of this reached Gaißmair he ended the siege at Radstadt and withdrew his army. In Salzburg, news of the impending arrival of fresh League troops under the command of Marx Sittich of Ems, to replace his cousin caused

1525 THE RISE AND FALL OF THE REVOLT

despondency amongst the insurgents. There would be no unification with Gaißmair's band who beat a tactical retreat over the Rauris pass into Swiss exile. With that the uprising in the Alpine lands ended. Chancellor Leonard Eck wrote to the members of the Swabian League that their Landsknechts could be stood down requiring only payment for the League's services and the appointment of executioners. The Prince-Archbishop allowed the soldiers of the Swabian League to plunder and burn down farmsteads. Entire villages, such as Altenmarkt im Pongau, were razed to the ground. Whole families – children, mothers and fathers – were put to death. In Radstadt, for example, 22 ringleaders were beheaded. All church bells in the archdiocese had to be taken down and delivered to the city of Salzburg, where they were cast into cannons. Soon a new tax to the sum of 100,000 florins was imposed, to be paid by the population in five annual instalments.

Elements of a Light-Cavalry armour made around 1505–1510 by the Austrian armourer Christian Schreiner the Younger (1499–1528). This originated in Mühlau or Innsbruck where Maximilian established his court armour making workshop in 1504. Particularly distinctive are the gracefully bold mitten gauntlets, which blend features of late Gothic design with the evolving German Renaissance style. (Metropolitan Museum of Art, with permission).

6

Aftermath

By the end of the summer of 1525, it is estimated that there were 100,000 peasant casualties. Vast parts of the countryside in Southern and Central Germany had been devastated – with castles and priories destroyed and/or ransacked and hundreds of villages burnt to the ground. It is difficult to estimate the number of refugees who were on the move – either expelled or seeking new settlement.

This civil war had shown its three sides – completely unrestricted and unregulated absolute conflict, periods of instrumental war according to considerations of expediency and agonistic warfare based on accepted norms.[1] These differences now manifested themselves in the way that the defeated peasants were to be treated. Any consensus which had prevailed within the ruling elites prior to the conflict had now been shattered.[2] This could be seen in the different approaches taken by the victors towards the punishment of the rebels. In the post-war turmoil, every authority from the poorest imperial knight to the most powerful prince and the strongest free imperial city claimed the right to treat and punish their own subjects according to their own discretion and resources. At the same time, however, there was distinct fear that reprisals might lead to renewed uprisings.[3] The need for a coordinated and uniform pacification policy seemed obvious at least to the members of the Swabian League which had played a significant role in supressing the uprisings in Swabia, the Black Forest, Württemberg, Franconia and parts of the Alpine lands. The League Council took on the task of drawing up uniform guidelines for the punishment and pacification of the defeated rebels. Three issues needed to be addressed – the prevention of renewed uprisings, the punishment of both the leaders of the uprising

---

1   Hans Speier, The Social Types of War, *American Journal of Sociology*, Volume 46, Number 4, 1941.
2   Thomas Sea, Predatory Protectors? Conflict and Cooperation in the Suppression of the German Peasants' Revolt of 1525) *Sixteenth Century Journal* (Volume: 39, Issue:1, 2008) pp.89–111.
3   Scott and Scribner, pp.319–320.

AFTERMATH

The practice of 'Brandschatzung' – extorting money from villages and towns to avoid being razed – not only terrorised the peasants but provided a clear and steady source of income or reparations for the authorities' war chest. The process was usually overseen by a designated officer known as the *Brandmeister*. The authorities were at pains to prohibit plunder but if the war chest was empty after a battle and the infantry were due an extra month's pay following a victory, then the likelihood of ill-discipline, if not mutiny in the ranks, would be high. On numerous occasions the victor's mercenaries cut loose to supplement their pay where they could. This not only wreaked havoc in the outlying countryside – it disrupted the work of the officer whose task it often was to fill the League coffers to meet its own mounting debts. Woodcut: Erhard Schön.

and the masses that had followed them, and the reimbursement of the costs of the campaign against the insurgents.

As a first step the League Council, in its role as the prime military contractor, insisted on its exclusive right to determine the terms of surrender and the extent of punishments in those territories covered by its membership. These far-reaching claims remained unchallenged. To conduct its policy, the council first demanded the unconditional surrender of the rebels and the immediate disbanding of their respective troops. As the campaign had progressed the terms of capitulation had been developed as each band had surrendered so that by the end of the war a standard formulation of some 10 points had been agreed:

The Surrender Terms of the Swabian League

All those who surrender unconditionally to the Confederation must surrender all arms, flags, and other military equipment. Anyone still apprehended with such items after surrender will receive severe corporal punishment and heavy fines – half of which will go to the Confederation and half to the authorities concerned.

All must again swear obedience to their lords and assure, under pain of death, never again to join any fraternity, covenant, or other association directed against their authorities.

All property illegally appropriated during the uprising must be returned; in addition, an agreement with the authorities is to be reached providing for compensation for all damage done. In disputed cases, the League Council will decide.

All looted church property is to be returned.

Leaders of the uprising and persons who incited rebellion shall be punished immediately by the Chief Field Marshal according to their guilt.

As a punishment and to avoid a fire-raid, each village and market town must pay six guilders per property (hearth) to the League. Those who do not deliver the required sum in the prescribed time will be subjected to plunder by the League's troops.

Those who have not participated in the uprising shall be exempted from the above-mentioned penalties.

Anyone who does not wish to submit to these conditions and prefers banishment shall be accompanied by his family. All his property shall be confiscated – one-half shall go to the League Council and the other half to the authorities. Whoever kills such a banished person shall be deemed to have not committed any crime.

All must again swear obedience to their sovereigns and assure, under penalty of death, never again to join any fraternity, confederation or other association directed against their authorities.

All subjects must swear not to support any banished person, but to pick him up, if possible, and hand him over to the appropriate authorities.

Should any subjects in the territories of the members of the League believe that they have been unjustly punished by their authorities, they shall have the right to bring their complaint before the League's Council. Obedience, however, may not be refused while this petition is pending. Decisions of the League Council in this regard shall be binding on both sides.[4]

---

4 Author's translation of the Swabian League's terms of capitulation from: Thomas S. Sea and G. Meyer 'Schwäbischer Bund und Bauernkrieg: Bestrafung und Pazifikation' in *Geschichte und Gesellschaft. Sonderheft Vol. 1, Der Deutsche Bauernkrieg 1524–1526* (Vandenhoeck & Ruprecht, 1975), pp.129-167 p.30

AFTERMATH

In enforcing these terms, the League showed no mercy but understood from the outset that its pacification programme could only be enforced with military support. At the end of July, the first steps were taken to retain some of its disbanding army. A force of 200 men on horseback and a troop of between 600 to 1,000 Landsknechts was stationed between Kempten and Ulm and tasked with keeping the peace and assisting in the collection of reparations to the League. This decision subsequently developed into a comprehensive plan for regular patrols of the territories of the members of the League with the formation of a troop of 800 mounted men-at-arms divided into 'quarters' to be stationed at Kaufbeuren and Kempten, Ulm, Heilbronn, and Bamberg. Beginning in September 1525 on a trial basis, there was to be a monthly muster of the necessary horsemen for this purpose. Although the reaction of the League members varied regarding this request, the use of mounted patrols primarily to hunt down insurgents still at large continued until April 1526.[5]

Peasant ring leaders being led before a summary court. Woodcut by Petrarca Meister. (Bavarian State Library with permission).

---

5   Sea T. & Meyer G. *Schwäbischer Bund* p.133

THE GERMAN PEASANTS' WAR 1524-26

The intention pursued with these League troops became evident in the first months of patrols as the means employed by the leaders of these troops for the complete subjugation of the insurgents consisted chiefly in an uncompromising campaign of terrorising the peasants and their families irrespective of involvement in the insurrection. Of notoriety was the League provost Berthold Aichelin, hired out by the city of Ulm to the League, who by the end of the war was responsible for the executions and maimings of hundreds of ring leaders.[6] It was the threat of extreme punishment and the use of torture which is responsible for the presence of detailed lists of peasants in the archives who participated in the revolt as the names of their fellow insurgents were extracted in confession generally under 'painful interrogation' (*peinliches Verhör*).

Finally apprehended by the League, Rohrbach was roasted to death along with Melchior Nonnemacher for his part in the massacre of the nobles at Weinsberg. Coloured drawing, originally from Peter Haarer's, *Wahrhafte Beschreibung des Bauernkriegs*, 1551. Peter Blickle has suggested that according to the account of the Truchsess von Waldburg's scribe this was in fact Melchior Nonnenmacher. (Signatur Cod. Karlsruhe 2476 Baden State Library with permission).

In some areas the retribution was fierce as at Hilzingen where the League commander Mark Sittich von Ems ordered the ringleaders to take down the church bell which they had originally tolled to mark their uprising and transport it to Lake Constance where they accompanied it over water to his residence at Bregenz. Here they were hanged. In the aftermath of certain

---

6   Blickle, Der Bauernjörg, p.440

battles as at Frankenhausen, the commanders had to order a stop to the killing in the town threatening those Landsknechts who would not desist with execution.⁷ In some cases the desire to humiliate the peasants would appear to explain the Landgrave Philip of Hesse's decision after the taking of the priory at Frauenberg near Fulda to hold 1,500 peasants in the moat for several days without bread and water for the amusement of the bystanders.⁸

A pattern emerged in the aftermath of victories of the nobility as far as seeking reparations was concerned. Joß von Laubenberg, commander of the League's *Rennfahne,* gained particular notoriety amongst the peasants of the Allgäu as he burnt down local farmsteads and any churches deemed to be of the reformist faith.⁹ The Margrave Casimir, for example, had entire villages burnt down, and rebels executed. He had 300 people killed in Feuchtwangen alone. In Kitzingen, he wanted to set an example.

Promising to spare the lives of the residents he punished them hard by chopping off their right-hand index and middle fingers (the 'oath fingers'), blinded some and sent others into exile. Some 58 villagers who had declared they 'wanted to see no more Margrave ' before the rebellion had their eyeballs removed. He also punished Rothenburg and wrung territorial concessions from the city. Contemporary reports claim that the market squares of Rothenburg and Schweinfurt were stained red with the blood of the beheaded rebels. Since Casimir was described as the imperial henchman, it can be assumed that he acted in accordance with the wishes of the Emperor or the Swabian League. He only ceased his punishments when it emerged in November 1526 that innocent people were affected as well.

This is an artist's impression of the forced transportation of the church bell of Hilzingen which appeared on a 50 billion mark note in the 1920s (City Archive, Singen, with permission).

---

7   Miller, *Frankenhausen 1525*, p.106.
8   Wiegand Lauze, Leben und Thaten des durchleuchtigsten Fursten und Herren Philippi Magnanimi, Landgraffen zu Hessen. (*Zeitschrift des Vereins für hessische Geschichte und Landeskunde, Zweites Supplement, Leben Philipps des Großmüthigen,* vol. 1), Kassel: Vereins für hessische Geschichte und Landeskunde,1841), p.82.
9   Cf. Miller, *The Army* op. cit. p.85.

THE GERMAN PEASANTS' WAR 1524–26

The princes were merciless in wiping out any further resistance. This coloured woodcut depicts summary executions of peasants following the Franconian uprisings. Some were more staged particularly where towns were involved. Note the quite plain garb of the mounted men-at-arms. (Photo: Gerald Raab, Bamberger Burgenbuch. Bamberg State Library, with permission).

Master Augustin's Bill to the Margrave for his Services[10]

80 beheaded	
69 eyes removed or fingers cut off	114 ½ florins
From this deduct	
Received from the Rothenburgers	10 florins
Received from Ludwig von Hutten	2 florins
Remainder	102 ½ florins
Plus 2 month's pay at 8 guilders per month	16 florins
Total	118 ½ florins

---

10   Scott & Scribner p.301

AFTERMATH

Such heavy repression took its toll on rebel resistance, but the rebellion most certainly shook the elites as reflected in the some of the albeit minimal concessions offered at the Imperial Diet held in Speyer in 1526. However, the peasants were far from cowed, and their recalcitrance soon provoked fresh complaints of disobedience from their lords. Some peasants were determined to stand firm on the evangelical principles with which they had launched the insurgency. There were soon fresh signs of renewed peasant truculence and possible rebellion most significantly in the Alpine lands, and the legacy of Thomas Müntzer was to endure in the rise of Anabaptism with an attempt in 1527 to raise the standard of an apocalyptically inspired rebellion.[11]

Extract from the Sheet VIII of the Weissenauer Chronik – depicts the capitulation of the Ummendorf peasants at Weingarten. Here they are swearing an oath to the Swabian League commanders to recognise once again the status quo. (Waldburg Zeil'sches Gesamtarchiv, Schloss Zeil ZAMs54, with permission).

In the aftermath of the war there was a curtailment of the rights and freedoms of the peasant class, with rights and privileges being removed from those municipalities which had supported their cause. Some representation emerged in the form of territorial assemblies at Kempten and Weissenau, but overwhelmingly the authority of the nobility remained intact as very few of the demands articulated in the 12 Articles could be enforced.

---

11   Scott and Scribner, pp.328–340

7

Conclusion

> It is inconceivable how all the nobility, knighthood and regents throughout Germany could be so desperate that as few as ten puny unarmoured farmhands could take an impregnable castle – and then for things to reverse with a single horseman being able to take on 10 peasants.[1]

This observation by the Lutheran reformer Frederick Myconius goes right to the heart of any assessment of the German Peasants' War. How do we account for the utter collapse of the insurgency given its extent and the lack of preparedness of the authorities? Within a few months the peasant uprising had spread like wildfire, with numerous cities having joined the cause. In the process, scores of castles and priories were occupied, looted and in some cases burnt to the ground. In the eleven-day period from 15 to 26 May 1525, within the borders of the high diocese of Bamberg alone, 197 castles and residences of the nobility and the clergy as well as well as six monasteries were attacked.[2] How do we account for the capitulation of so many castles during this early phase of the war?

It is widely held that by the turn of the sixteenth century the knighthood was becoming a spent force both socially and militarily. The rebellion most certainly exposed the knighthood's economic and political vulnerability. Few knights could afford the necessary garrison or weaponry to protect their property against the sudden appearance of unorganised and organised bands of peasants. In the early phases of the conflict, an exposed knighthood

---

1 Author's translation of Es ist nicht wohl zu glauben, wie alle Herrschaft, Ritterschaft und Regenten in ganz Deutschland so verzagt wurden, daß auch zehen Bäuerlein ohne Harnisch ein ungewinnlich Schloß einnehmen konnte. – Darnach kehret's sich wieder um, daß ein einziger Reuter zehen Bauern gefangen nehmen konnt. Friedrich Mykonius, *Geschichte der Reformation*, ed Otto Clemen, Altenburg reprint 1990, p.62.
2 Opitz, *Militärgeschichtliche Aspekte*, p.19.

and clergy were unable to form a united front against the insurgents, who were able to take control of key routes of communication. Keen on self-preservation in the face of an unexpected troop of peasants at their gates, many succumbed to their demands even joining the rebel ranks fearful that their property would be ransacked or destroyed. We can identify a second group, which did not join the peasants, but at first followed the actions of the insurgents with sympathy. This group included, for example, the Franconian knights whom Wilhelm v. Henneberg had united in 1523 into the Schweinfurt Knights' League with the aim of defending the remaining political and economic position against the encroachments of the princes, especially the bishop of Würzburg. Von Henneberg, and with him men like Götz von Berlichingen, made no secret of the fact that they were using the unfortunate situation in which some bishops and princes had found themselves in order to consolidate and improve their position.

Henneberg was typical of those nobles who believed that they could control the 'rebellion' by entering into negotiations with the peasants,[3] but he had misjudged his position, and especially the character of the insurgency. In Franconia the uniting of the bands and resolution of a field ordinance (see Appendix I) which demonstrated their military intent, coupled with the fear of meeting the same fate as Count Ludwig of Helfenstein in Weinsberg provoked him into swearing on the Twelve Articles.[4]

Most of the knighthood still fought in the ranks of those armies raised by the princes: in addition to Sebastian v. Rotenhan and Sylvester v. Schaumburg, members of the best-known Franconian noble families were part of the garrison of the Marienberg fortress at Würzburg. Of note here are Zobel, Thüngen, Bibra, Aufseß, Castell and others. Ambrosius Geyer, a relative of Florian Geyer at Giebelstadt, was one of the commanders under George III, Truchsess at Waldburg. At the massacre at Weinsberg some 13 nobles were named as having perished under a gauntlet of pike.

While the knighthood was in the throes of losing its significance as a conventional military force on the battlefield, the absence of mounted troops on the rebels' side gave it a renewed purpose even though the first quarter of the sixteenth century had seen greater emphasis placed on the use of light horse to undertake scouting and skirmishing duties as part of an army's vanguard. In the Swabian League campaigns, the Truchsess of Waldburg made increasing tactical use of the so-called *Rennfahne* when launching an assault on peasant positions. Since the rebels would often be ensconced behind a wagon fort, it was necessary to soften up the defensive position with artillery fire as at Frankenhausen, or to deploy a forlorn hope to clear a way through for the horse as at Scherwiller. As the code of chivalry

---

3   There were similar reactions within the nobility in Thüringia cf. Miller, *Frankenhausen* 1525, pp.53–54.
4   When the princes' counter-offensive at Frankenhausen bore fruit, he joined forces with the Elector Prince Johann and sought to restore his authority particularly against the Bildhausen band at the battle of Meiningen.

THE GERMAN PEASANTS' WAR 1524-26

Women and priests retrieve the dead bodies of Swabian soldiers just outside the city gates of Constance after the Battle of Schwaderloh during the Swabian War 1499. This image from the so-called Lucerne Chronicle was produced by Diebold Schilling the Younger in an illuminated manuscript of 1513 depicting the history of the Swiss Confederation. It gives a sense of what the battlefields must have looked like following the victories of the nobility during the Peasants War. (Creative Commons).

dictated it necessary for the knight to achieve glory on the battlefield, some knights may have discarded their heavy horse armour (bards) to be part of the fighting with the light horsemen.

How were the tables turned on the rebels such that they were crushed militarily? In the history of peasant uprisings very few have proved successful in achieving their aims,[5] and the German Peasants' War was no different. Apart from the single rebel victory at Schladming which can be explained by miners and peasants using their local knowledge of the terrain to their advantage[6] every military engagement on open ground ended in

---

5   For an overview cf.< https://en.wikipedia.org/wiki/List_of_peasant_revolts> last accessed 5 September 2022.
6   von Clausewitz C. 1984, *Vom Kriege*, Hamburg: Reinbek Verlag p.173.

CONCLUSION

a crushing defeat for the rebels. How are we to explain the turnaround referred to by Mykonius in their military fortunes?

Although substantial numbers of Landsknechts flocked to the peasant bands, these men in some cases still demanded pay which the peasant bands were at pains to accommodate – relying on booty from their occupied properties. A plan for the better use of mercenaries was developed by Wendel Hipler, chancellor of the Odenwald troop. He proposed to create a core company out of the individual Landsknechts present in the ranks of the band but failed to get this adopted by the Ring.

Instead, they were used for drills and training and held key offices within the ranks particularly in maintaining formation in battle. One can only speculate about the tensions which may have existed between experienced mercenaries and democratically elected band leaders on matters military. Except for Hans Müller von Bulgenbach, Jäcklein Rohrbach and Florian Geyer who had military experience, the leadership of the peasant bands came from a broad spectrum of society: urban notables, officials, members of the nobility, rural artisans, farmers, and clerics. This already provided for some tension between the leadership and rank and file as in the case of Matern Feuerbacher and Georg Schenck of Schleusingen who were charged with deliberately assuming leadership to defuse the uprising.[7] [8]

The tactics of the rebels on open terrain were defensive in the main. In most of the military engagements the rebels deployed their wagons and carts into a defensive fort. In the absence of contemporary imagery, one has to visualise how these defences would have appeared. Some efforts may have been made to construct and link war wagons in Hussite style, but it is more likely that some wagon forts would have been improvised structures with

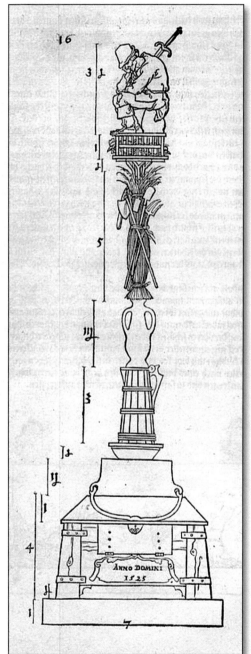

In 1525, Albrecht Dürer included the woodcut of the 'Peasant Column' in his 'Manual of measurement of Lines, Areas and Solids by means of compass and ruler'. three years before his death. He accompanied the woodcut with the words 'If someone wishes to erect a victory monument after vanquishing rebellious peasants, he might use paraphernalia ……. upon which sits a melancholy peasant with a sword stuck into his back'[8] leaving a contradictory message behind – were the peasants betrayed or did they receive their just punishment? (Photo: Gerald Raab, Bamberg State Library, with permission).

---

7   Cf. Scott & Scribner pp.141–142 and pp.247–248 respectively.
8   Greenblatt S.1990 *Learning to Curse* Abingdon: Routledge p.137.

wagons and carts overturned on their side or equipped with boards hanging on the side facing the enemy. These would have offered little protection from artillery but would have nevertheless presented an obstacle to a charge of armoured horse.

From contemporary accounts it tended to be the light horse which was able to penetrate these defences before the arrival of the infantry forlorn hope and main battle (*Gewalthaufen*). In this respect it can be said that the tactical superiority of the princes owed much to the deployment of cavalry and a greater supply of ordnance both of which were lacking on the rebel side. Although accounts from the victors describe the insurgents as being in panic and disarray once defence lines were broken through, we know of hard-fought rearguard actions at Königshofen, Ingolstadt, Lupstein (Saverne) and Scherwiller.[9] However, constant movement of the bands throughout the countryside to find supplies would have curtailed the prolonged weapons drills necessary for those rank and file who had had no experience in the militias. When it came to mortal combat the experience of having survived numerous battles was critical. For many peasants the necessary combat experience could usually be gained only once, on the day of their defeat.

One of the striking features of the war was the rapid nature in which the initial rebellion spread from district to district and then simultaneously across regions. Discontent had of course been simmering for years but the publication, reprinting and distribution of the 12 Articles and word of mouth were major factors behind the spread. What was absent was an overarching leadership capable of determining military strategy. Hans Müller von Bulgenbach made strenuous efforts to hold the Black Forest and Hegau bands together traversing the southwest and there was strategic liaison between the Württemberg and Kraichgau leadership.[10] However, the one attempt to bring the Franconian, Swabian and Rhineland leadership together was undertaken by Wendel Hipler and Hans Berlin who convened a parliament in Heilbronn in early May. Having begun to debate a set of common goals and coordinate further action they swiftly dissolved the parliament following news of defeat of the peasant army at Böblingen. What remains under researched is the impact of communications (or rather the lack thereof) on the insurgents' ability to coordinate action. One can only speculate that the absence of horsemen generally would have hampered liaison while the nobility would have relied on a steady stream of despatch riders crisscrossing the region to keep each other informed. This was facilitated by an already existing postal system created by the Thurn und Taxis dynasty[11] and promoted by Maximilian and Charles V by appointments of family members to the rank of postmaster general.

---

9   For this reason, low casualty figures reported by the victors must be viewed with some caution.
10   Klebon, *Im Taumel* p.73.
11   Cf. < https://en.wikipedia.org/wiki/Thurn_und_Taxis> accessed 20 September 2022.

CONCLUSION

In the end the rebels who had wrenched themselves away from their manor or municipality were defeated by mobile armies of mercenaries well used to travel[12] and to supplementing their monthly *Sold* with plunder from villages held to ransom under threat of fire raising. The savagery which followed the victories of the princes only mirrored the existing regime of commercialised warfare and the existence of state terrorism where extreme violent and disproportionate forms of punishment were meted out for material rather than human damage.[13] It would be centuries before the freedoms the insurgents craved could be attained.

---

12   Most aptly described by the Swiss word *Reisläufer*.
13   Cf. Thomas T. Müller 2021 *Mörder ohne Opfer* (Murderers without victims) (Michael Imhof Verlag, 2021. See also Johannes Hasselbeck 2012 *Die Folgen des Deutschen Bauernkriegs im Hochstift Bamberg* (Bamberg: University of Bamberg Press, 2012), pp.127–202.

Colour Plate Commentaries

Plate A

Imperial circles and the Holy Roman Empire
The Holy Roman Empire of the German Nation was formalised in a decree following the Diet of Cologne in 1512, to emphasise the new importance of the German Imperial Circles following its reform. The primary purposes of the circles were the organisation of a common defensive structure and the collection of imperial taxes. They were also the administrative groupings for convening of the Imperial Diet and the Imperial Chamber Court – the highest representative assemblies within the Empire.

Plate B

Map showing the overall area of the uprising in 1525.

Plate C

The Bishopric of Würzburg at the time of the Reformation. The maintenance of order and rule was not an easy task. The map shows the fragmentation of the prince-bishopric which was surrounded and penetrated by territories of other rulers.

Plate D

The Palatinate after the Cologne Arbitration Treaty 1505

Plates E-I: Peasant Banners

These representations of peasant banners are based on written descriptions as no banners have survived the efforts of the nobility to eradicate them. Consequently they cannot be seen as categorically accurate renderings. We do have some contemporary images however. The Bundschuh banner does appear in two contemporary images: on the stained-glass window in Überlingen town hall and in an iconic but later 1539 woodcut by Hans Weiditz showing a knight surrounded by a group of peasants brandishing

COLOUR PLATE COMMENTARIES

a banner with the Bundschuh motif. A Peasants' War Museum in Nussdorf in Rhineland-Pfalz displays a reproduction black banner bearing a white Bundschuh emblem.

5 1 Bundschuh banner, 2 Upper Swabian Peasants, 3 Hegau band
6 1 Bebenhauser band, 2 Deiningen Band, 3 Bright Band
7 1 Odenwald band, 2 Eichsfelder band, 3 Gerstungen band
8 1 Mühlhausen band, 2 Sundgau band, 3 Ebersheimmünsterer Band
9 1 Herbitzheimer band, 2 Salzburg crucifix, 3 Austrian peasant banner.

Plate J: Demi Lancer attacking a Peasant

This armoured demi lancer is wearing Maximilian style armour noted for its decorative edging and flutings (grooves in the armour to provide extra protection from blows). The knight is wearing a cloth base over his armour – most probably the extension of his *Wappenrock* worn under his breastplate. The horse is not barded as the extra weight of the horse armour would have hindered the need for mobility as the demi llancers were found in the vanguard of horse. The peasant is wearing a knee length woollen jerkin which in turn is worn over a long white undershirt. The peasants would have worn woollen hose and leather boots (for those who could afford) split up the side to allow easier fit. Longer leather leggings/boots would have been doubled over – as here. He has a cleric's stole tied around his waist – contemporary accounts from the aggrieved clergy decribe how the peasants were not averse to stealing clerical garments and adorning themselves with them.

Plate K: Peasant Drummer and Landsknecht Standard Bearer

For both sides in the war the drum and fife were not only a means of signalling and communicating for both the march and battle, they also possessed the function of an 'acoustic flag'. In the city, the drum in particular had the function of a signalling instrument, and in this respect, like the church bell it was an instrument of power whose misuse was punishable by law. For the insurgents, the drum and whistle came to symbolise their fight against the nobility. Drumming was an important means to initiate an uprising and for this after their defeat the peasant bands had their drums hunted down and confiscated and drummers and ensigns were severely punished. Perhaps this accounts for the absence of any surviving drums to this day. This drummer wears a steel pot helmet and chainmail mantlet over his jerkin. The characteristic peasant knife or *Rugger,* as it was known, varied in length. This has a wooden handle.

The ensign here is a Landsknecht and wears a breastplate. Some would have made do without a backplate although the role of the standard bearer was so important they would require maximum protection. The ensign is wearing striped hose and a feathered bonnet and a white ribbon tied around his upper sleeve to denote his affinity with the peasant cause. He is armed with a Katzbalger short sword.

THE GERMAN PEASANTS' WAR 1524-26

Plate L: Italian Handgunner and Stradiot

Accounts of Giovanni de' Medici so-called Banda Negra[1] arquebusiers describe how 'sleeves' of handgunners began to outnumber pike in Italian condottieri armies. They would operate separately from the block of pikemen but always remained at a distance that allowed them to operate in open formation, supported by groups of halberdiers. They soon gained a reputation. The main equipment of the hand gunner, in addition to his arquebus and accessories, was a sword and/or knife. He usually wore an open sallet, a padded doublet and/or a buff coat. Of course, an arquebusier could wear any piece of armour he could buy or loot, but he had to remember that speed, lightness, and agility remained his best assets. The low rate of fire and the limited effective range of his weapon required him to operate as close as possible to the enemy which accounts for the tactic at Lupstein (Saverne) of using the light horse to transport the arquebusiers as near to the peasant position in the village as possible. What singled the Italian skirmishers out from other was their willingness, to engage their opponents in savage melees in which all sorts of weapons could be used including the butts of their arquebuses.

Although any kind of standardisation in size and calibre was still very far off, the barrel of a 'typical' Italian arquebus would be approximately 1 metre in length and fired shots that weighed one *oncia* (28.29 grams) or somewhat less, using a charge of about the same weight. The accessories usually included a pouch for the balls, two flasks of powder, a large one for the main charge to be poured in the barrel and a smaller one for the finer powder to be poured in the firing pan, a few lengths of match cord and a ramrod. According to Arfaioli there is no evidence of Italian arquebusiers using bandoliers of wooden cartridge apostles.[2]

Stradiot

These mounted troops of Albanian and Greek origin initially entered military service during the Republic's Wars with the Ottoman Empire in the fifteenth century, but soon found employment in Southern Germany and France. Louis XII recruited some 2,000 stradioti in 1497, two years after the battle of Fornovo. Among the French they were known as estradiots and argoulets. The term 'argoulet' is believed to come either from the Greek city of Argos, from where numbers of them originated. They pioneered hit and run light cavalry tactics and could well have been used at Saverne by the Duke of Lorraine to carry the Italian hangunners in his army's ranks to fire on the peasant troop ensconced in the village of Lupstein. The stradioti

---

1   Maurizio Arfaioli, The Black Bands of Giovanni. Infantry and Diplomacy during the Italian Wars (1526–1528) (Pisa: Plus-Pisa University Press, 2005), p.17
2   Arfaioli, The Black Bands, p.18.

used javelins, swords, maces, crossbows, bows, and daggers and wore a mix of Ottoman, Byzantine and European garb. Their armour was initially a simple mail hauberk, replaced by heavier armour in later eras. The figure here wears a long striped cloak and a distinctive beaver skin tall hat. Note also the concave shield which also had a characteristic outline shape.

Plate M People on the Move

This extract from one of the final sheets of the Triumph of Maximilian by Albrecht Altdorfer et.al. presents a cross section of costume of the time. The group is part of the baggage train and depicts Landsknechts mingling with artisans and peasants. Note the plain garb worn by the mercenaries and muted colours. (Hispanic Digital Library, with permission).

Plate N Banners of Palatinate

Banners of Palatinate allies Mainz, Trier, and the United Duchies of Jülich, Cleves and Berg. Source: Wapen des Heyligen Römischen Reichs Teutscher Nation or Arms of the German nation of the Holy Roman Empire. Wapenbuch der Heilig Roemischer Reich Deutscher Nation by Jacob Köbel. Frankfurt am Main, 1545. (Bavarian State Library, with permission).

Plate O Banner of Lorraine.

Source: *Wapen des Heyligen Römischen Reichs Teutscher Nation* or *Arms of the German nation of the Holy Roman Empire*. Preface by Jacob Köbel. Frankfurt am-Main, 1545. Courtesy: Bavarian State Library München, with permission.

Plate P

1.Stained Glass Window Überlingen

This stained glass window in the municipal hall of the old imperial city of Überlingen, which lies in the northwest corner of Lake Constance, is one of the few remaining contemporary images of the peasant war. On the left-hand side are the forces of the Swabian League with their main banner whose knights are engaging with the peasant bands on the left – note the yellow flag bearing the Bundschuh emblem and the striped banner emblazoned with a ploughshare. (Überlingen City Archive, with permission).

2. Coat of Arms of the Elector Palatine.1500

Wernigeroder (Schaffhausensches) Wappenbuch; (Bavarian State Library, Cod.icon.308 n, with permission).

Appendix I

Extracts from the Ochsenfurter Field Ordinances, 24–27 April 1525[1]

This is one of the few examples remaining of a field ordinance (*Feldordnung*) in which the command structure of the army would be laid down. This example was drawn up by the Franconian peasants and is clearly modified but based on a typical letter of articles of the day.

9. ... it is considered that the supreme commander shall have four aides appointed alongside him, and the lieutenant two, to serve alongside them day and night, and loyally to follow their requests and orders.

10. The supreme commander (*Oberster Befehlshaber*) and the lieutenant (*Leutinger*) shall have their lodgings and tents near the cannon, so that they can be found by day or night in case of need.

13. A captain is to be elected[2] by each troop, to whom those in the troop may reveal their needs and grievances. Afterwards, the same captains shall present these grievances to the supreme commander in the presence of the appointed captains and councillors, which will be discussed by them, and so all disorder and trouble will be kept in check.

14. From each company comprising around 500 men, one man shall be elected[3] as colour-sergeant. And the elected colour-sergeant shall be obliged, as is fitting, to exercise his office truly and honourably, as far as his honour and bodily power permit.

15. A judge (*Schultheiss*) is to be appointed ... and he is to administer justice each day, as often as the need arises, alongside the appointed assessors or jurors who have been or may in future be appointed, and to punish the evil and advance and protect justice. And in this he shall let

---

1 Scott & Scribner pp.160–163.
2 League captains would have been appointed.
3 Again this officer would have been an appointee.

himself be influenced by no bribes, fees, friendships, or enmities, but keep before his eyes ... only God and his justice. The judge shall have two aides appointed to assist him.

16. One man is to be appointed ... as provost marshal (*Profoss*). He shall exercise his office in the following manner. First, whenever camp is pitched, he shall immediately erect a gallows for the punishment of the wicked ... He shall arrest all evildoers and transgressors and hold them in secure custody, and afterwards present the misdeeds of each to the captains and councillors. Whatever orders are sent to the provost marshal after the presentation and assessment of the accused, he is to implement. The provost marshal shall have no power of his own to do violence to or to levy anyone, ... but only on the orders, and by the will and knowledge of the supreme commander and the appointed councillors. He shall on his oath hand over the confiscated or acquired goods or money to the captains and councillors, or whoever else has so entrusted him, and not retain them in his power.

17. The provost marshal shall also, as soon as camp is pitched, assess all the provisions brought into the camp according to fair prices, whether it be bread, wine, meat, or other victuals If corn, wheat, or oats are brought in, he shall also price them fairly and shall take a shilling from each wagon and three pence from a cart as his fee ...

18. For the office of master of artillery (*Oberster Zeugmeister*), armourer, and master of the arsenal, ... shall be in sole command of the cannon and keep it in good order and security ...

19. A master of the wagon fort (*Wagenburgmeister*) is to be appointed, and his command is that when camp is struck and moves off, the wagons are to move off and proceed according to his orders. However, he orders them to proceed, they shall keep that order, and the carts are not to be mixed in among the wagons.

20. The office of master of the watch shall have four appointed to it, who are to use their true diligence so that when camp is pitched, watch will be kept as necessary.

21. Four sergeants shall be appointed ... to make a battle-order ...

22. Then there shall be appointed a sergeant for each troop, to march alongside the ranks, and whoever shall fall out of the ranks he shall drive them back into them. On the march everyone is to remain where he has been ordered and not leave the ranks, on pain of punishment.

23. Two quartermasters are to be elected to supervise the kitchens and cellars, so that they can be kept in good and uniform order.

24. A master of the spoils is to be appointed in each company, so that booty will be distributed equally and no one receive more or less advantage than another.

25. A paymaster shall be appointed, and everyone shall pay him for provisions consumed and the like.

Appendix II

Ordinance Of the Upper Swabian Peasantry, March 1525[1]

This document is preceded by a list of the councillors and envoys of the three bands from the Allgäu. Lake Constance, and Baltringen.

The worthy community (*Landschaft*) of this Christian Union is ordered and divided into three parts as follows:

One part or quarter by name Baltringen, the second part Lake Constance, the third part the Allgäu, and each part shall have an appointed leader

The leaders specified by name:

In the Baltringen part, Ulrich Schmid from Sulmingen.
In the Lake Constance part, (left blank).
In the Allgäu part. Waiter Bach from Oy
The leaders shall have agreed a special password and procedure with each other.

When the abovementioned three parts are divided into bands, there is to be in each band an appointed leader with four councillors.

It has been discussed and decided that no one shall allow any despatch, whether written by word of mouth, to pass from one-quarter or part to another without the leader's command. so that alarm and unnecessary disturbance be avoided: if such is reported by others, it shall not count and no one shall act on it.

If a quarter is attacked and requires the aid of another quarter then the other two parts shall on receiving the call from the first. send every tenth man on the first call, every sixth on the second, and every fourth man on the third.

For each quarter attacked, the assault shall extend no further than to aid the band which is attacked. It should mobilise as strongly as it for the salvation of land and people and admonish the other bands by means of despatches.

---

1   Scott and Scribner pp.133–135.

The banner shall be red and white. and the sign or cross shall be red and white also. and sewn onto it as a saltire.

Each part and quarter shall appoint and uphold its own government as appropriate. according to military law.

Each leader in the individual parts shall determine a procedure and password with his government, deputy commanders, and other councillors as is appropriate.

Whatever the officers and junior officers. council, and government undertake. perform order, and negotiate shall be obeyed by the common man in Christian loyalty

It is especially amicable plea that each man in the brotherhood should act fraternally towards everyone so that the rich should not think that the poor should do as much as they can but they should act equitably as should be done when a feudal tax is levied, so that there will be fraternity. Everyone Should heed his company commander, and those who remain at home should man the watch. so that we can advance our cause. and each person should fervently pray his beads.

When the alarm is sounded, each person shall come to his appointed place on his oath and honour, and whoever does not appear shall be dealt with by the court according to these articles

All disputes are to be set aside. and no one is to take revenge on another. If anyone commits a crime, no one shall support or rescue him, but allow him to be dealt with by the provost marshal or his assistants, according to the judgement of the court and the common man …

When two or more settle a dispute, the other side shall keep the peace and abide by it and if anyone is called upon to keep the peace three times and does not observe it his life and goods shall be forfeited. No one may strike another with a long weapon such as a halberd, or strike them without warning when they are prostrate, or from behind

When camp is pitched, no one shall desert by his honour and oath, At a call to arms, whether by day or night. if anyone will not join the ranks and deserts, the sergeant shall have power to round them up with forcer whether with an arquebus or whatever is necessary.

Further. in dealing with the enemy. any spoils shall be placed in the common booty oath and honour. If we have to plunder our enemy during a campaign. this shall be done only through the corporals (*Rottmeister*), unless permission is given otherwise

Whether they be townsfolk or villagers. each shall obey whatever is requested and instructed.

When on the march. no one, of whatever rank, shall break ranks or disobey the leaders. particularly the corporal, captain, or quartermaster to what he has been assigned, in order to pitch camp; similarly. no one is to approach the baggage train. but is to remain where he has been placed by the sergeant,

Nothing shall be sold in the camp unless it has been taxed by the provisioning officer and the provosts-marshal.

Appendix III

Extracts from the Ordinance of the Rhineland Peasants,[1] 10 May 1525

The column is to be organised as follows:

The vanguard shall consist of two companies of men made up of two men from each squad (*Rotte*) and these shall rotate daily with the rear-guard.

These two companies shall precede the main column (*Gewalthaufen*) which shall be followed by the artillery.

The latter shall be protected by two companies in the rear-guard on a rotating basis.

No one may stray from this formation without express permission of the commander.

The master of the train shall be accompanied by two quartermasters whose task it is to organise the erection of the camp.

Day and night sentry duty shall be organised by two masters of the watch.

Each company shall have its own commissary.

Where city, castles or property is seized these shall have their contents duly itemised by appointed officers. Removal of any items without permission of the entire band shall be severely punished.

13. All artillery, shot, gunpowder, wagons and horses seized from cities, castles and other property shall be solely commandeered by the master of the train.

21. Failure to show officers, standard bearers and sergeants due respect shall be severely punished.

Matters relating to provosts:

22. Failure to show the provost and his officers including the executioner due respect shall be severely punished.

---

1   Bensing M. Hoyer S. 1982 *Der Deutsche Bauernkrieg* Berlin: Militärverlag der Deutschen Demokratischen Republik. pp 239–241 Translation by the author.

23. The provost or his executioner shall not take the life of any man without due process involving an appointed judge. Where a capital crime has been committed the supreme commander, his officers and the ensign shall sit in judgement.

24. The provost and his men shall be paid from the booty – for every florin value one-half of a Batzen[2] or the equivalent in grain, wine or wheat or animal. To avoid double counting no wares paid to the provost shall be returned to the booty.

25. Should the provost be required to put a man in irons he and his officer shall be paid one Batzen.

26. The executioner shall receive a monthly pay of four florins, be entitled to the same provisions as others and any property belonging to the condemned.

27. The officers shall inform the whole band every two days whether they have appropriated any gold and submit accounts regarding the same every fortnight to the men.

28. Any man engaging in plunder without the knowledge of the supreme commander shall be severely punished.

29. Two commissaries shall be appointed.

30. The officers and war council shall be assisted by two Christian chaplains to perform daily prayers.

31. 4 mounted messengers shall be appointed to maintain contact where it is needed with other bands.

---

2 The Rhineland florin was the equivalent of 15 Batzen which equalled 60 Kreuzer, which in turn amounted to 240 Pfennig or 480 Heller.

Bibliography

Alter, Willi, *Pfeddersheim um 1525,* (Verlag Stadtarchiv, Worms, 1990)
Arfaioli, Maurizio, *The Black Bands of Giovanni. Infantry and Diplomacy during the Italian Wars (1526–1528)* (Pisa: Plus-Pisa University Press, 2005).

Bach, Volker, Markets for Mercenaries: Supplying Armies in Sixteenth Century Germany in McWilliams M. (ed.) *Food & markets: proceedings of the Oxford Symposium on Food and Cookery* 2014 (London: Prospect Books, 2015) pp.33–45.
Barthhold, Friedrich Wilhelm, *Georg von Frundsberg oder das deutsche Kriegshandwerk zur Zeit der deutschen Reformation* (Hamburg: Friedrich Perthes, 1833) pp 357–362.
Bartlau, Christian, *Der Weingartner Vertrag. Eine verpasste Chance?* BA-Arbeit, (Universität Potsdam: Historisches Institut, 2007).
Baumann, Reinhard. *Georg von Frundsberg: Vater der Landsknechte* (Munich: Süddeutscher Verlag 1984)
Baumann, Reinhard, *Landsknechte,* (Munich: C.H. Beck Verlag, 1994).
Baumann, Reinhard in Bröckling Ulrich, Protest und Verweigerung in der Zeit der klassischen Söldnerheere in *Armeen Und Ihre Deserteure: Vernachlässigte Kapitel einer Militärgeschichte der Neuzeit* (Göttingen: Sammlung Vandenhoeck,1998) pp.39 – 44.
Baumann, Reinhard, Böhmische Söldner; in: *Historisches Lexikon Bayerns,* 2010 <http://www.historisches-lexikon-bayerns.de/Lexikon/BöhmischeSöldner> accessed 13 August 2018.
Belfort Bax, Ernest, *The Peasants' War in Germany 1525–1526* (London: Swan Sonnenschein, 1899).
Blickle, Peter, *Der Bauernjörg. Feldherr im Bauernkrieg* (Munich: C.H.Beck Verlag, 2015).
Boell, Balthasar: *Der Bauernkrieg um Weißenburg Anno 1525* (Johann Ohleyer, Weißenburg 1873)
Bumiller, Casimir, Der Bauernkrieg im Hegau 1524/5 Rekonstruktion einer revolutionären Bewegung in *Hilzingen Geschichte und Geschichten, Band 1* (Gemeinde Hilzingen,1998), pp 251 – 431
Brunner, Jean-Claud, The Siege of Salzburg. The Prince-Archbishop vs the People in *Medieval Warfare,* Vol. 6, No. 6, 2017, pp.20–25

Delbrück, Hans, *The dawn of Modern Warfare, History of the Art of War Vol. IV* (Lincoln: University of Nebraska Press 1990)

Frisch, Ernst von, *Der "Salzburger Bauernkrieg"des Egidius Rem in seiner ursprünglichen Fassung von 1525* available at <http://www.zobodat.at/pdf/MGSL_82_83_0081-0091.pdf> (accessed 9 October 2018) .

Gerstacker, Oliver, *Was waren die Gründe für das Scheitern des "gemeinen Mannes" im Bauernkrieg 1524–26?* GRIN Verlag,2016.

Grosse, Fritz, *Ottheinrich von der Pfalz (1502–1559) Studien zur politischen Ikonologie*, PhD Thesis, Martin-Luther-Universität Halle-Wittenberg, 2003.

Haarer, Peter, *Eigentliche und Wahrhaftige Beschreibung des Bauernkriegs 1531*, (Halle: Max Niemeyer 1881, Kessinger Legacy Reprint)

Hasselbeck, Johannes, *Die Folgen des Deutschen Bauernkriegs im Hochstift Bamberg* (Bamberg: University of Bamberg Press, 2012)

Hertle, Werner, Hans Halm, der Stadtschreiber von Aalen und seine Zeit, *Aalener Jahrbuch* (Aalen: Geschichts – und Altertumsverein, 1996).

Hoyer, Siegfried, *Das Militärwesen im deutschen Bauernkrieg 1524–1526* (Berlin: Deutscher Militärverlag, 1975).

Huber, Barbara, *Im Zeichen der Unruhe: Symbolik bäuerlicher Protestbewegungen im oberdeutschen und eidgenössischen Raum 1400–1700*, PhD Philosophisch-historischen Faculty of (University of Berne, 2005), pp.172–178.

Hutter, Franz, *Geschichte Schladmings und des steirisch-salzburgischen Ennstales*, Moser Publishing, 1906.

Johann, G.A., Enkevoerth B., von Falke J. McNealy M. (eds.), *Landsknecht Woodcuts: Kriegsvölker im Zeitalter der Landsknechte* (Quakenbrück: Nadel und Faden Press, 2013).

Kratts, Alison, *German Peasant Clothing 1510–1540* The Compleat Anachronist, #168 <https://amiesparrow.wordpress.com/kasf-2015/german-peasant-clothing–1510–1540/ > accessed 26 September 2022.

Klein, Herbert, 1952 Die Kämpfe um Radstadt am 24. Juni 1526 und daß Ende des Salzburger Bauernkriegs, *Mitteilungen der Gesellschaft für Salzburger Landeskunde*, Bd. 92, Salzburg S. 124 ff.

Klüpfel K. (ed), *Urkunden zur Geschichte des Schwäbischen Bundes (1488–1533)* (Stuttgart: Literarischer Verein, 1853).

Köchl Karl. *Die Bauernkriege im Erzstift Salzburg in den Jahren 1525 und 1526.* (1814) Available at <https://www.zobodat.at/pdf/MGSL_47_0001-0117.pdf > accessed 9.October 2018.

Ludwig, Karl-Heinz (2009): Bergleute im Bauernkrieg 1525/26: Salzburger zwischen Habsburg und Wittelsbach — oder politisch darüber hinaus? – *Mitteilungen der Gesellschaft für Salzburger Landeskunde*, 2009, pp.191–248. Available at <www.zobodat.at> accessed 28 April 2022)

BIBLIOGRAPHY

Maurer, Hans-Martin, Bauernkrieg 1524/25 – Heereszüge der Aufständischen und des Schwäbischen Bundes, Beiwort Zur Karte 6, *Historischer Atlas von Baden-Württemberg: Erläuterungen* (Stuttgart: Kommission für geschichtliche Landeskunde in Baden-Württemberg 1980), pp.1–8.

Miller, Douglas, (2003) *Armies of the German Peasants War* (Oxford: Osprey 2003).

Miller, Douglas, *Frankenhausen 1525*, (Seaton Burn: Blagdon Publishing, 2017)

Miller, Douglas, *The Army of the Swabian League 1525* (Warwick: Helion Publishing, 2019)

Moxey, Keith, *Peasants, Warriors, and Wives* (Chicago: Chicago Press 1989).

Müller Karl & Peikert Gernot, Die Rolle der Glocken im Bauernkrieg 1524/2 in *Hegau-Geschichtsverein, Kriege, Krisen, Friedenszeiten im Hegau*, Jahrbuch (Hegau-Geschichtsverein e.V. Singen/Hohentwiel 2014). S. 49–64.

Nef, John U., Silver Production in Central Europe, 1450–1618, *Journal of Political Economy* Vol. 49, No. 4 (The University of Chicago Press:1941), pp.575–591.

Neumann, Franziska, Der selektive Blick. Frauen im Bauernkrieg zwischen Frauen und Geschlechtergeschichte, in: Schattkowsky, Martina (Hrsg.): *Frauen und Reformation. Handlungsfelder, Rollenmuster, Engagement*, (Leipzig Universitätsverlag 2016), pp.153–170.

Oakeshott, Ewart, *European Weapons and Armour* (Suffolk: Boydell Press, 1980).

Opitz, Eckart, Militärgeschichtliche Aspekte des Bauernkrieges in Deutschland *Militärgeschichtliche Zeitschrift* Volume 28, Issue 2, 1980, pp.1–34.

Pichler, Georg Abdon, *Salzburgs Landes-Geschichte: Allgemeine Geschichte. 1*, (Salzburg: Oberer Verlag, 1865).

Rogg, Matthias, *Landsknechte und Reisläufer: Bilder vom Soldaten: Ein Stand in der Kunst des 16. Jahrhunderts* (Paderborn: Verlag Ferdinand Schöningh, 2002).

Sea Thomas & Meyer G. Schwäbischer Bund und Bauernkrieg: Bestrafung und Pazifikation in Geschichte und Gesellschaft. Sonderheft Vol. 1, *Der Deutsche Bauernkrieg 1524–1526* (1975), pp.129–167.

Seger J. *Der Bauernkrieg im Hochstift Eichstätt*. Friedrich Pustet Verlag, 1997.

Scott T. & Scribner R. (Eds), *The German Peasants' War. A History in Documents*, Amherst: Prometheus Books, 1991.

Sieber, Siegfried, 1963 Der Joachimsthaler Aufstand 1525 in seinen Beziehungen zu Sachsen, *Bohemia*; München Vol. 4, (1 January 1963) pp 40–53.

Stockmann, Erich, „Funktion und Bedeutung von Trommeln und Pfeifen im deutschen Bauernkrieg 1525/26. *Beiträge zur Musikwissenschaft* 21, 1979, pp.105–24.

Stulz, Jodok, *Bericht des Landeshauptmanns Sigmund V. Dietrichstein An Den Erzherzog Ferdinand über den Überfall Zu Schladming Am 3 Juli 1525* (1858) (Kessinger Publishing 2010) .

Schäffer, Roland, Der obersteirische Bauern – und Knappenaufstand und der Überfall auf Schladming 1525 *Heft 62 der Militärhistorischen Schriftenreihe des Heeresgeschichtlichen Museums* (Vienna: Österreichischer Bundesverlag,1989).

Speier Hans, The Social Types of War, *American Journal of Sociology*, Volume 46, Number 4, 1941.

Übel Rolf, *Nussdorf und der Bauernkrieg* <https://www.landau-nussdorf.de/mains/geschichte.html#krieg> accessed 8 May 2022.

Vice, Roy. L. The Leadership and Structure of the Tauber Band during the Peasants' War in Franconia: *Central European History*, Vol. 21, No. 2 (Jun. 1988), pp.175–195

Vogt, Wilhelm, Die Correspondenz des schwäbischen Bundeshauptmanns Ulrich Artzt von Augsburg a. d. J. 1524 und 1525. Ein Beitrag zur Geschichte des Bauernkrieges in *Zeitschrift des Historischen Vereins für Schwaben,* vols. 6 and 7(1880) 9 (1882) 10 (1883).

Wagner, Emil, die Reichsstadt Schwäbisch Gmund in den Jahren 1523–25 aus: *Württembergische Vierteljahrshefte für Landesgeschichte* 2 (Stuttgart, 1879,) p.26–33, 81–101.